Taunton's
BUILD LIKE A PRO™
Expert Advice from Start to Finish

INSULATE and WEATHERIZE

Expert Advice from Start to Finish

INSULATE and WEATHERIZE

BRUCE HARLEY

The Taunton Press

The Taunton Press
Inspiration for hands-on living®

The Taunton Press, Inc., 63 South Main Street, P.O. Box 5506, Newtown, CT 06470-5506
e-mail: tp@taunton.com

EDITOR: ANDREW WORMER
JACKET/COVER DESIGN: Lori Wendin
INTERIOR DESIGN: Lori Wendin
LAYOUT: Jeff Potter/Potter Publishing Studio
ILLUSTRATOR: Ron Carboni

Taunton's Build Like a Pro® is a trademark of The Taunton Press, Inc.,
registered in the U.S. Patent and Trademark Office.

Library of Congress Cataloging-in-Publication Data
Harley, Bruce, 1964–
    Insulate and weatherize your home : expert advice from start to finish
/ Bruce Harley.
        p. cm. -- (Taunton's build like a pro)
Includes index.
        ISBN 1-56158-554-8
    1. Dwellings--Insulation. 2. Buildings--Airtightness. 3. Sealing
(Technology) I. Title. II. Build like a pro.

        TH1715 .H35 2002
        693.8'3--dc21

                                            2002006060

Printed in the United States of America
10 9 8 7 6 5 4 3

The following manufacturers/names appearing in *Insulate and Weatherize* are trademarks: 3M® tapes, Aquastat®, Comfort Foam®, Corbond®, Duro Dyne® Corporation, General Electric®, HEPA®, Icynene®, IECC®, International Energy Conservation Code®, Juno®, Kichler®, Low-e™ coatings and paint, Maxlite®, Metlund® "D-Mand System," Plexiglas®, Progress®, Sealection®, Styrofoam®, Tapcon® screws, Teflon® tape, Thermo-Ply®, Typar®, Tyvek® tape, v-seal®, Voyager®

Homebuilding is inherently dangerous. Using hand or power tools improperly or ignoring safety practices can lead to permanent injury or even death. Don't try to perform operations you learn about here (or elsewhere), unless you're certain they are safe for you. If something about an operation doesn't feel right, don't do it. Look for another way. We want you to enjoy the craft, so please keep safety foremost in your mind whenever you're in the shop.

To Winifred Jewell Harley and George Way Harley, my grandparents, who dedicated their lives to helping others and sharing the tools to build better lives.

Acknowledgments

MY HOPE IS THAT the success of this book will be in providing real and lasting benefit to many people. If it helps you, please consider it a small payment "forward" for the huge gifts others have given me. Without every one, I really couldn't have done it. Please pass it on.

Many thanks to:

Terry Brennan, Tom Downey, Chris Derby-Kilfoyle, Dave Keefe, Joe Lstiburek, Mark LaLiberte, John Proctor, Bill Reed, Marc Rosenbaum, Bill Rock Smith, Stephen Strong, David Weitz, and many others for teaching me lessons about buildings and building science and for modeling a thoughtful and humorous approach to teaching people about buildings and the people who live in them.

Rich Andelman, Caitriona Cooke, Steve Cowell, Bob Eckel, Adam Gifford, Mike Guerard, Shirley Harris, Karen Hourigan, Randy Joyce, Erin Martinez, Jack Morris, Adam Parker, Nat Peplinski, Barb Smith, and everyone at Conservation Services Group for being supportive in every way.

Mieke Kohl, my life partner, for the ultimate encouragement and support, for laughter, Reiki, movement, patience, and helping me get my vegetables along the way.

My mother, Barbara Harley, for teaching me to trust; my father, Bob Harley, and my brother, Mark Harley, for instilling in me a hunger for how things work and hands-on learning; my sister, Carol Harley, for lots of sympathy and encouragement and for helping me cultivate gratitude; and Catherine Harley, for cheering me on.

Scott Carrino, Carol Hansen, Andy Gaines and Bill McCully, Julia Butterfly Hill, Chungliang Al Huang, Stephen and Ondrea Levine, Meredith Monk, Gary Sachs, Ramsay Drew Steward, and Andrew Weil, for inspiration and openheartedness, which have helped me to survive and even flourish—physically, spiritually, emotionally—through this arduous process, and for helping me find my voice.

Andy Wormer, my editor; Helen Albert, Jenny Peters, Jennifer Renjilian, and everyone at The Taunton Press.

Molly Kerns, for amazing, healing massage. Joe Bamburg, Paul Fisette, Ron Jackson, Karen Kane, Roland Kohl, Maria Loring and Al Wroblewski, Blake McClenachan, Kent Mikalsen, Ken Nardone, Dave Roberts, Brian Starr, Buck Taylor, and Wild Oats Community Market. Special thanks to Dan Berube.

And to many others unnamed . . . this work is truly an expression of all those who have nurtured, influenced, and helped me along the way.

Contents

Introduction

WHY IS energy efficiency so important? You can't see energy efficiency, but it can make a big difference, both for your budget and for the environment. Here's how. First, increasing your home's energy efficiency puts money right back in your wallet. The average American family living in a single-family home spends $1,500 on energy for the home every year. How much of that can you save? From a few dollars per year to more than 50%, depending on the existing condition of your home and the level of weatherization you undertake. And an investment in energy savings not only reduces your operating costs but also helps shield you against future price increases. In addition, the money saved generally benefits the local economy, helping neighbors and local businesses rather than oil and utility companies.

Of course, comfort is important, too. Weatherizing does not mean turning down the thermostat and freezing in the dark. It means using less energy for the same level of comfort—or even more. My customers are often amazed to discover how much more comfortable they are when their energy culprits are found and fixed.

Indoor air quality is a big deal. U.S. Environmental Protection Agency studies have found that indoor air pollution levels are typically two to five times worse than outdoor air pollution levels. This book emphasizes the concept of the home as a dynamic system. Chapters 1 and 3 cover the basics of energy, moisture, air quality, combustion safety, and ventilation in houses. Other books may focus only on energy savings, but careless weatherization can aggravate or create moisture, air quality, and combustion safety problems. I try to show you how to avoid those problems and provide guidance about when to get professional help.

Building problems related to energy, moisture, and airflow can lead to chronic paint problems. Condensation in wall and roof cavities may lead to mold growth and structural damage. In cold climates, ice dams on roof eaves and freezing pipes are commonplace; they are often caused by hidden air leaks. The house system approach and weatherization techniques that form the foundation of this book can help you reduce or eliminate those problems.

Energy, moisture, combustion safety, health, and indoor air quality are all interrelated. Although this book is intended to provide a balanced, overall view of managing the interactions among these factors, and to point out areas of concern, it is impossible to anticipate all possible situations that could lead to trouble—including structural failure, carbon monoxide poisoning, or chronic indoor air problems. Because of the potential moisture issues involved, you should not undertake any of the projects outlined here unless you are sure that you have a sound, reliable roof and a solid structural frame. If you feel that the descriptions and background information offered here are not adequate to understand your situation or do not cover the specifics of your home, hire a professional who is skilled in building science, diagnostics, and/or building performance to evaluate your home.

This book shows many practical ways to improve your home's energy efficiency, ranging from small, simple projects to comprehensive weatherization. The subject of energy conservation is too large to fit into one book. I hope that this volume provides enough information so the advanced do-it-yourself homeowner can make substantial improvements. I also hope it will steer you to professional help when that's appropriate. Weatherization can be very satisfying. Although the results are largely invisible, the increase in comfort and the decrease in monthly costs are well worth the effort.

How to Use This Book

IF YOU'RE READING THIS, you're a doer, not afraid to take on a challenging project. We designed this book and this series to help you do that project smoothly and cost-effectively.

Many doers jump in and do, reading the directions only if something goes wrong. It's much smarter (and cheaper) to start by knowing what to do and planning the process, step by step. This book is here to help you. Read it. Familiarize yourself with the process you're about to undertake. You'll be glad you did.

Planning Is the Key to Success

This book contains information on designing your project, choosing the best options for the result you want to achieve, and planning the timing and execution. We know you're anxious to get started on your project. Take the time now to read and think about what you're about to do. You'll refine your ideas and choose the best materials.

There's advice here on where to look for inspiration and how to make plans. Don't be afraid to make an attempt at drawing your own plans. There's no better way to get exactly what you want than by designing it yourself.

After you've decided what you're going to undertake, make a list of materials and a budget for yourself, both in money and in time. There's nothing more annoying than a project that goes on forever.

Finding the Information You Need

This book is designed to make it easy to find what you need to know. The main part of the book details the essential parts of each process. If it's fairly straightforward, it's simply described. If there are key steps, they are addressed one by one, usually accompanied by drawings or photos to help you see what you will be doing. There are also other elements, such as sidebars, to help you understand the process better, find quicker or smarter ways to accomplish a task, or do it differently to suit your project.

Alternatives and a closer look

The sidebars and features included with the main text explain aspects in more depth and clarify why you're doing something. In some cases, they describe a completely different way to handle the same situation. You'll learn when you may want to use a particular method or choose another option, as well as the advantages of each. Photos or drawings usually accompany the sidebars to help you visualize the tasks described. The sidebars are meant to help, but they're not essential to understanding the process or completing the task.

Heads up!

Always read the "Safety First" and "According to Code" sidebars. "Safety First" gives you a warning about hazards that can harm or even kill you. Always work safely. Use appropriate safety aids and know what you're doing before you start working. Don't take unnecessary chances, and if a procedure makes you uncomfortable, try to find another way to do it. "According to Code" can save you from getting into trouble with your building inspector, building an unsafe structure, or having to rip your project apart and build it again to suit local codes.

There's a pro at your elbow

The author of this book, and every author in this series, has had years of experience doing this kind of project. We've put the benefits of their knowledge in quick tips that always appear in the left margin. "Pro Tips" are ideas or insights that will save you time or money. "In Detail" is a short explanation of an aspect that may be of interest to you. Although it is not essential to the job, it is meant to explain the "why."

Every project has its surprises. Since the author has encountered many of them already, he can give you a little preview of what they may be and how

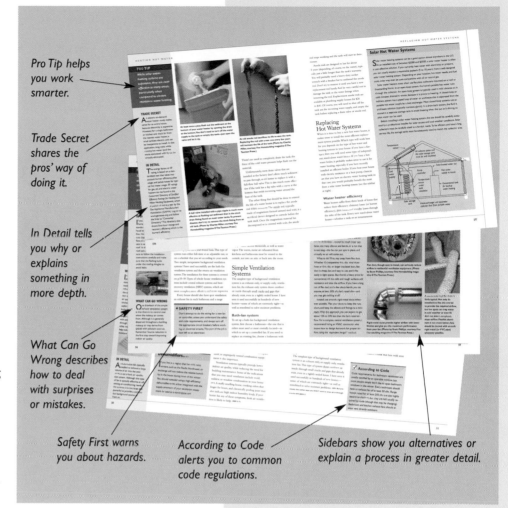

Pro Tip helps you work smarter.

Trade Secret shares the pros' way of doing it.

In Detail tells you why or explains something in more depth.

What Can Go Wrong describes how to deal with surprises or mistakes.

Safety First warns you about hazards.

According to Code alerts you to common code regulations.

Sidebars show you alternatives or explain a process in greater detail.

to address them. And experience has also taught the author some tricks that you can learn only from a pro. Some of those are tips include tools or accessories you can make yourself or materials or tools you may not have thought to use.

Building Like a Pro

To make a living, a pro needs to work intelligently, quickly, and economically. That's the strategy presented in this book. It presents options to help you make the best choices in design, materials, and methods. That way, you can adjust your project to suit your skill level and budget. Good choices and good planning are the keys to success. And remember that all the knowledge and every skill you acquire on this project will make the next one easier.

Energy Basics

CHAPTER ONE

There is a lot of misconception, tion, folklore, and conflicting information about the consequences of weatherizing a house: "A house has to breathe—you don't want it *too* tight," "Too much insulation will make your house rot," "Insulate your attic because heat rises." While some of these statements are based on fact, they tell only part of the story.

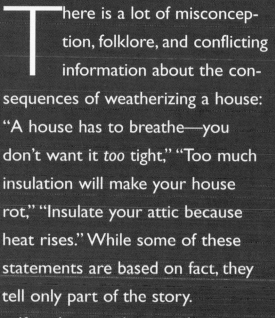

If you're considering making energy improvements to your home, it is important to look at the big picture. Houses are complex systems: Energy, moisture, air, people, structure, and mechanical systems all influence and affect each other. In this chapter, I'll give you a basic overview of the "house system" approach and outline the basics of energy and moisture movement. I'll also explain the key concepts so you'll know *why* it's important to view the home as a system. With this information, you can plan and prioritize your weatherization projects; maximize your comfort, health and safety; and minimize building maintenance.

PRO TIP

Insulation and air leakage both play a big role in the energy usage of most houses. Always seal air leaks when you insulate a house.

IN DETAIL

The greater the temperature difference between one area and another, the faster heat moves. A cup of hot tea cools quickly at room temperature because the temperature difference is large: about 90°F. Iced tea takes about twice as long to warm up, because the temperature difference is about half (40°F). If you were trying to keep a cup of tea hot with a heating element, the heater would need to produce twice as much heat to maintain the cup at 160°F as it would to keep it at 115°F (assuming the room is 70°F).

IN DETAIL

The largest energy use in most houses is heating and cooling (about 55%). Therefore, improvements to the building envelope and mechanical systems have the most potential to save energy. Next are hot water heating (15%), refrigeration of food (10%), and lighting (7%). It's easy to notice when lights are left on or when someone stands in front of the refrigerator with the door open, but the things we don't see have the biggest impact on our home energy use.

Understanding Heat Transfer

You don't need to be a heating engineer to know how to install insulation. But by understanding how the mechanisms of heat transfer work and their relative importance in your home, you can better decide how to approach to any weatherization project that you undertake.

Heat transfer is the movement of heat from indoors to outdoors in the winter, and from outdoors to indoors in the summer. If heat transfer didn't occur, your house would always keep you cozy and warm in the winter and cool and comfortable in the summer, without the use of a furnace or air conditioner. In a way, the function of your furnace or air conditioner is less to "make heat" or "make cold air" than it is to replace the

It is important to seal air leaks when you insulate. (Photo by Andrew Wormer, courtesy *Fine Homebuilding* magazine, ©The Taunton Press.)

Steel studs, joists, and headers are straight, strong, and superb conductors of heat. Unless they have an effective thermal break, such as rigid insulation, they conduct far more heat than conventional wood-framed walls. (Photo by Bruce Harley, © Conservation Services Group.)

heat that escapes in the winter and remove the heat that enters in the summer.

There are three forms of heat transfer: conduction, convection, and radiation. Of the three, conduction and convection are larger in magnitude—how *fast* the heat moves—and radiation can have a big influence on the comfort inside a house. Let's look at how each of these mechanisms operates and affects your home.

Heat flows toward cold

Conduction refers to the movement of heat through solid materials. Conductive heat loss always moves from the warm side to the cold side of a material. For example, if you have a cup of hot coffee outside on a cold day, the heat will move through the cup and out into the cold air around it (or into your hands to help keep them warm). On the other hand, if the weather is hot and you have a cup of iced tea, the heat will move *from* the warm air, through the cup, and *into* the tea, warming it.

Different materials allow conduction to happen at different rates. For example, we may use a steel pan on the stove to efficiently transfer heat from the stove burner to our food because steel is a very good conductor of heat. For the same reason, steel framing in an exterior wall performs poorly from an energy-efficiency standpoint. *Thermal insulation* describes a number of products designed to slow conductive heat loss in walls, ceilings, and floors. Common types of insulation, such as fiberglass, cellulose, and polystyrene foam, are poor conductors of heat (for more on insulation, see chapter 4).

It is important to remember that heat flows through solid materials toward cold *in any direction.* A house may lose more heat *down* through an uninsulated floor in a sunroom than it loses *up* through the moderately insulated ceiling of the same room. The reason attics are usually insulated to a higher degree than walls or floors is not because heat rises; it is simply because the ceiling usually contains more space to hold thicker layers of insulation more cheaply and easily than anywhere else in a house. The old saying "heat rises" is misguided—heat actually moves in every direction. However, that saying does have some truth to it, which brings us to the next subject: convection.

Heat moves on air

To an engineer, *convection* describes heat transfer through the movement of fluid. Convection, to an engineer, is a much more complex subject than we need to understand for weatherizing homes. For our purposes, convection can be thought of as heat transfer through air movement. What causes air to move? Three main forces cause air to move through your house: the stack effect, mechanical systems, and wind. In a typical house, convection is almost as important as conduction and, because it is often misunderstood, I will go into some detail discussing it here.

The stack effect. The first convective force, the stack effect, is what is meant by the saying

These infrared scans show a house before and after it was insulated (above and below, respectively). In the "before" image, the white areas represent the most heat loss; the black areas, the least. Note the hot areas in the walls and gable of the left dormer, in the walls below the dormer (under the porch roof), and under the rake overhangs, as well as the plume of heat coming out of the main gable vent. (Photo © Bruce Harley.)

Although this house is insulated, there's still some heat loss; the windows haven't changed. The chimney is quite warm because of the steam boiler, which stays hot all the time. Note the wall of the shed dormer on the right appears to have lightened. It had been insulated when the dormer was added and wasn't touched. Because the scanner auto ranges for good contrast, most of the walls in this "after" image show up a bit lighter than they would otherwise. (Photo © Bruce Harley.)

PRO TIP

Don't just pack the ceiling with insulation because you can access the space. Remember that heat can just as easily escape through a poorly insulated floor.

IN DETAIL

Most combustion appliances, such as furnaces, water heaters, and fireplaces, draw their combustion air from inside the house. When they're working properly, they act like exhaust fans, drawing in air to supply oxygen for combustion, then exhausting combustion gases up the chimney or out the vent pipe. Some appliances, known as *power vent* or *induced draft*, have blowers that push the combustion gases out. These blowers (shown below) are even more similar to the simple exhaust fans found elsewhere in the home.

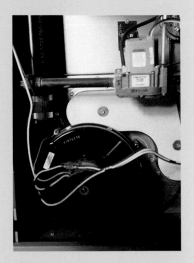

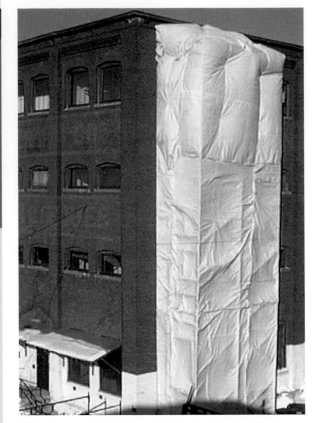

This photo of a building under construction displays the air pressure pushing the tarp *out* at the top and *in* at the bottom. This clearly shows the pressures that move air through a building in winter. (Photo © David Keefe.)

"heat rises." What is really meant is, "warm air rises when surrounded by cold air." In the winter, a house is very much like a hot-air balloon that is too heavy to lift off from the ground. If you were the pilot and wanted the balloon to go up, you would turn on the burner and add more heat; this would intensify the force pushing up the balloon by increasing the temperature of the air inside the balloon. Similarly, the amount of force pushing air through your house is proportional to the temperature difference between the indoor air and the outdoor air. This is an important concept for understanding the basics of air leakage in relation to indoor air quality and fresh-air ventilation. Because the stack effect is driven by temperature, it is a more important force in severe climates than it is in mild climates.

If you were piloting a hot-air balloon and wanted to descend, you would let some hot air escape by opening a flap at the top of the balloon. When you open the flap, warm air escapes from the top and cooler air rushes in from the bottom to replace it. Similarly, when you heat your house in the winter, warm air leaks *out* of holes at the top, and cold air leaks *in* at the bottom to replace it. Another way to picture this is to imagine holding a cup of air upside-down in a pan of water. The air in the cup, like the warm air in your house, is lighter—more buoyant—than the water, which is heavy like the cool, outdoor air. If you poke a small hole near the top of the cup, the air will leak out slowly, and the water will come in from the bottom at the same rate to replace the air (see the sidebar on the facing page).

Wind. People think that the wind causes most drafts, but in most houses, the effect of wind is quite small. Although the pressure may be greater than the stack effect when the wind is blowing, it is a part-time occurrence; the stack effect operates 24 hours a day, 7 days a week, all year long. If your house is perched on a cliff or smack in the middle of a treeless plain, the wind may have a larger effect but, for most homes, the stack effect dominates the air movement.

One way to compare the seasonal impact of the stack effect versus the wind effect is to ask yourself whether you would rather have me give you $10 a month or $1 a day. The $10 feels like more on the day I give it to you, but you'll be about three times richer if I give you $1 every day. So it is with the stack effect: Although it is perhaps not as dramatic a source of energy loss as windy days are, it adds up over time to be a far greater energy cost.

Mechanical systems. In addition to the stack effect and wind, fans move air through houses. Exhaust fans, combustion appliances, and furnace air handlers move air in predictable and

A central vacuum system, if it vents to the outside, can also act as an exhaust appliance in the home.

unpredictable ways. Exhaust fans push air out of a house—when they are working properly—and that air is replaced by outdoor air leaking in through openings in the building. Typical exhaust fans include kitchen and bathroom exhaust fans, dryers, and occasionally central vacuum systems (when they are vented to the outside). Combustion appliances, especially furnaces and boilers, contribute even more to air exchange when they are operating, which is when the weather is at its coldest.

Even more significant than exhaust fans are duct systems. Furnace and air conditioner fans are not intended to move air in and out of a house; however, if the ducts are leaky—and many are—your furnace fan may push a lot of air through your home. Like the furnace combustion air, an air handler runs the most when the temperatures are extreme, so ducts leak the most when it costs the most to reheat all the air that leaks out.

Whether the mechanical systems or the stack effect moves more air in a year varies from house to house, depending on the climate, the construction of the home, the size and location of leaks in the ductwork, and many other factors. In many homes, the air exchange caused by mechanical systems, though mostly unintentional, is the dominant force of convective heat transfer. (See chap-

The Stack Effect in Summer

One misunderstood aspect of the stack effect is that it *reverses* in hot weather. If the outdoor air is hotter than the indoor air, the heavier air in the house tends to *sink* and leak out through the bottom; it is then replaced by warmer outdoor air that comes in through the top of the house.

To use the cup analogy, a house in the summer is like a cup full of water that is held upright. If you poke a hole in the bottom of the cup, the water (which is heavier) dribbles out the bottom and the cup fills from the top with air (which is lighter) at the same rate. People who leave upstairs windows open on a hot day thinking that the hot air will escape because "heat rises" are mistaken—they are actually opening a large hole through which hot outside air can be drawn into the house.

Although it's true that the upper floor of a home tends to be much warmer on a summer afternoon, that is not because the heat is rising inside the house. It is because superheated air is being drawn from the attic and roof deck into the upper part of the house through hidden air leaks—and through open windows and skylights.

The Stack Effect Is Reversed in Hot Weather

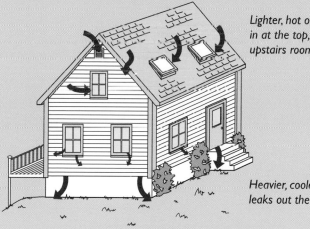

Lighter, hot outdoor air is drawn in at the top, heating the upstairs rooms (red arrows).

Heavier, cooler air leaks out the bottom (blue arrows).

ters 2 and 3 for more information on controlling air movement in homes; see chapters 6 and 8 for more on combustion equipment; see chapters 6 and 7 for more on sealing duct leaks.)

Heat moves through space

Radiation is heat transfer from one object to another through space. Like conduction and convection, radiation depends on a temperature dif-

PRO TIP

Glass is usually the coldest interior surface in winter and the warmest in summer. Rooms with a lot of glass may be uncomfortable in both seasons.

WHAT CAN GO WRONG

Furnace air handlers should not move air *in and out* of a house; they are designed to move air *around* the house. Normally, as air is heated, it is released into the house through supply ducts; house air is brought in through return ducts to begin the cycle again. However, leaky ductwork in attics, basements, and other areas can push air outside the house, acting like an unintentional exhaust fan. In fact, research has found that, in many homes, duct leakage accounts for the majority of air moving in and out of the house when the furnace blower is running.

Mechanical Systems Contribute to Air Movement

Makeup air is drawn in from the outside through cracks and gaps (blue arrows). House air is drawn into combustion equipment and exhaust fans (black arrows).

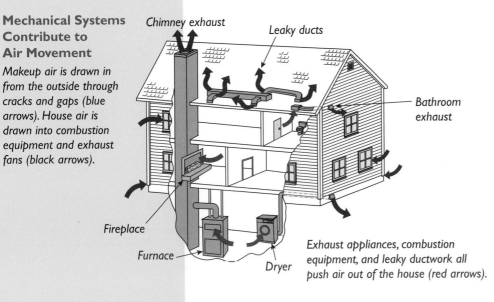

Chimney exhaust

Leaky ducts

Bathroom exhaust

Fireplace

Furnace

Dryer

Exhaust appliances, combustion equipment, and leaky ductwork all push air out of the house (red arrows).

ference, but this time between the surfaces of objects rather than across a material. While conduction moves heat through solid materials and convection depends on air movement, radiation happens only when there is a direct line of sight between two objects of differing temperatures.

Radiation plays a much smaller role than conduction or convection in the heat loss from a house in the winter. The type of window glass can influence radiative heat loss to some extent (see chapter 5). Radiation is, however, the primary factor in solar heat gain. Solar gain is a good thing in the winter (it adds some heat from the sun to your house for free), but it is also the largest driver of air-conditioning loads in the summer (see chapters 5 and 7). In any season, radiation has a large impact on comfort. A person's comfort level actually depends more on the average temperatures of the surrounding surfaces than it does on the air temperature in the room (see the top drawing on the facing page).

The biggest role radiation plays in a home's comfort is due to the surface temperatures of glass. In the winter, glass is usually the coldest surface in a house; in summer, it is the warmest. A room with lots of glass may be uncomfortable in both hot *and* cold weather. Uninsulated or poorly

A room with lots of glass is likely to be uncomfortable in hot or cold weather, especially if it has a southwestern exposure.

insulated walls, ceilings, and floors also create cold surface temperatures in the winter (or hot ones in the summer). Cold surfaces add to the problem of conductive heat loss by making people feel less comfortable. When people are chilly, they turn up the thermostat, driving the heat loss even faster and costing them even more.

Defining the Thermal Boundary

The *thermal boundary* (also called the *thermal envelope*) refers to the parts of a building that separate indoor space, which is heated or cooled with a furnace or an air conditioner, from the outdoors and other spaces that are not heated or cooled. The spaces in your home that are heated or cooled are called the *conditioned space*, and the purpose of your furnace or air conditioner is to maintain those spaces at a comfortable temperature.

The thermal boundary is not the same as the *weather shell* of the house. Although it may coincide in many places—for example, most exterior walls are part of both the thermal boundary and the weather shell—they have different purposes and are often not in the same place. The purpose

Mean Radiant Temperature

The mean radiant temperature in a room is the average temperature of all the surfaces in the room weighted by the percentage of the room that each surface occupies.

(NOTE: The temperatures around the edges refer to the surface temperatures of the wall, ceiling, floor, and windows)

A. Even though the room temperature may be 70°F, the person sitting in the middle experiences a mean radiant temperature of 67°F. The window, because it is both large and cold, is the surface that has the most effect on lowering the mean radiant temperature.

B. If the room has twice as much window area, the radiant temperature drops to 63°F—too cold for comfort! This happens even though the room temperature is still at 70°F. To keep this room comfortable, the thermostat will need to be set higher to compensate.

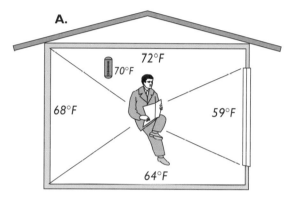

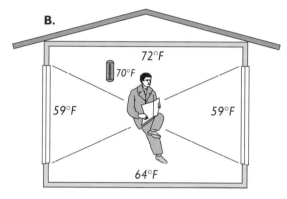

The thermal boundary of a ceiling is typically made up of drywall or plaster, thermal insulation, and ceiling joists or truss members. If the attic space is vented to the outside, temperatures in the attic will be close to outdoor conditions, and the rafters, sheathing, and roofing materials play virtually no role in the thermal boundary.

of a building's weather shell is to shed rain and snow and keep the building and its contents dry. It also is able to resist forces that try to break it down, such as sun and wind. The roof is usually part of the weather shell of a building, but most roofs are not part of the thermal boundary, unless they are built as an insulated cathedral ceiling. Usually, the thermal boundary is the flat ceiling, and there is some type of open attic space between it and the roof. A garage is another example; the exterior walls and roof of the garage form a weather shell, but the wall between the garage and the home is the thermal boundary (see the drawing at right).

Like the weather shell, the thermal boundary is not usually made of a single material, and some materials may play more than one role. Walls may consist of siding, building paper, sheathing, studs, thermal insulation, and drywall or plaster. All of those materials contribute in some way to the thermal properties; some of them are also structural, and some make the building weather resistant.

For the greatest comfort and energy efficiency, it is important that the thermal boundary of the home be clearly defined. Sometimes it is unclear whether or not a space is part of the conditioned area. For example, a basement may be comfortably warm in the winter due to heat loss from the fur-

The Thermal Envelope

The boundary between the conditioned space and anything that's not conditioned is called the thermal envelope (or thermal boundary). Like an envelope, it is supposed to surround its contents neatly and completely. The shape may be complex, and it usually does not include attics, garages, or crawl spaces.

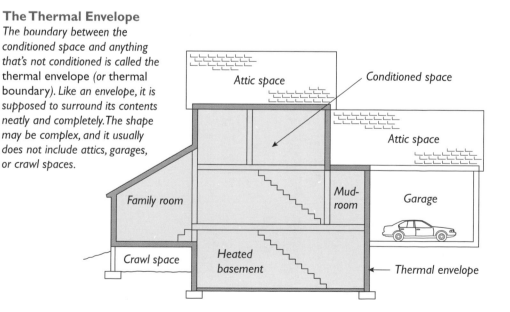

WHAT CAN GO WRONG

The thermal boundary should always be continuous, and you should be able to draw an imaginary, uninterrupted line around your house, in any direction, that represents the thermal boundary. Every part of that line should represent some type of insulation material—either that exists now or that you plan to install.

Even though this attic area behind a kneewall has insulation in the floor, wall, and rafters, it's unclear whether the area is inside the conditioned space. In this example, the thermal boundary is ambiguous.

nace and ducts, even though there is no insulation on the foundation wall. One might think that the thermal boundary is the foundation walls. What if that same basement opens into a crawl space underneath the family room that was added on later? The crawl space may have louvered vents (which are often required by code), and it is defi-

nitely an unconditioned space. Perhaps the best place for the thermal boundary is at the foundation wall, between the full basement and the crawl space. On the other hand, if the inhabitants never go into the basement and don't mind it being rather cold in the winter, it may make more sense to put the thermal boundary between the basement and the house. To do that, you must insulate and seal the heating ducts and the floor over the basement; then the entire basement and the crawl space are considered unconditioned.

Insulation does not stop air

Although all parts of the thermal boundary should include some type of insulation material, they must also incorporate some type of air barrier. Most insulation does not stop air. Let me repeat that: *Insulation does not stop air.* Although there are exceptions, the most common types of insulation materials—fiberglass and cellulose—do not stop air from moving under the driving force

Some Thermal Boundary Problem Areas

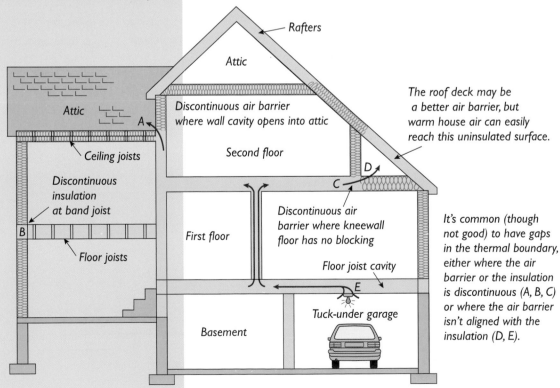

Rafters

Attic

Attic

Discontinuous air barrier where wall cavity opens into attic

Ceiling joists

Discontinuous insulation at band joist

Floor joists

Second floor

Discontinuous air barrier where kneewall floor has no blocking

Floor joist cavity

First floor

The roof deck may be a better air barrier, but warm house air can easily reach this uninsulated surface.

It's common (though not good) to have gaps in the thermal boundary, either where the air barrier or the insulation is discontinuous (A, B, C) or where the air barrier isn't aligned with the insulation (D, E).

A. Where the ceiling height changes
B. At the band joist
C. At the kneewall
D. Warm air between the floor joists can easily move to the wrong side of the insulation in an unvented kneewall attic.
E. Air from a tuck-under garage can get in through unblocked joist bays.

Tuck-under garage

Basement

of a pressure difference. Fiberglass, in particular, does almost nothing to stop air movement under the forces of convection. People often think that if they put a lot of insulation in a house it will be airtight; this is simply not true.

When you define the thermal boundary of your home, it is critical to think about where the air barrier is located in relation to the insulation. Think of insulation as a sweater or fleece pullover: On a cold, windy day, it doesn't keep you warm because the air moves right through it. A windbreaker has very little insulating value but, by stopping the air, it makes the sweater much more effective. Similarly, stopping air leaks makes insulation much more effective.

Air barriers and insulation

Another thing to consider when defining the thermal boundary is whether the air barrier is close to the insulation. It is usually best to align them whenever you can; for example, it does not

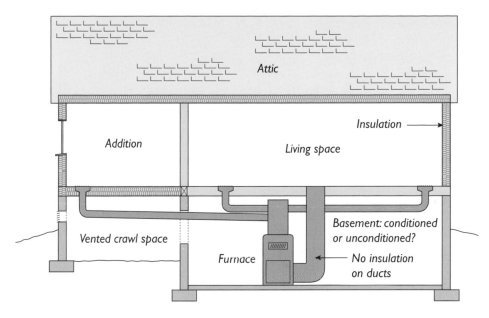

Where Is the Thermal Boundary?
In this common scenario, the thermal boundary is unclear. The crawl space is clearly outside, but the rest of the basement could be conditioned (by insulating the foundation walls) or unconditioned (by insulating and sealing the furnace ducts and insulating the floor). Either way, it would be smart to seal off the opening between the basement and the crawl space.

Unlike fiberglass batts, rigid foam insulation can provide a good air barrier, but all of the seams must be sealed carefully. (Photo courtesy Joe Lstiburek, Building Science Corp.)

make sense to insulate the flat ceiling of a house and then create an air barrier at the roof sheathing. If you did, warm air from the house would circulate through the insulation, warming the attic and increasing the heat loss through the roof.

If you're not sure, knowing a place where it is easy to make a good air barrier can help you decide where to put insulation.

However, there may be places where the insulation and air barrier need not be aligned. The most common example is a basement, because it can be very difficult to provide a continuous air barrier between a basement and the first floor. Even if you wanted to insulate the floor over the basement and make it a cold space, if you have a solid concrete foundation wall, it may be much easier to air-seal the foundation walls and the sill area instead. If you can effectively stop cold air from leaking into the basement, that will prevent it from moving up into the house through the floor.

PRO TIP

Most common insulation materials do not stop air movement. Fiberglass batts act like an air filter, stopping only the dust.

TRADE SECRET

Fiberglass does not stop air under pressure, but it does stop dust. This photo shows a piece of fiberglass that has been sitting on top of a plumbing chase where warm air constantly escaped into the attic during the winter. The black color isn't mold but particles from the air that were trapped by the insulation as the air passed through it.

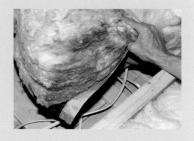

IN DETAIL

Some of the biggest air leaks are at the top of the house, but people don't tend to notice them because there is no cold air leaking in. Those leaks actually draw warm air to that part of the house on its way out, so they are not noticed. They also cause more cold air to be drawn in from the bottom, increasing discomfort on the lower levels.

Older homes "breathed" because they were so full of leaks and lacked insulation. While moisture didn't get trapped by the walls, neither did much heat, making these homes energy hogs.

Energy, Moisture, and Building Durability

One key issue in the field of building science is the relationship between moisture and energy; another is the effect of moisture on building durability and indoor air quality. We've all heard horror stories about brand new buildings that are rotting because moisture gets trapped inside them, or houses that are "built too tight" so that the air inside becomes dangerously polluted with combustion gas. These stories make good headlines and have some basis in fact, but they typically oversimplify situations and perpetuate myths about the relationships among energy, moisture, air quality, and building durability.

So, let's clear up some of the misconceptions about energy efficiency and moisture damage. One way to do that is to compare the moisture performance of new, energy-efficient homes to the performance of old, inefficient ones.

Energy and moisture: myth and reality

Older homes usually had little or no insulation and were quite leaky. They are the basis for that pearl of wisdom "a house has to breathe" (more

Now that buildings are constructed with continuous sheathing materials and insulation, moisture that makes its way into a wall cavity takes much longer to dry, potentially causing structural and health problems. (Photo by Steve Culpepper, courtesy *Fine Homebuilding* magazine, © The Taunton Press.)

on that later). These homes were basically flow-through systems; heat, air, and water vapor could move easily through walls and roofs. If the exterior wall sheathing got wet, heat loss through the wall cavity would dry it out quickly. These homes were quite forgiving of moisture, but they were also uncomfortable energy hogs.

The way we construct buildings has changed dramatically in the past 50 years. The sheet materials we use as exterior sheathing—plywood and oriented strand board (OSB)—slow air movement and act as a condensing surface for water vapor in cold weather. Unfortunately, insulated wall cavities are much slower to dry out when they do get wet. Although energy efficiency by itself does not cause moisture problems, air-sealing and insulation can change the moisture dynamics in a building and may make it less forgiving of moisture that is already being generated inside or leaking from outside the house.

Damp basements have more effect on a house than just damaging the walls; they can also be a major source of moisture that causes damage in the rest of the building. "Moisture-resistant" greenboard didn't help much here. (Photo by Bruce Harley, © Conservation Services Group.)

Water in the basement is not only annoying, but it can also add a lot of moisture to the air in a house. (Photo by Bruce Harley, © Conservation Services Group.)

One approach to dealing with these issues is a head-in-the-sand stance: *Let's not make this house "too efficient" in the hope that it will "breathe" and stay healthy.* A much better approach is to control moisture intelligently and avoid those problems deliberately.

The importance of managing water

Unwanted water can be a real scourge in any house. We need water in our homes; plumbing systems are designed to bring water into the house

These photos show the difference between water resulting from a roof leak (top) and water caused by interior water vapor that condenses on the roof sheathing in cold weather (bottom). A roof leak, besides being more likely to show on the ceiling below, often does not have the broad impact that moisture rising through an air leak has. Moisture from indoors often has a more damaging impact over time, partly because it's less likely to be detected until it's too late. (Top photo © Kevin Kennefick; bottom photo courtesy Stephen Smulski, Wood Science Specialists, Inc.)

and remove it in a controlled way. But too much water in the wrong places contributes to mold growth, which is not only annoying but also potentially hazardous. Water can contribute to structural and furnishing damage; damp basements are renowned for slowly turning everything that's left there into a soggy, stinky mess. To understand how

✔ According to Code

Most states have adopted some version of the International Energy Conservation Code® (IECC) or its predecessor, the Model Energy Code (MEC). Focused on new residential construction, these codes also apply to additions to existing homes in most states. Although the energy-efficiency requirements of state or local codes may be less stringent for remodeling, check before starting an energy project to see whether there are any minimum requirements and whether you need a building permit for the work.

How Much Water Vapor?

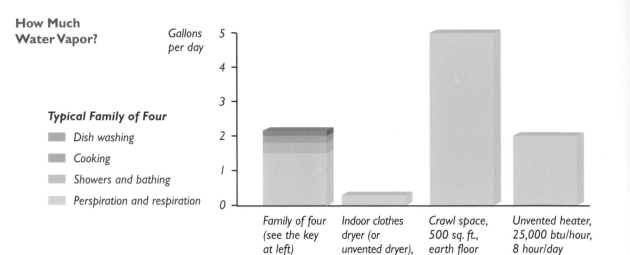

Typical Family of Four
- Dish washing
- Cooking
- Showers and bathing
- Perspiration and respiration

Gallons per day (y-axis: 0, 1, 2, 3, 4, 5)

Categories:
- Family of four (see the key at left)
- Indoor clothes dryer (or unvented dryer), per load
- Crawl space, 500 sq. ft., earth floor
- Unvented heater, 25,000 btu/hour, 8 hour/day

TRADE SECRET

Even though your basement may appear to be dry, it can be a significant source of moisture. To find out whether this is true, tape a piece of 2- to 3-ft.-sq. clear polyethylene to your basement walls or floor. Stretch it tightly; if the surface is damp, you may need to brace some pieces of wood around the edges to keep it in place. Leave it for a few days; if water droplets form on the side you can touch, then the moisture is coming from humid inside air condensing on the cool concrete. If water collects under the poly, then moisture is migrating through the concrete.

(Photo by Steve Culpepper, courtesy *Fine Homebuilding* magazine, © The Taunton Press)

to control the movement of water, we must understand where it comes from and how it moves.

Where does unwanted water come from?

Unless you live in the desert, one of the largest sources of water is from outside the house: rain and groundwater. Rain can enter through roofing, siding, or flashing defects and soak into roof, ceiling, and exterior wall materials. Although roof leaks are usually pretty obvious (if not always easy to fix), water that enters sidewalls may go unde-

tected for years (see chapter 9). Water that enters foundations and crawl spaces may also be obvious. However, groundwater can also enter a house through evaporation, and it can be difficult to detect in its vapor form.

Water in the ground under a crawl space, in a full basement, or even in a slab foundation can evaporate before it reaches the surface. Concrete is capable of wicking up moisture from an underground water source and "pumping" it into a house. Even though the floor and walls may *appear* dry, they can actually be the source of moderate-to-large moisture loads in a building. In hot, humid weather, water vapor also comes from outdoors, when humid air seeps into the house through air leaks (this is called a "latent load" in air-conditioning).

In cold weather, the other common source of water vapor is the people and activities in the house. People generate water vapor through perspiration and respiration. Everyday activities, such as showering, bathing, and cooking, also add vapor to the air. If you have a gas or propane cookstove, the combustion process adds water vapor to the air as well.

Many damaging moisture problems have at their root large or unusual sources of water vapor.

This moisture may find its way into exterior walls or roof framing in cold weather, then condense on cold surfaces, causing rot, deterioration, or mold growth. These conditions may go undetected for years and have the potential to cause major structural damage or health problems.

If you are insulating and sealing your home, you will probably be crawling through the attic, basement, and crawl space, which will give you the opportunity to identify existing moisture problems in the house. In all cases, you'll want to be sure to identify the source of any water or vapor and correct it before continuing your weatherization project.

Managing water vapor

The first step in managing water vapor in your house is to eliminate large sources that can be removed, then deal with sources you cannot remove with proper spot-ventilation (for more on ventilation, see pp. 20–22). The next step is to control vapor movement. Traditionally, water-vapor control has focused on diffusion. Water

vapor is made up of individual molecules suspended in the air, and they actually move through solid materials; this movement is called diffusion.

In cold climates, vapor primarily moves from indoors (warm and humid) to outdoors (cold and dry). In hot, humid climates, vapor moves from hot, humid outdoors to cooler, dryer indoors, especially with the use of air-conditioning. Trouble is avoided as long as the rate of vapor diffusion is low, but problems crop up when the concentration of moisture is large enough—or vapor movement is fast enough—that condensation occurs in walls or roof structures.

The most common method for reducing vapor transmission is to use *vapor retarders*, materials that slow the rate of vapor diffusion to very low levels, generally low enough to prevent condensation. In cold climates, vapor retarders are traditionally installed on the inside of the thermal envelope to keep water vapor from entering the wall cavity and reaching the cold exterior surfaces of the building.

The kraft-paper facing found on some brands of fiberglass insulation is an effective vapor barrier and should be installed facing the inside of a house in mixed and cold climates. In hot, humid climates, the vapor barrier must face the outside. Polyethylene sheeting should be used only in cold climates. In mixed or cold climates with humid summers, an air-conditioned home is better off with a kraft-paper vapor barrier rather than poly. (Photo © Kevin Kennefick.)

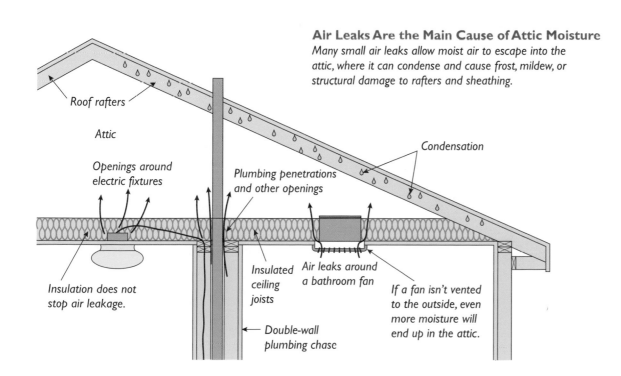

Air Leaks Are the Main Cause of Attic Moisture
Many small air leaks allow moist air to escape into the attic, where it can condense and cause frost, mildew, or structural damage to rafters and sheathing.

Roof rafters

Attic

Openings around electric fixtures

Plumbing penetrations and other openings

Condensation

Insulation does not stop air leakage.

Insulated ceiling joists

Air leaks around a bathroom fan

If a fan isn't vented to the outside, even more moisture will end up in the attic.

Double-wall plumbing chase

PRO TIP

To manage water vapor, eliminate the large sources that can be removed, ventilate the ones that can't, and control the movement of remaining water vapor.

IN DETAIL

Large sources of water vapor from inside buildings are called *moisture loads*. These can include exposed dirt floors in crawl spaces or basements, indoor pools or spas without proper ventilation or dehumidification, foundation drain access pipes and sump pits, unvented or improperly vented combustion appliances, firewood drying indoors, fish tanks, attached greenhouses, and even small plumbing leaks.

IN DETAIL

The force that pushes water vapor through solid objects is called *vapor pressure*. Water molecules move from high concentrations (humidity) to low concentrations (dryness). Vapor also moves from warm areas to cold ones. One example of such vapor diffusion is a loaf of bread, tightly wrapped in a paper bag, left out for a couple of days. Even if the bag is tightly wrapped, water molecules will escape right through the bag (from a higher concentration to a lower one). A waxed bag will keep the bread fresh longer, and plastic will slow the moisture loss the best.

In all but the coldest climates, it is helpful to provide drying ability in both directions. Drying ability does not depend on air leaks, and it is necessary to use only materials that are relatively permeable to water vapor (these include drywall, polystyrene foam board, solid wood, felt papers, and housewraps). The presence of a vapor retarder on the cold side can result in moisture condensing in a wall, roof, or floor, leading to mold, moisture damage, and structural decay. Unfortunately, the driving force is reversed in hot, humid weather in any home that has air-conditioning. Fortunately, kraft paper (typically used on kraft-paper-faced insulation) is much more forgiving than polyethylene and allows drying to the interior under summer conditions. Hence, it is the best interior vapor barrier to use in mixed humid climates (roughly from Kentucky and North Carolina to central Texas) and in cold climates in homes that have central air-conditioning.

Water vapor moves on air

Although the focus on water-vapor control has traditionally been vapor retarders, a much more important effect is air leakage. This cannot be overemphasized! Although vapor retarders are important, they do no good if warm, humid air can leak into the attic or an exterior wall in the winter (see the drawing on p. 19). Building scientists have found that, over the course of a winter, small air leaks actually move far more water into cold building assemblies than vapor diffusion does. This air movement is the result of the same convection forces we have already discussed, with the stack effect, duct leakage, and other mechanical systems typically being the largest factors. In fact, the lack of a vapor retarder in an insulated wall or a ceiling is secondary—in all but the most extreme climates— *if* air leakage into those areas can be controlled. This should come as a relief to anyone who wants to insulate a poorly insulated house to which it is difficult to add a vapor retarder.

Air Barriers and Indoor Air Quality

Perhaps the most widely misunderstood aspect of the house-system approach is the relationship between air leakage control and healthy indoor air. Conventional wisdom says "a house has to breathe," but what exactly does that mean? People and animals need to breathe. Houses are complex systems, but they are not living organisms, so I prefer not to use the term "breathing"

Indoor Air Quality

Building scientists have found that there are several important steps to ensure good indoor air quality, and they are generally consistent with energy conservation. These basic steps are:

1. Create a good, tight boundary between indoor and outdoor air.

2. Minimize or eliminate pollutant sources within the house (see the sidebar on p. 23).

3. Maintain indoor humidity within a healthy range.

4. Provide adequate fresh air ventilation for people in the home.

This approach cuts heating and cooling energy losses, reduces uncomfortable drafts, permits better moisture control, and maintains an indoor environment that is healthier *and* more energy-efficient.

for a house. There is still some underlying wisdom behind that statement, however. As we have already seen, it *is* vitally important to allow wall assemblies the opportunity to dry; this is done by using building materials that are permeable to water vapor. But this is not breathing; vapor diffusion does not depend on air movement. To understand the dynamics of air quality, let's first look at air barriers.

What is an air barrier?

Although it may seem obvious, an air barrier stops air. We've already seen that most types of insulation don't stop air movement. Another myth that has taken root over the last decade is the idea that housewrap makes a house airtight. Most housewraps are good air barriers, but the biggest air leaks occur in places where housewrap is not installed, where it is installed improperly, or where

Treat Air Like Water

We work hard to keep water out of our homes. Foundations, siding, windows, doors, roofing, and flashing represent a substantial investment in keeping out water. Then we purposefully bring water into the house through plumbing supply and drainage systems, which are another large price tag in our homes. Clean water is essential to our health, so we control it carefully. Fresh air is also essential, but in most residential buildings, we pay no attention to controlling it. If we treated air as we do water, by keeping out unwanted air and intentionally introducing fresh air, we would provide much healthier indoor environments for our families.

Attic and Crawl Space Venting

Most building codes have minimum requirements for attic, cathedral-ceiling, and crawl space venting. It is important to remember that this passive venting is different from fresh-air ventilation. Venting is designed to carry excess moisture out of those spaces so it does not damage the building structure. These venting strategies actually have nothing to do with indoor air, but they are often called "ventilation," which leads to confusion. Remember that there is a thermal boundary between the conditioned spaces and the attic or crawl space. Ideally, there should be no air exchange at all between those spaces and indoors.

Basically, attic, roof, and crawl space venting are "Band-Aids" that attempt to carry away moisture that should not be there in the first place. Good air sealing at the thermal boundary and proper water management of basements and crawl spaces (with vapor retarders and footing drainage) are more important to a building's health. Some building codes are just beginning to recognize the importance of these concepts, and venting requirements are beginning to change.

Passive roof ventilation is designed to transport moisture out of attics, but in certain circumstances, it can also be a point of entry for water or moisture-laden outside air.

Crawl space vents do little to reduce moisture loads in the living space, and they can introduce warm humid air into the crawl space during the summer.

WHAT CAN GO WRONG

One example of misguided building science is the application of a vapor retarder on the inside of houses in a hot, humid climate. Although most model codes have been updated to discourage this practice, it is not unusual to see vinyl wallpaper—an excellent vapor retarder—in hot, humid areas. If the exterior sheathing is vapor permeable, this can lead to big problems as outdoor moisture condenses on the inside surface of the vinyl. In general, vapor retarders should be installed on the outside of houses in these climates, and they must be avoided on the interior of outside walls. Such climates include Florida and the southern half of other Gulf Coast states, including southeastern Texas, and the eastern coast north to Maryland.

IN DETAIL

In hot, humid climates, vapor retarders do not need to be separately applied; instead, they may be integrated with the wall sheathing or exterior insulation materials by using foil-faced rigid-foam insulation or low-permeability, thin structural sheathing, such as foil-backed Thermo-ply.®

Controlling Humidity

In winter, excessive dryness can be controlled by a tight building envelope. People often think their heating system is what dries out the air in winter, but actually it is the dry outdoor air constantly seeping in and needing to be heated that lowers the humidity indoors. Many people use humidifiers, but these devices need a lot of maintenance, and some types may create health problems of their own. Excess humidity in winter is best handled by mechanical ventilation, particularly by fans that exhaust moisture at its source: in bathrooms and kitchens.

In the summer, air leakage tends to add humidity to the indoor environment. The best way to control this is with a tight building envelope and air-conditioning or other mechanical dehumidification. Air-conditioning dehumidifies better when it is sized properly (see chapter 7), and it will work better if the building envelope is tight, because excessive air leakage in humid weather brings moisture into the house. Of course, spot ventilation in bathrooms and kitchens is also important in the summer. (For more on humidity, see the top In Detail on p. 26.)

It is important that bathroom fans work properly and exhaust air to the outside, not just into the attic.

Kitchens are another source of moisture; range hoods should always be vented directly to the outside.

it is not detailed well. Chapter 2 details ways to create good air barriers in existing homes, and there is more discussion of housewrap in chapter 9. With this information, you should be well equipped to create a very good air barrier in your house.

Can a house be "too tight"?

Let's go back to the axiom "a house has to breathe." We certainly need fresh air in our homes, but where does that fresh air come from? Leaving your fresh air supply to enter through random air leaks in the house—which may include gaps and holes in dirty, damp, moldy, pesticide-treated basements, crawl spaces, and attics—has been compared to pulling air into our lungs through holes punched through our abdomens. Most people would prefer to breathe through the openings—the nose and mouth—that were intended for that purpose. Similarly, every home should have an *intentional* provision for fresh air in the form of a mechanical ventilation system.

Creating a tight building envelope that minimizes air leakage has many benefits beyond energy savings: It increases comfort, reduces the chance of moisture damage in the building structure, discourages mold growth in wall and ceiling cavities, and reduces the likelihood of ice dams in snow country. Most important, it allows the operation of mechanical ventilation systems to control the indoor environment for better health and under varying weather conditions.

Remember that the forces that move air through a house—the stack effect, wind, and mechanical-draft systems (especially combustion equipment and duct leakage)—move the most air when outdoor weather conditions are extreme. This is also the time when it costs the most to heat or cool that air. On the other hand, even a leaky house tends to be underventilated in mild weather, when those forces are minimal and windows and doors are closed. The ideal house is tight enough that it has just enough fresh air leaking in when outdoor conditions are the most extreme; then the difference can be made up with mechanical ventilation for the rest of the year.

Mechanical ventilation

Mechanical ventilation, as opposed to random air leaks, ensures the right amount of air exchange *year round, under all conditions.* When I talk about

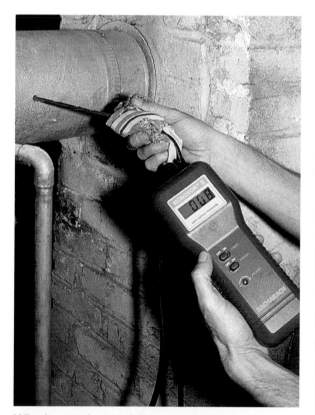

Whether you have a tight or a leaky house, any natural-draft combustion appliance may produce deadly carbon monoxide. The only way to know is to have a professional test the flue gases.

Minimizing Pollutants in the Home

■ **Source reduction** is the most important way to deal with toxins; keep them out of the house whenever possible! Learn which household products are the most toxic, get rid of any you don't use, and substitute less toxic products whenever you can.

■ **Separation of toxic materials** from everyday living spaces is another useful strategy. Don't just put dangerous chemicals in a childproof cupboard; keep them in a metal cabinet in the garage, and make sure the garage is separated from the rest of the house. Better yet, store them in a locked, outdoor storage shed.

■ **Dilution of toxins** is helpful, too. Installing a mechanical ventilation system helps bring in fresh air regardless of the weather conditions; such a system helps reduce concentrations of harmful substances.

■ **Combustion appliances** must be vented properly. Don't use unvented heaters of any kind, including "vent-free" fireplaces.

■ **Humidity control** reduces mold sources by keeping indoor surfaces warm and maintaining relative humidity.

■ **Radon testing** can detect this invisible, cancer-causing underground soil gas, which can occur anywhere. The only way to tell whether you have dangerous levels in your house is to test for it. Use an EPA-certified laboratory and follow the directions carefully for an accurate test.

A radon test kit like one of these can tell you how much radon is in your house. (Photo © Kevin Kennefick.)

An important rule of thumb: To maintain good indoor air quality, provide about 15 cu. ft. per minute (CFM) of fresh air per person.

IN DETAIL

Unlike water molecules, air can't leak through solid materials. Air leaks through cracks where different parts and materials of the building are connected together. Gaps between window and door frames and rough framing, places where exterior walls make a jog or are interrupted by a cantilever, and connections between dormer walls and roofs are areas often missed by housewrap. And the biggest leaks (as you'll see in chapter 2) are often hidden in attics, basements, and crawl spaces where housewrap is never installed.

IN DETAIL

Although outdoor air pollution is significant in many parts of the country, research done by the U.S. Environmental Protection Agency indicates that indoor air is typically 2 to 5 times more polluted than outdoor air. This includes most urban areas, most of the time. In some cases, research shows that indoor air can be as much as 100 times more polluted than outdoor air. Bringing in less polluted outdoor air in a *controlled* way is important for improving indoor air quality.

mechanical ventilation in this book, it is very important to understand that I am referring to ventilation of indoor spaces to provide fresh air and remove unwanted moisture. A mechanical ventilation system always consists of one or more fans, usually with ductwork, which either bring fresh outdoor air into the living space, or exhaust indoor air to the outside, or do a combination of both. It can also include filtration of incoming air. This is very different from passive (or fan-induced) venting of the roof, attic, or crawl space, but people often assume that the purpose of those attic and crawl space vents is to ventilate the entire building (i.e., "let the house breathe"). See chapter 3 for a discussion of installing basic mechanical ventilation systems.

Indoor air quality

Controlling the indoor environment through tight building and a mechanical ventilation system offers other health benefits as well. One of these is control of the indoor relative humidity. How do you control humidity? The simple answer is by controlling air exchange.

There are, of course, many sources of indoor air pollution besides moisture and its related effects. Volatile organic compounds (VOCs) can be found in paints, stains, cleaners, solvents, wood preservatives, and carpeting. Formaldehydes are found in manufactured wood products, such as interior-grade plywood, medium-density fiberboard (MDF), carpets, and furniture. Fuel and automotive products stored in the home or garage can also be toxic.

Many common household chemicals, such as cleaning products, aerosol sprays, moth repellents, pesticides, and herbicides, can be toxic. Pesticides, herbicides, and radon gas can be drawn into the house from underground (yes, air moves underground in many places). Running automobiles and improperly vented (or unvented) combustion

appliances can send deadly carbon monoxide (CO) into the home. How can you deal with these pollutants? Isn't it bad to tighten a house with these substances present?

The answer is definitely "yes" but, also, "not at all." If you tighten a house that already has a significant source of toxic fumes, the concentration of pollutants will probably increase. Therefore, source reduction is important, and separating unavoidable toxins from the living space is critical. At the same time, unintended airflow can also contribute to indoor pollution. Sealing air leaks between the house and the garage, for example, can improve air quality by cutting off the path for auto exhaust to migrate indoors. Meanwhile, a mechanical ventilation system that introduces fresh air helps dilute any toxins that remain. There's a slogan in the building-science industry that sums up these ideas: "Build tight, and ventilate right!"

Weighing Costs and Benefits

Typically, one of the first things people ask when they are thinking about energy improvements to a house is, "What is the payback?" I find this interesting, because most of us make hundreds of other purchase choices—buying a car, paying for a vacation—every year without ever asking that question. But one of the obvious reasons to conserve energy is to save money, so it is understandable that homeowners think about how much they will save and how long it will take to reclaim that investment. I believe this also happens because energy-efficiency improvements are not things that can easily be seen—it's much easier to show off a new deck, patio, or kitchen countertop, so people want to be able to justify energy conservation by some objective means.

Value beyond energy saved

A cost-benefit analysis can be a useful tool, but payback should not be the only criterion for deciding how much to spend and what to do. As I've pointed out in this chapter, there are many nonenergy benefits that may be realized simply by treating the house as a whole system, which means doing a thorough, thoughtful analysis. These benefits include improved health and reduced building maintenance, both of which are likely to have economic benefits for your family. However, the influence is difficult to measure; both also have the potential to greatly improve your quality of life.

There are other, noneconomic, factors that may affect your decision to invest in energy improvements. The most obvious noneconomic benefit of energy efficiency is comfort. Actually, I think that more comfortable people are likely to be happier and healthier, characteristics that probably create some economic benefits as well. Aesthetics and convenience are also important factors, for example, in the choice of whether to replace windows.

If you know the cost of a project and the energy savings, it's not difficult to calculate the payback; however, predicting energy savings is more complex. (Photo © Kevin Kennefick.)

Financing Energy Improvements

Instead of focusing on payback, cash flow can be a more useful way to look at financing energy improvements. Shown here are the estimated savings from air-sealing and insulating a house financed with a home-equity loan, as shown on a Home Energy Rating report. The annual cost of financing the work is less than the annual energy savings, and the annual cost for energy plus financing the improvements is less than the preimprovement cost of energy alone. The monthly payment on the loan eats up most of the energy savings, leaving about $5 per month in positive cash flow to the owner; however, the house is more comfortable, has less environmental impact, and is better protected against rising energy costs.

Energy costs ($/yr.)

End-Use	As Is	With All Improve- ments	Savings
Heating	$1,371	$1,002	$369
Cooling	0	0	0
Hot Water	453	454	0
Lights and Appliances	475	475	0
Service Charge	200	200	0
Total	$2,500	$2,131	$368

As Is: $2,497 — Improved: $2,440

- Energy
- Loan payment

Courtesy Architectural Energy Corporation, Boulder, CO

Net Present Value

You can think of savings from your current energy expenses as a tax-free income stream every month. A savings of $10 per month for 10 years has a net present value (NPV) of about $950, assuming an interest rate of 5%. This means that it would be an economic benefit to invest as much as $950 on a project that will save you $10 per month. The NPV is less than you would think—isn't $120 a year for 10 years worth $1,200? But NPV includes the interest earnings you have given up for the money you invested in the project. On the other hand, a savings of $10 per month represents about $14 per month before taxes; if you factor that in, the NPV increases to more than $1,300.

IN DETAIL

There are a number of negative health effects associated with very dry or very humid conditions. Dust mites and mold growth—common respiratory irritants and asthma triggers—thrive in high-humidity conditions. To minimize the negative health effects of very high or low humidity levels, The American Society of Heating, Refrigeration and Air-Conditioning Engineers (ASHRAE) recommends maintaining residences at a relative humidity of between 30 and 60 percent.

IN DETAIL

Although a comprehensive look at health issues in homes is beyond the scope of this book, a number of other books have been written about indoor air quality and health issues. See Resources on p. 194 for a list of resources that I've found to be useful for helping identify and deal with sources of pollution in your own home.

Environmental issues may also be a motivating factor. More and more people are taking time to recycle, or they are willing to pay higher prices for "green" or environmentally beneficial products, even if there is no direct payback whatsoever. Energy consumption in housing is one of your family's biggest environmental impacts (transportation and food consumption are the largest), so reducing your energy budget by a significant chunk will also help the planet and reduce our dependence on nonrenewable fuels.

Cost-benefit calculations (So, what is the payback?)

The basics of cost-benefit analysis are pretty easy. If you invest $100, and it saves you $10 per year, the payback is 10 years. This is called *simple payback*. There are many other methods for calculating payback and cost-effectiveness; some of them take into account the interest you could earn on that same money if you invested it. Other methods express future income streams in terms of net present value (NPV). Note that future increases in

Home Energy Ratings

Most states have programs called Home Energy Rating Systems (HERS), which can provide technical assistance and financial tools for home energy improvements. Local utility companies, state agencies, contractors, or private companies may run these programs. There are national standards that govern the activity of energy raters, and I recommend that you find a certified rater from an accredited program. You can find information on accredited HERS programs at www.natresnet.org.

An energy rating can provide the following benefits:

- **A professional assessment** of your energy situation and recommendations for cost-effective upgrades.

- **Special equipment** and diagnostic tools to test your house for air leakage, duct leakage, and other energy problems.

- **Referrals to contractors.** Note that some states and financing programs limit the ability of raters to recommend themselves as contractors to work on your house.

- **Access to preferred financing** for energy upgrades.

An energy rating may cost between $250 and $400, and some raters provide contract management services for an additional fee. In some cases, a local utility company or the lender (through project financing) may pay for part or all of the cost of the rating.

This Home Energy Rating report tells you how your home scores on a scale of 1 to 100, and it estimates the energy consumption in your house. (Photo © Kevin Kennefick.)

fuel prices make any conservation investment more cost-effective. Energy prices are generally rising, but how quickly is fairly unpredictable over time. Getting a truly objective picture of payback is more guesswork than most people may think.

It is also difficult to predict what the savings will be. Some people in the energy industry use simple rules; their accuracy is highly dependent on the experience of the user, the age and geometry of the home, the energy-improvement details, and the climate. Even professional energy analysts who use complex engineering calculations to estimate savings can make mistakes.

For the average do-it-yourselfer, it's not practical to account for all these variables. Generally, the approach I advocate is to plan for the available budget; to prioritize, given the information in this book and the specifics of your house; and to try to balance energy savings with a whole-house approach. For example, don't ignore fresh-air ventilation just because it doesn't result in energy savings. Also, contact your local utility companies, and find out whether they can offer technical or cash assistance for energy conservation. Electric and gas utilities often provide energy audits, and some even contribute money toward energy improvements for their customers' homes. Many community action agencies and other aid organizations run weatherization-assistance programs for income-qualified homeowners. Find out what is offered, and take advantage of any available help when planning your home weatherization project.

Opportunity savings

One other element to consider when thinking about payback is what I call *opportunity savings*. This is sort of the opposite of what economists call *opportunity cost*, which refers to the negative impact of benefits consumers may forego (for example, interest earnings on investments) when

If you are already replacing a boiler or furnace, the added cost to upgrade to a high-efficiency unit is relatively small; don't miss the opportunity.

they decide to spend money in a certain way. Opportunity savings is the reduction in cost of energy upgrades when you plan those upgrades to coincide with other necessary building maintenance or equipment replacement.

For example, adding a significant amount of insulation to an insulated cathedral ceiling may be expensive, but if the roof shingles need replacing anyway, that cost may be reduced substantially. Insulating exterior walls with extra layers of rigid-foam insulation is rarely cost-effective unless you are already re-siding your home anyway. When heating or cooling equipment breaks, the added cost to replace it with high-efficiency equipment is much less than it would be otherwise, because you are already paying someone to take away the old machine and put in a new one. Remodeling—one room or an entire house—provides an unparalleled opportunity for including energy upgrades. Try to take advantage of these opportunities when planning your energy retrofit projects.

Sealing

CHAPTER TWO
Air Leaks

Almost every house has a large number of hidden air leaks that rob it of heating and cooling energy. Although sealing these leaks is not the easiest job, it is probably the most cost-effective thing you can do to increase your home's energy efficiency. You'll want to do this before adding any insulation, since finding air leaks is much more difficult once extra insulation is installed. In addition to saving energy and making your home more comfortable, sealing air leaks also reduces ice dam problems and helps control moisture movement that can contribute to mold and structural damage.

People often think that windows and doors are the source of most air leakage in a house, but the largest leaks are almost always hidden in attics, basements, crawl spaces, and other unexpected places. This chapter will show you where to look for common air leaks and how to seal them properly.

PRO TIP

To create a comfortable environment quickly, find the big leaks first and seal them. Then look for smaller leaks.

WHAT CAN GO WRONG

Furnace ductwork located in an attic can be a major cause of ice damming on the roof. Warm air leaking from air handlers and ducts, as well as heat getting through uninsulated ducts via conduction, can melt snow on roof sheathing. As the snow melts, water runs toward the eaves, where it freezes again and creates a dam of ice that can push water underneath the shingles. All attic ductwork should be air-sealed and insulated to help prevent ice dams. (For more on insulating and sealing ducts, see chapter 6.)

TRADE SECRET

The biggest air leaks in the attic typically occur at places where the ceiling plane is interrupted. This can occur wherever there is a change in ceiling height or where there is a dropped soffit. Duct, plumbing, and chimney chases are also prime suspects when hunting down large avenues of air leakage (see the sidebar on p. 33.)

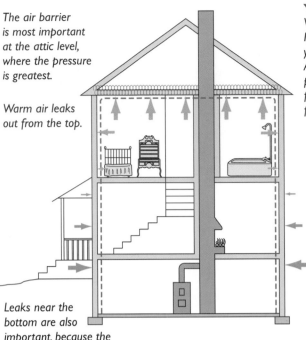

The air barrier is most important at the attic level, where the pressure is greatest.

Warm air leaks out from the top.

The pressure is less in the middle of the house.

Cold air seeps in from the bottom.

Leaks near the bottom are also important, because the pressure is greater there.

(Green dotted line = Air barrier)
(Gold arrows = Warm air)
(Gray arrows = Cold air)

Sealing the Attic Keeps You Warmer Down Below
Warm air pushes hardest to escape at the attic level. If you can keep the air from leaking out from the top, you will prevent cold air from seeping in from the bottom. A glass under water (see inset) demonstrates the same principle: If the lighter air is prevented from leaking out from the top, the heavier water will not be able to get in from the bottom.

The upside-down glass is a good air barrier, preventing exchange between the inside air and the outside water.

(Red arrows = Air inside glass)
(Blue arrows = Water outside glass)

Air-Sealing Priorities

With air-sealing, as with any job, it's useful to know what your priorities are. My strategy is first to always find the big leaks; sealing them makes the biggest difference in comfort levels. Then I look for the smaller leaks.

Air movement and leakage areas are not always intuitively clear, but the most important thing to remember is that air does not move through solid objects. Air leaks through connections and spaces between building materials.

First find the big leaks

Although it may sound obvious, the most important holes to seal are the largest ones. Not every house has every type of hole, but as you read through this chapter, you may recognize some of these big leaks—called *bypasses*—where indoor and outdoor air mix. I've actually seen bypasses that are big enough to crawl through!

Sealing just one of these large bypasses may make a greater difference than replacing every leaky, rattling window in your house. Most bypasses are small but still big enough for a cat to crawl through. When you head up into your attic to hunt for them, make sure your cat doesn't follow you, or he may get lost.

Seal the high and low leaks

Remember the stack effect, which pushes out air at the top and pulls in air from the bottom during the winter? (If not, see the sidebar on p. 11.) The greatest pressure differences are those at the highest and lowest points in your house, so your top priority should always be the attic. Doing a complete job of sealing leaks between the house and the attic will help prevent cold air from seeping in from the bottom of the house (see the drawing above).

When I sealed the leaks in my own attic, I was amazed at how much more comfortable my living room became. Sealing the attic also helps keep out moisture, reduce ice dams, and prevent hot air from leaking in from the attic and roof in the summer. Sealing leaks in an attic is hard work, but it is the best place to access the thermal boundary at the top of the house.

Once you have sealed the attic, the next priority is the basement, crawl space, or slab—the home's foundation. Sealing leaks there will help prevent cold air from coming in during the winter and cool air from escaping during the summer. Then you can spend some time with the sidewalls and smaller leaks in other parts of the house.

Attic Air-Sealing

When walking around your house, you're likely to see only the plaster or drywall. What you don't see are all the connections where building materials meet (or don't meet). The biggest leaks are hidden behind the walls, where you can't see them. The key to air-sealing an attic is to block off the large openings and seal the smaller ones as completely as possible—from one end of the attic to the other.

The best way to start is to walk through the top story of your house, noticing the location of all the partition walls. Also note the location of ceiling mounted light fixtures, changes in ceiling height, stairwells, hallways, closets, plumbing fixtures, and other features where leaks occur. Then put on your protective gear and head up into the attic to take a closer look.

Start with partition-wall top plates

It's best to be organized when working your way through an attic, so I usually start at one end and work my way to the other in an orderly fashion. This prevents me from getting mixed up or missing things, particularly when I have to move existing insulation out of the way as I go. And when

the attic is cramped (as it often is), it's better to limit your movements.

In most homes, it makes sense to start by first sealing the top plate along one gable end, then work your way down the center, load-bearing wall. Seal the top plate to the plaster on both sides, and seal any wiring holes with spray foam or caulking (see the top photo on p. 32). As the center wall meets intersecting partition walls,

Ice Dams

If you live in snow country, you've seen houses with ice dams clinging to the eaves. The most common solutions to ice dam problems are self-stick rubberized membranes and/or roof ventilation, such as soffit and ridge venting. Other fixes include mounting electric heater cables, shoveling snow off the eaves area, and installing strips of metal roofing near the eaves. Unfortunately, none of these fixes deals with the *cause* of the melting snow. Most ice dams form when heat loss into the attic warms the underside of the roof sheathing. This heat loss occurs when insulation is compressed or poorly installed near the eaves; it is also due to air leakage, one of the major causes of ice dams. To help prevent ice dams, thorough attic air-sealing should always be a top priority.

How Ice Dams Form
Air leakage is the biggest source of the heat loss that causes ice dams; poorly installed insulation comes in second. Ice dams form when snow melts and runs down the roof to the eaves, where it refreezes and backs up into the eaves or the house, causing damage.

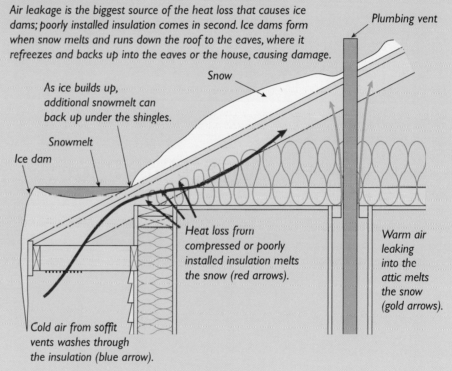

Plumbing vent

Snow

As ice builds up, additional snowmelt can back up under the shingles.

Snowmelt

Ice dam

Heat loss from compressed or poorly installed insulation melts the snow (red arrows).

Warm air leaking into the attic melts the snow (gold arrows).

Cold air from soffit vents washes through the insulation (blue arrow).

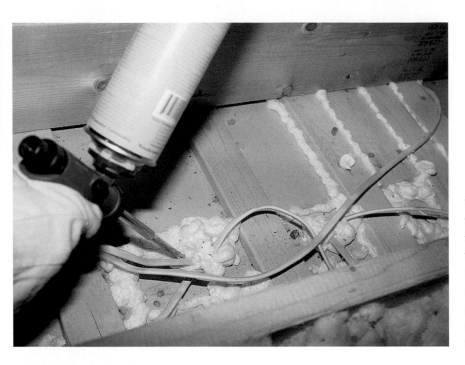

PRO TIP

Don't depend on a fiberglass insulation batt lying across an opening to act as an air barrier. Regardless of the type of facing, it will not stop air movement.

Sealing the gap between the top plates and the drywall or plaster with foam insulation is tedious, but it's a critical part of any attic air-sealing job. This is a good time to seal wiring holes as well.

TRADE SECRET

My first choice for attic air-sealing is a professional foam gun, which I use to apply low-expansion foam with precision control to a wide range of holes and gaps. Hardware-store foam cans are cheaper and smaller, but they are also awkward to use and difficult to control. Once you start a can, you must use it up quickly or throw it away. Caulking is inexpensive for small jobs, but it can't bridge gaps wider than 3/16 in., and most caulks don't stick well to dusty or dirty surfaces. Although useful in many places, caulk is not recommended for most sealing jobs in the attic.

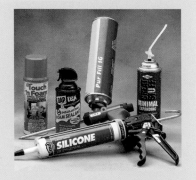

+ SAFETY FIRST

Attics can be nasty places—dusty, uncomfortable, and sometimes hazardous. At a minimum, always wear a tight-fitting, paper dust mask. I prefer a good-quality respirator (one with an HEPA® filter); it works better and is more comfortable because of the valves—you're not breathing right back into your nose. It's also a good idea to wear coveralls or other protective clothing and gloves.

You should always wear at least a dust mask when working in an attic. Although a HEPA (High Efficiency Particulate Arresting) respirator (left) is more expensive, it is also more effective. (Photo © Kevin Kennefick.)

follow each partition toward the eaves as far as you can reach. Be sure to find all the closet and hallway walls, which can be confusing.

As you pass each room, closet, or hallway, find any light fixtures that may be in the center of the ceiling and seal the electrical boxes (be careful not to squirt any foam inside the box). Treatments for recessed lighting fixtures are covered on p. 37. If your attic already has insulation in it, be sure to let the foam or caulking set before putting the insulation back in place.

Along the way, you will probably find some larger leaks, such as duct or plumbing chases, chimneys, and the like. Some of them can be sealed with foam or caulk as you go, but most will require some type of blocking. Make a note of what and where those larger leaks are, so that you can return with the right materials. Also make a note of any electrical junction boxes where wires are spliced. This will be useful later, particularly if you are going to add more insulation. If your house is insulated with fiberglass batts, you may be able to identify some leaks by the black or brown discoloration on the insulation above them, indicating that air has leaked through.

ATTIC AIR LEAKAGE DETAILS

The greatest attic air leaks typically occur where the ceiling is interrupted: at changes in ceiling height or dropped soffits (A) and at duct and chimney chases (C). Also, check openings around the attic hatch (B); at plumbing vent stacks (D), which vary in size; wiring holes (E); light-fixture boxes (F); and other electrical penetrations, which are small but fairly obvious. Less obvious is the crack that almost always occurs between the top plate and the plaster (G) when the framing lumber shrinks. You may also find walls with no top plate (especially gable-end walls) (H) or gaps of a few inches between the exterior wall's sheathing and the exterior wall's top plate (I).

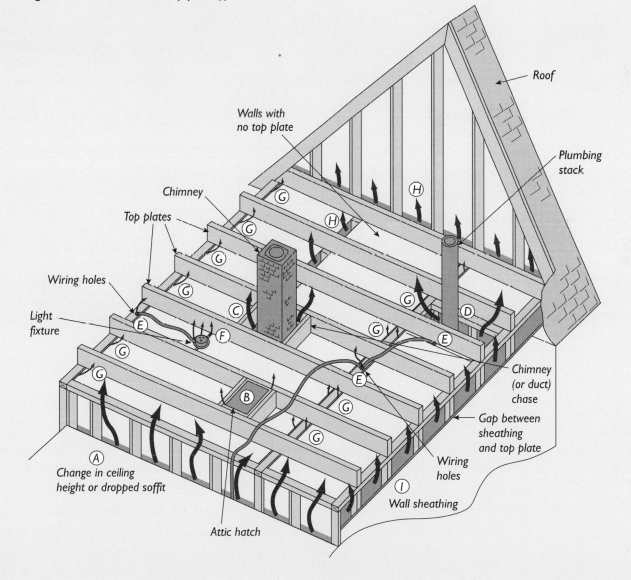

Roof

Walls with no top plate

Plumbing stack

Chimney

Top plates

Wiring holes

Light fixture

Chimney (or duct) chase

Gap between sheathing and top plate

Wiring holes

Change in ceiling height or dropped soffit

Wall sheathing

Attic hatch

PRO TIP

After cutting blocking material to fit and setting it in place, be sure to caulk or foam around all four sides for an airtight, permanent seal.

WHAT CAN GO WRONG

If your furnace is in a closet with an attic above it, there may be combustion air openings from the closet into the attic. Don't seal those openings; if the furnace can't get adequate combustion air, it can generate deadly carbon monoxide gas. Codes require high and low combustion air inlets, and the low one may be fed by a stud bay that opens into the attic, so be sure to leave that unobstructed as well.

WHAT CAN GO WRONG

Bathrooms and kitchens are the rooms where most moisture is produced, and each one usually has one or more penetrations in the ceiling for light fixtures, fans, and plumbing vent stacks. Pay particular attention to air-sealing the attic space above these rooms.

Some contemporary homes have cathedral ceilings flanking both sides of a small attic over the hallway. The studs framing the hallway walls often open into the attic. This one has a plumbing vent, too. Stuff some fiberglass into the opening before sealing it with foam.

One potentially leaky area is the gap between the housing on a bathroom ventilation fan and the ceiling drywall or plaster. However, don't seal this area up yet if you are planning to replace the fan as part of your ventilation strategy.

If there is enough clearance between the top plates of the eave walls and the roof sheathing, seal them between the rafter tails. This may be difficult to do. You may want to wait until you have finished the interior partitions and other leaks, then put back any existing insulation you have disturbed before tackling the exterior walls.

Through-framing into attics

Now that you are thoroughly familiar with your attic, you should have an idea of where the big holes are located. These holes typically occur wherever framing members, such as wall studs or floor joists, run from the conditioned space to the attic space. These bypasses require a little more thought to seal properly, and they are usually the largest and most important leaks.

The key to creating a good air barrier between the conditioned space and the attic is to make sure you bridge all the gaps and spaces between the plaster and the framing members that you *can't* see from the inside. Your job is to find every place where there is a space and then patch it. Follow the plane of the plaster or drywall along the ceiling and any connecting walls. This is sort of like playing a three-dimensional "connect-the-dots" game where someone has already filled in some of the links but left out a bunch of them. Wherever the ceiling plane is interrupted or changes levels, you need to supply the connecting link.

Keep in mind that insulation batts with paper or foil facing that lie across one of these openings do *not* constitute an air barrier. Insulation does not stop air! In fact, it's best to ignore the insulation when assessing and fixing an attic's air boundary.

Be aware of some other important issues. First, don't inadvertently seal combustion air openings (see What Can Go Wrong on p. 34). Second, use only noncombustible materials against a chimney. Third, recessed lights and some of the situations listed below require special attention.

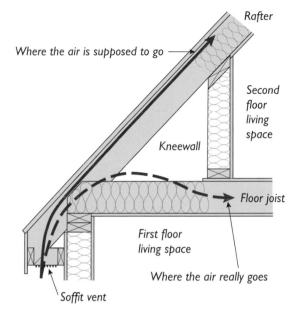

Airflow in a Cape-Style Kneewall
Floor framing that extends into a side attic, such as the kneewall spaces commonly found in Cape-style houses, and doesn't contain blocking is an open invitation for cold air to flow between the floor joists.

Cape kneewalls

One of the most common through-framing leaks is found in Cape-style houses. As you can see in the drawing above right, the floor joists between the first and second floors usually open into the kneewall attic area, allowing outdoor air to circulate between the floors. Even if there is no access into the kneewall space, it is worth cutting a temporary access through the wall to get in there and block off the joist bays. There are usually many joist bays; you can cut pieces of foam board to fit each one, making them slightly undersized, or cut long strips, notching for the joists. Wedge them into place, and foam or caulk all the gaps. If there is a subfloor in the kneewall area, you will have to pull up some boards to reach that area.

This type of open floor framing occurs in other places. For example, an ell or an addition with a lower roofline, or a finished room over a garage, may be built the same way, so they need the same type of draft-stopping. Also, floor framing between the first and second floors may open into a porch roof or the attic over a single-story addition or garage. Many of these areas are not normally accessible, so you may need to cut

+ SAFETY FIRST

When working in an attic, make sure you support your weight on the ceiling joists. Otherwise, you may fall right through the ceiling drywall or plaster. It's a good idea to bring a 4-ft. length of 1×12 or a small piece of plywood to help support your weight. Kneepads can also help with the awkward jungle-gym moves.

ATTIC BYPASSES

Although there are a number of variations, here are some common attic bypass situations:

A. Dropped, or soffited, ceilings are common in kitchens above cabinets, in bathrooms over showers or vanities, and sometimes over stairways. (See the photos below and at right).

B. Plumbing chases (see the bottom photo) can be much larger than the pipes that run through them.

C. Chimney chases often run all the way to the basement of a house (see the photo below).

(Photo © Kevin Kennefick.)

D. Tri-level homes often have wall studs that extend from the lower level into the attic; these stud spaces are bypasses, as are the large openings that may occur near the stairs. (see the photo at right).

E. Older homes and row houses with brick exteriors may have wood furring strips that extend from the attic to the basement. Walls above pocket doors may also have gaps, which open into the channel in which the door slides.

(Photo by Daniel Berube, © Conservation Services Group.)

an access through the drywall or plaster to get into them (see chapter 4); because the leaks are so large, it is worth the trouble. Seal these leaks the same way you would a cape kneewall—foam board or similar blocking material, foamed or caulked in place between the floor joists.

Recessed lights

Recessed "can" fixtures are often big air leaks. Most common styles are full of holes to vent the fixture so it doesn't get too hot. These lights act like little chimneys when they are on; the heat from the lamp drives warm indoor air into the attic even faster than it would move on its own. If you have a lot of them, the result can be an energy disaster.

The best approach is to replace them with air-tight fixtures that are rated for insulation contact, or "IC." Not all IC-rated fixtures are airtight; new construction energy codes in many states require airtight IC fixtures, so they are not difficult to find. Look for a label that says IC and another one that references the Model Energy Code, MEC, Washington State energy code, or ASTM™ E 283-91. An airtight retrofit kit is also available for existing recessed cans.

As an alternative to replacing your light fixtures, you can build airtight boxes over them using 1-in.-thick duct board. The box must fit between the joists and be large enough to dissipate the heat

emitted by the light. For typical 16-in. o.c. framing, for example, make a box that is about 14 in. square and 20 in. high.

Cut out the fiberglass in a "V" behind the corners, being careful not to break through the foil facing, and hold it together with aluminum tape. Make sure the surfaces are clean and free of dust. Clean off any insulation and dust around the recessed light, and cut openings for wires and mounting brackets. Set the box over the light, foam or caulk it in place, then seal the seams with duct mastic (see the photos on p. 39).

WHAT CAN GO WRONG

Recessed lights are very popular, but they can be a major source of air leakage and heat loss, particularly when they are located in a ceiling that has an attic space above. While the light shown here is insulation contact (IC) rated, it's not airtight, as you can see by the dark fiberglass around it.

TRADE SECRET

Polyethylene sheeting has a slippery surface, and it's difficult to get anything to stick reliably to it. Two products I've found that work well are 3M®'s builder's sealing tape and Tyvek® sheathing tape. Make sure that the poly is clean, then firmly press the tape in place with a rubbing motion. This tape also sticks to housewraps; plywood sheathing; and clean, dry framing lumber.

The floor framing behind this kneewall is open right into the attic. Unless these gaps are blocked, outdoor air will circulate between the first and second floors.

Other special situations

Attic air-sealing is complicated by the fact that there are so many types of houses, but there are some fairly common situations. First, don't miss hidden attic areas. Sometimes, an addition, dormer, or an ell may have a separate attic that you can't see, because the new roof was built right over the first roof. Cut an access in the roof sheathing once you know where the second attic area is. If you aren't sure, use a tape measure. The nail pattern may give you a hint as to where the valley rafters were nailed. Use a reciprocating saw

Sealing the floor bays with foam board is the air-sealing equivalent of closing up two to four large windows.

Use airtight recessed lights that are certified as meeting current codes. Look for a label that says IC and another one that references the Model Energy Code, MEC, Washington State energy code, or ASTM E 283-91. (Photo © Kevin Kennefick.)

and start low. Begin with a small hole, so you can see how far up you can safely cut, and make sure you don't cut into any rafters.

Suspended ceilings can hide tremendous leakage areas, particularly if they have attic spaces above. In older houses, such ceilings are often installed to hide deteriorating plaster. There may be large holes in the ceiling or high on the walls

Duct board, or rigid fiberglass with foil on one side, is available at HVAC supply houses. The foil facing is the air barrier and is noncombustible. Be careful not to cut through the foil.

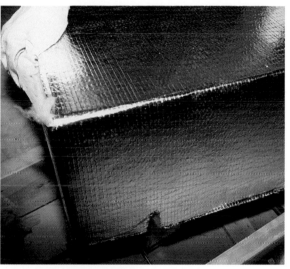

Make the box narrow enough to fit between the joists but large enough to dissipate the heat of the light it will cover. Notches at the bottom fit over the light's mounting brackets.

You can use foam to seal a light box to the ceiling, but be careful not to squirt it in under the box. Duct mastic is not combustible and should be used on the other seams. If the light is not IC rated, you must keep all materials at least 3 in. away from the light's housing.

PRO TIP

Suspended ceilings can hide tremendous leakage areas, particularly if they have attic spaces above them.

IN DETAIL

Cathedral ceilings are difficult to air-seal and add insulation to. But not all ceilings that appear to be cathedral are. If the slope of the ceiling is shallower than the slope of the roof, the roof was probably built with scissors trusses and is not a true cathedral ceiling. With these roofs, it may be possible—although difficult—to gain access through the attic to reach some of the larger leaks and install more insulation.

WHAT CAN GO WRONG

Acoustical tile ceilings present a potentially large air leakage problem. These 1-ft.-sq. tiles are basically made of compressed paper with tongue-and-groove edges, and the cracks between them leak like crazy. The only reasonable solution is to drywall right over them. If they are on sloped- or cathedral-ceiling areas where there is limited room to add insulation, this is the perfect opportunity to install some rigid-foam insulation prior to the drywall.

that are hidden by the dropped ceiling. If you are restoring or renovating the house, the best approach is to remove the suspended ceiling and repair the plaster, or install new drywall over the plaster. Or you can leave the suspended ceiling in place and patch the holes with drywall scraps. Cut pieces that are large enough to cover the holes. Be sure to drive plenty of screws into the lath or ceiling joists, and caulk around the edges to obtain a good seal.

Sometimes, a suspended ceiling hides open framing that is insulated with only faced fiberglass batts. This is a huge air leak; the insulation facing does not constitute an air barrier and, of course, the suspended ceiling does not either. There are two ways to deal with this problem. If you plan to do some remodeling, it's best to remove the suspended ceiling and install new drywall. If this is not an option, you can remove ceiling tiles and

staple an air barrier to the underside of the joists. Use 6-mil poly in cold climates or nonperforated housewrap in mixed or hot climates. This can be a tedious task, depending on how many hangers, wires, and other obstructions are in the way, because you must cut and fit the material around each penetration. Be sure to use good-quality tape for the seams. Also, tape the air barrier to the walls or top plates on all sides, and use a sealant (preferably foam) for all penetrations.

Another potential air-leakage disaster is a wooden tongue-and-groove ceiling. Whether the ceiling is flat or cathedral, if there is no air barrier behind the planks (which is typical), the hundreds of lineal feet of cracks in even a small room can add up to a big leak. If the aesthetic value of the wood ceiling is important, the only reliable way to add a good air barrier is to carefully remove the planks, create an air barrier, and reinstall the

The milled tongues and grooves on these boards provide a nice rustic look and blind nailing, but they are notoriously leaky. Always be sure to mount an air barrier on the inside before installing the boards. (Photo © Kevin Kennefick.)

Sometimes, small dormer attics may be hidden behind the roof sheathing; in this case, fortunately, the attic is visible and easily accessed.

wood. The air barrier can be taped polyethylene (in cold climates) or rigid polystyrene insulation (in any climate). The latter also adds R-value (see p. 64). If the wooden ceiling is not important to you, drywall (an effective air barrier) can be installed over the boards. This is also a good opportunity to add rigid insulation, especially if it's a cathedral ceiling with limited room for insulation in the rafter cavity.

Before you pull apart a wooden ceiling, check to see whether there is an air barrier behind it; if there is, you may have a much smaller problem on your hands. Poke around a bit at the cracks where the wood fits together; there are almost always some places where the tongue is cracked, the wood is split, or the ends don't butt tightly. Use a small flashlight to see past the wood. If you don't see polyethylene, drywall, or some other solid material (kraft paper or foil facing doesn't count), you probably have no air barrier.

Occasionally, air leaks occur in places that are virtually impossible to reach. If your house has a lot of cathedral-ceiling areas, you may have many plumbing vents and wiring holes that lead from partition-wall cavities up into the roof. These provide a path for warm, humid air to escape in winter and for hot attic air to leak into interior walls in summer. Unless you are planning to gut those partitions in a remodel, your best two options involve dense-packed cellulose insulation. The first option is to dense-pack from indoors the partition walls near the roof, which is messy but very effective (see p. 80). The second option is to dense-pack the roof cavity from outdoors; this adds R-value to the roof, but it may be difficult to do if the roof cavities are already full of batt insulation (see p. 74).

Other hard-to-reach areas include gambrel and mansard roofs. Structurally, they are very similar to the cape kneewalls (see p. 35), but the kneewall area is far too narrow to access. Small eyebrow

The high, narrow kneewall areas in gambrel and mansard roofs can be a big source of air leakage, and they are often difficult to seal.

Small roofs like this one can hide big air leaks; they often have no wall sheathing behind them.

roofs, or overhangs in the middle of two-story walls, can also be a problem. It may be possible to access the area from the exterior by removing the soffit; if the space is small, you may also be able to fill it with dense-packed cellulose.

IN DETAIL

Stepped foundation walls are often built on hillsides in cold climates. The vertical parts of the steps are often particularly leaky. These can be sealed from inside or out with silicone caulking. Stuff in some fiberglass as a backing, or use spray foam (indoors) if the gap is large.

The vertical joints where foundation walls are stepped often leak badly. (Photo © Conservation Services Group.)

Basement/Crawl Space Air-Sealing

After the attic, the basement or crawl space is the next most important area to seal for several reasons. Like the top of a home, the bottom typically has the largest air pressure pushing air in or out of the house, so sealing those leaks results in larger energy savings. Second, though often smaller than attic leaks, basement and crawl space leaks tend to be larger than those in exterior walls. More important, in most climates, air leaks *in* from the bottom much of the year—particularly in cool or cold weather. This leaking air can carry radon gas, mold spores, gases from pesticide treatments, water vapor, and any other subsoil nasties that may become airborne. Sealing leaks at the lowest level of your home helps prevent these undesirable elements from entering your home. Finally, most pipe-freezing problems result from cold air leaking in around the sills, where the pipes are often located.

Basement walls

As I pointed out in chapter 1, if you have a concrete foundation wall, it is probably easiest to create a good air barrier between the basement and the outdoors by sealing the walls. This is true even if you intend to insulate the floor over the basement. There are four common leakage areas

+ SAFETY FIRST

Attached garages can be a source of deadly carbon monoxide and other toxic fumes, as well as cold air, so it is very important to seal the boundary between the house and the garage. Make sure that all joist spaces over garage walls are blocked and sealed. If drywall is in the way, try dense-pack cellulose in the garage ceiling (see pp. 71–74).

All service penetrations in a basement should be sealed with caulking (if the gap is small) or foam (if the gap is large).

in basement walls: service penetrations, stepped-wall transitions, bulkhead doors, and the sill/band joist area.

Service penetrations. Every home has basic service penetrations, including (at a minimum) those for electricity, telephone, and plumbing. Fuel lines and cable-TV services are also common. Often, these penetrations are made in the band-joist area, also called the box sill or ribbon joist in conventionally framed houses (in older homes, this may be one large sill beam). Sometimes, penetrations come through the foundation (especially plumbing drainpipes, which are always below grade). Seal all penetrations from the inside, the outside, or both with caulking or foam. Any below-grade penetrations must be sealed from the inside. And don't assume that air can't leak in from underground; soil is often surprisingly porous to air movement.

If other joists are in the way, services that run through the band joist may be difficult to reach from the inside, so you may need to seal them from the outside. If your basement is finished, the

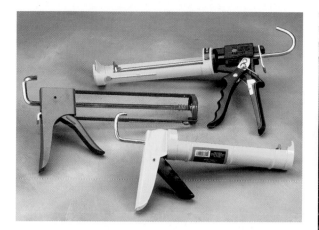

Here are three grades of caulking guns. From bottom to top, they sell for about $4, $8, and $20. You get what you pay for—stay away from the $4 guns. (Photo © Kevin Kennefick.)

Although a typical steel bulkhead basement door sheds water, it barely slows cold air from leaking inside.

Be sure to seal between the door frame and the foundation wall. Remember to use only treated wood in contact with concrete.

exterior may be the only area to which you have access. Caulk or seal these openings, being careful to seal all the way around.

Bulkhead doors. Another common source of basement leakage is the bulkhead door. Bulkheads are designed to keep out rain but not to stop air. If your basement is unfinished, the best way to deal with this is to install a new exterior door at the foundation wall inside the bulkhead. Use treated wood where the door contacts the foundation, and be sure to tightly seal between the framing around the door and the concrete. If your basement is fully or partially finished and already has a door inside the bulkhead, you may still have a large air leak at the top and sides. Be sure to put solid blocking in the gap between the door frame and the foundation, then caulk around all the edges.

Sills and band joists. When I started doing blower-door testing in 1990, I didn't expect to find a lot of air leaking in from the sills, particularly in relatively recently built houses. You may think, as I did, that the massive weight of a house would flatten out the framing in that area. Was I ever mistaken! Even with all that weight, wood can really have a mind of its own. And, of course, the tops of foundation walls are often far from flat.

An insulated, weatherstripped door is essential inside any bulkhead basement opening.

+ SAFETY FIRST

Although air-sealing a home can theoretically increase radon levels, it is unlikely. Sealing leaks and slowing the stack effect is more likely to *reduce* the amount of soil gas—including radon—that is pulled into the house from underground. The *only* way to tell whether you have dangerous radon levels is to test your home. Because of the potential health risks, it is a good idea to test for radon before and after air-sealing. If elevated radon levels are confirmed by at least two tests, find a certified professional to install a mitigation system.

PRO TIP

If you want to use your basement as living space, you should plan to completely air-seal and insulate the exterior basement walls.

WHAT CAN GO WRONG

When air-sealing a basement, be careful not to interfere with combustion air required by the furnace, boiler, or hot water heater. All combustion equipment needs enough air to provide oxygen for the fire, and sealing a house can sometimes interfere with that process. If the equipment is not working properly, it can lead to the production of deadly carbon monoxide.

WHAT CAN GO WRONG

In some cases, it's possible to seal sills from outside by caulking the space between the bottom edge of the exterior sheathing and the foundation wall. In some places, there may be gaps so large that you need to fill them with foam instead of caulk. Trim off the extra foam so you don't create any ledges that can trap water running down the siding and direct it inside.

Blower-Door Testing

Air-sealing is a job that requires much more labor than material, which often suggests a do-it-yourself approach. However, air-sealing does require attention to detail and (in many homes) a willingness to squeeze into difficult places. If these qualities don't describe you, it may be worth hiring a building performance professional. Experienced professionals use a blower door to help find air leaks and measure the tightness of the building envelope. The blower-door fan blows air into (or out of) the house, measuring how well the building envelope contains pressure. This can be very handy, especially in a house with complex air leakage paths.

You can make your own blower door if you can obtain a powerful fan (a regular box fan won't work). You won't be able to measure the air leakage, but you can use it to feel the air leaks. Set the fan to blow air *out,* and you will be able to feel air leaking *in* from the basement or from elsewhere inside the house. If you do this, be sure to set any combustion appliances to pilot, so that they can't turn on (don't forget the water heater). If you have, or suspect, asbestos on pipes or ducts, do not use this method until it is properly removed.

A blower door is used to measure how airtight a house is. It's also useful in helping identify where the air leaks are.

Note the gap between the sill and the band joist. Even after this building is finished and the frame settles, there will still be a big leak here.

Sealing the band joist (in this case, with foam-board blocks) from the inside is the most effective approach... if you can reach it. (Photo © Kevin Kennefick.)

The gaps may be small, but spread around the perimeter of a home, they really add up. Even recently built homes that have a foam sill sealer between the sill and the concrete may leak a lot of cold air at that location.

There are usually three or four framing members that are stacked on top of each other between the foundation wall and the first floor's subfloor, and each of those junctions can leak. You can seal this area from the inside or from the outside; if you have access, you may want to do both.

Sealing the band joist from the inside, when done properly, yields the best results, but it may be difficult to reach. To do this, cut blocks of rigid-foam board (I recommend extruded polystyrene). A 2-in. thickness provides a good amount of insulation, as well as air-leakage control. Cut the blocks to fit snugly in height, but leave them about ½ in. narrower than the joist spacing. Wedge them into place, as close as possible to the band joist, then foam or caulk them on all four sides. Be sure to seal the area between each block at the bottom, where the joist rests on the sill. You can do the same thing on the gable ends of the house, using long strips of foam board that are sealed on all four sides.

Sealing the floor deck

Although it is typically more difficult than sealing foundation walls, sealing the floor deck between the basement and the first floor may make sense. If you want to use the basement as living space, it's almost always better and easier to insulate and seal the exterior basement walls. But if the basement is not finished, sealing the floor may be the best option, especially if your house has a fieldstone foundation, which may be impossible to seal well.

Even if the exterior basement walls are sealed and insulated, sealing the floor deck slows the path

of air leaking into the main part of the house. It is also beneficial, particularly if the basement is damp or musty, to isolate it from the living space. If you plan to insulate the floor, seal it first. Note that sealing the floor deck can be very difficult if you have a finished-plaster or drywall ceiling in the basement. In this case, focus your efforts on the sill and the exterior foundation walls.

Most floors have many service penetrations, which make them difficult to seal well.

This tub trap is a big air leak from the basement into the house. Note that the duct chase (another big air leak) in the lower right corner should also be sealed.

✔ According to Code

Code (and common sense) says not to use foam or other combustible materials around active chimneys or heating-equipment vent pipes. These penetrations can be sealed with high-temperature caulking; use metal flashing or duct board if you have large spaces to fill. Also, avoid using foam around heating pipes, particularly if you have steam heat.

PRO TIP

For the best results, include a crawl space in the conditioned space by sealing and insulating the exterior walls— just like a basement.

TRADE SECRET

I often use acoustical sealant when I'm installing poly in a crawl space, particularly to seal it to the walls. While it is messy to work with, it sticks well to poly sheeting and works even better than high-quality tape. It's also a good choice when the work area is dusty, because I've found that it sticks fairly well even in those marginal conditions.

IN DETAIL

If you have an older house with a plank subfloor instead of a plywood subfloor, air-sealing the floor can become quite complex. In addition to the obvious holes, be sure to fill the gaps between the plank boards, as well as the penetrations. You must also seal any gaps underneath the cabinets and anywhere else that lacks a finished floor.

Even better than regular poly are products such as Tu-tuf, Tenoarm, and Tuff-poly. These sheets are thinner but much stronger and more puncture resistant than regular polyethylene. (Tu-tuf and similar products are available from Energy Federation, Shelter Supply, and other dealers that sell energy-efficient building products; see Resources on p. 194). (Photo © Kevin Kennefick.)

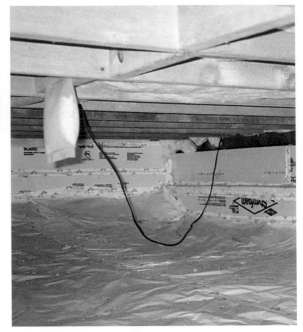

The insulation on these crawl space walls was carefully sealed to the vapor barrier on the floor, creating a warm, dry space. (Photo by Bruce Harley, © Conservation Services Group.)

The basic idea behind floor air-sealing is the same as attic air-sealing: to create an uninterrupted air barrier between levels. Typically, this is done at the subfloor. First-floor decks have many holes in the subfloor for plumbing drains, supply piping, wiring, ducts, and chimney chases. Bathtubs and showers often have large cutouts underneath the drain trap. Those holes require a

---

✓ According to Code

Most codes require crawl space vents, which are supposed to allow moisture to escape. But these vents bring in cold air in winter; they don't really mitigate the moisture loads from the ground; and, in warm, humid weather, they actually introduce moisture that can condense on cool framing members and contribute to mold and rot. For years, building scientists have been advocating sealed, insulated crawl spaces, and some building codes are beginning to show signs of allowing this approach.

---

material that can span large spaces. The materials listed for attic bypasses will work. Also, look for openings or penetrations under kitchen and bathroom cabinets and built-in furniture.

Crawl spaces

Crawl spaces are nothing more than short basements, usually just deep enough for the footings to be below the frost line. Unlike basements, they often have exposed dirt floors. Building code requirements for vapor retarders are typically inadequate, even when they are followed properly. Crawl spaces can be pretty nasty places; they often have footing drainage that is inadequate. Building codes that require these spaces be vented to the outdoors may make matters worse.

The best treatment for a crawl space is to include it in the conditioned space by sealing and insulating the exterior walls, just like a basement. Of course, any standing water must first be eliminated. Install a sump pump if necessary. Next, where code permits, existing crawl space vents should be closed; I recommend cutting a piece of 2-in.-thick polystyrene to fit in the vent from inside the crawl space, then caulking it in place.

Crawl spaces should have a superbly sealed vapor retarder. The earth is such a large source of moisture and other unwanted substances that you can't expect a few pieces of poly scattered on the floor to do a good job. Use full sheets of 6-mil polyethylene or, better yet, one of the varieties of cross-laminated poly that are now on the market. This must be laid across the entire floor, with overlaps of 12 in. to 24 in., and taped at the seams with a good-quality tape. Seal around any penetrations, such as water pipes or support piers, with spray foam or acoustical sealant.

Next, insulate the crawl space walls with 2-in. extruded polystyrene, tape or seal every joint, and then seal the vapor retarder to the insulation around the perimeter. In this case, the insulation around the walls is your primary air barrier, so be sure to caulk or seal the polystyrene insulation to the sill and seal the band joist carefully, as described on pp. 43–45.

Slab-on-grade

If your home (or part of your home) has no basement or crawl space, it is probably a concrete slab-on-grade. Those homes are somewhat simpler to seal because there are fewer connections among building materials at the foundation. Your primary job with slab-on-grade construction is to caulk or otherwise seal the exterior walls where the house framing meets the slab. Caulk any gaps between the baseboard and the floor from the inside. With carpeting, this may be more complicated. If you pull up the edge of the carpet, you may have a tough time embedding it neatly in the tack strip around the perimeter of the room. You can also caulk the exterior, where the siding or sheathing meets the slab, but that may be difficult if the slab is very close to the ground.

Sidewall Air-Sealing

Exterior walls are not typically the leakiest parts of a house. Leaks occur in walls where services enter the home, where the framing of the house makes transitions, around rough openings for windows, and through and around window sashes. (Windows will be covered in more detail in chapter 5.)

Service penetrations

Sealing cable, wiring, plumbing, and telephone service penetrations is fairly easy. Such openings are usually accessible from the exterior and are often small because some effort is made to weatherproof them during installation. I usually use caulking to seal any gaps where services enter through the siding.

Caulk for Air-Sealing

I generally use two types of caulk: 100% pure silicone and siliconized acrylic latex. My preference is pure silicone caulk. Although it's more expensive and harder to clean, pure silicone is much more adhesive, more flexible, and less prone to shrinkage as it cures. It's a must anywhere you are trying to seal wood, metal, or concrete to one another, because the differential movement of these materials will tear acrylic caulks apart. It can safely be used on gaps up to about 1/4 in. wide; wider gaps require you to stuff in some spongy material or insulation as a backing. Pure silicone is also much more durable, so it's better for exterior applications that aren't too visible; however, it is not paintable. Once it cures, almost nothing will stick to its slick surface. Acrylic can be painted easily, so I generally reserve it for interior spaces and conspicuous exterior areas. However, because it shrinks more, don't use acrylic on any gap or crack wider than 3/16 in. unless you install backing.

Both kinds of caulk are available in a number of different colors; try some in an inconspicuous place and wait until it cures to check the match (especially browns!). And stay away from clear acrylics. They come out white, then dry clear, but the clear material has a shiny surface that can be quite noticeable. Clear acrylics also contain fewer solids than pigmented acrylic caulks do, so they shrink more. Be sure to store any type of caulking at room temperature; if it gets too cold, it can be very difficult to squeeze out, and it may not cure properly.

IN DETAIL

Pull-down attic stairs are especially difficult to insulate and seal. You can buy a prefabricated kit like this Therma-dome, which is made of 1½-in.-thick foil-faced insulation, or you can make one yourself. Make sure you have a nice, flat deck around the stairway opening on which the box can sit (the deck needs to be only 1 ft. wide), and caulk the deck to the rough opening for a good seal.

This pull-down stair kit comes with adhesive, weatherstripping, aluminum tape for the edges, and hook-and-loop tabs on each end to tie it down tightly.

TRADE SECRET

If you are using a nail-in type of weatherstrip, leave the nails protruding slightly until after you check that the door operates normally. This way, you can adjust the fit of the weatherstrip, if necessary.

This cantilever can be a source of cold-air leaks; be sure to caulk around it carefully.

Transitions in exterior wall framing

One common example of a wall transition is a cantilevered floor, typically an overhang of 1 ft. to 3 ft. that is common on raised ranches and colonial-style homes. Often, the plywood soffit at the bottom of the overhang is not sealed tightly, and air can leak through these gaps, which are easy to caulk. If the cantilever is finished with aluminum or vinyl soffit material, the leakage is even worse. I've seen cantilevers finished with perforated vinyl and no air barrier at all! In that case, you should carefully remove the soffit and add a solid material, such as plywood. Caulk around all four edges, and replace the vinyl or aluminum soffit, if you wish.

Other places where walls make transitions can be leaky, but they often take the form of a roof or an attic interrupting a vertical wall. Most of those cases are covered under Attic Air-Sealing on pp. 31–41.

Most weatherstripping available at hardware stores is not worth the packaging it comes in. Here, from left to right, are some high-quality ones. V-seal® can be used for doors and windows. Silicone rubber bulb, which stays flexible and soft at low temperatures, works well for doors with a narrow clearance. My personal favorite is the vinyl-covered V-section (Q-lon is one brand name). It is available without backing for stapling onto unfinished areas, such as attic hatches, and with aluminum or wooden backing for stapling onto finished areas. (Photo © Kevin Kennefick.)

Weatherstripping Doors and Hatches

Most modern doors and windows have good weatherstripping built in, but older ones usually don't. In addition, many homes have at least one less-finished, or even makeshift, door or hatchway as part of the thermal envelope. This section discusses replacing or repairing weatherstripping on hinged doors, access panels, and attic hatches. Window weatherstripping is covered in more detail in chapter 5.

Weatherstripping a door

To seal any standard swinging exterior door, install a flexible, spongy weatherstrip on the top and both sides. First, remove old weatherstrip that may be in the way. Take note of any storm-door hardware that may need to be moved out of the way while you work. Start with the top piece, cutting it to fit into the corners of the doorstops. If you are using one with a wooden backing strip, prestart a few

4-penny finish nails in the wood strip. Press the piece against the door so that the spongy side is slightly compressed, then nail or screw it in place. Then cut the side strips to length. Install those pieces the same way. Starting at the top, hold a piece in place so the spongy part is slightly compressed against the door, then drive a nail or screw. Work your way down until you reach the bottom. The trick is to compress the spongy part enough to ensure that there will be contact year-round, as the door shrinks and swells, but not so much that it interferes with the door's closing and latching. If the door doesn't latch properly, you may need to move back the weatherstrip or adjust the door's strike plate.

If you have an insulated steel door with magnetic weatherstripping that is falling apart, you may be able to replace it with unbacked vinyl-covered V-section strips. Those strips often fit in the same rabbeted groove in which the magnetic strips were mounted.

Door sweeps

For a crack at the bottom of a door, a door sweep may be just the thing. If you plan to install weatherstripping on the sides of the door opening, be sure to do so first. Buy a heavy-duty door sweep that will sit flat against the door and last for a while. Cut it to length (if it will be installed on the side of the door with the stops, cut it about ⅛ in. short, so it doesn't get jammed between the stops). Hold it in place, again with just enough pressure to make sure it will always be in contact with the threshold, and screw it in place.

If your door has a low threshold, or if there's a thick rug or an irregular floor in front of it, a flat sweep will scrape and prevent the door from working. In that situation, use a hinged sweep, which flips down snugly when the door is closed. A few pointers: Be sure to cut the sweep ⅛ in. shorter than the doorstops, so the sweep doesn't bind.

Pull out the flexible rubber strip, and use a hacksaw to cut the sweep to length on the end that will be at the hinge side of the door. Reinsert the strip, then cut it to length with a utility knife. Next, squeeze the ends of the aluminum track to pinch the rubber strip in place. I recommend predrilling a hole for the stop button, because the doorstop is likely to split. Open and close the door a few times to make sure everything works properly.

Weatherstripping an attic or a crawl space hatch

Attic hatches are often quite leaky, and it can be difficult to seal them well. I recommend using vinyl-faced weatherstripping with an aluminum carrier strip. Usually, a kit designed for a door will do at least one access hatch, sometimes two, depending on the size of the hatch(es). Cut the pieces with a pair of sharp tinsnips and screw them in place. Generally, the weatherstripping should be attached to the jamb or trim around the opening; in some cases, it may be easier to attach it directly to the door. If the hatch door is too lightweight or too warped to make a good seal, replace it with ⅝-in. A/C plywood or another sturdy flat material. Either way, you may need to add a pair of eye hooks or a barrel bolt to keep the hatch snug against the weatherstripping. Don't forget to insulate the door with rigid foam insulation.

This door sweep lifts out of the way when you open the door, riding clear of carpets and uneven floors.

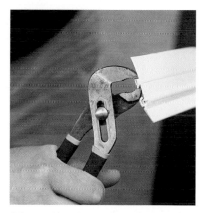

After trimming a door sweep to size, crimp the ends to hold the rubber strip in place.

A regular door sweep works well if the door has a prominent threshold or the floor slopes away from the door.

Ventilation

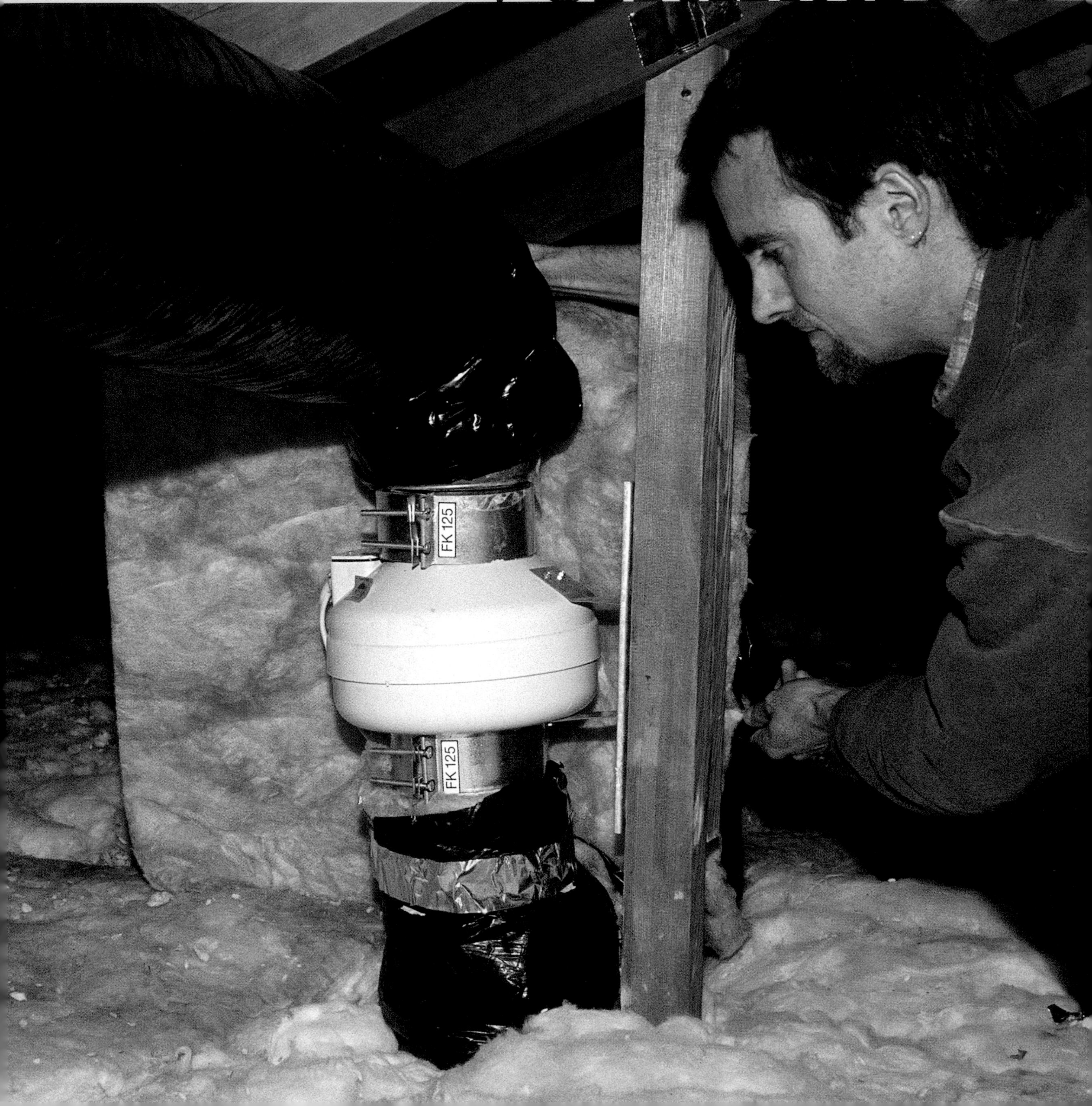

CHAPTER THREE
Systems

Ventilation systems are important to a healthy, comfortable indoor environment. After sealing a house as tightly as you reasonably can, I strongly recommend installing a simple mechanical ventilation system to provide controlled air exchange. This system should include local spot ventilation in bathrooms and kitchens, as well as some type of automatic, full-time background ventilation. The background ventilation may be easily and inexpensively integrated with bathroom exhaust fans or with a heating or cooling system. More comprehensive, whole-house ventilation systems are the best choice for controlling air exchange and filtration, but they can be considerably more expensive. This chapter will outline the basic options for house ventilation systems and describe how they are installed.

51

WHAT CAN GO WRONG

In hot, humid climates, ventilating a house with outdoor air may actually introduce moisture. Although fresh-air ventilation is still important, including spot-ventilation in the kitchen and bathrooms to exhaust moisture, ventilation rates should be lower. It is also important to supplement ventilation with adequate dehumidification, through air-conditioning or other mechanical systems.

IN DETAIL

A whole-house fan, typically installed to exhaust a large volume of air into the attic, is often effective at offsetting air-conditioning needs in the summer, but it is too large and powerful to provide a continuous background source of fresh air.

Do I Need a Ventilation System?

Why make a house tight, and then spend money to ventilate it? Doesn't it make more sense to just leave it a little bit leaky? The short answer is, "No." A leaky house experiences haphazard ventilation that may or may not be appropriate or adequate. A good ventilation system, on the other hand, allows you to control the introduction of fresh air into a home.

Fresh-air ventilation can help dilute pollutants in the home, manage moisture, and improve air quality. It is not something you install to compensate for a tight house. It should be installed in every house, and the house must be tight—that is, properly air-sealed and insulated—before ventilation can work properly. A tight building envelope is an essential part of a ventilation system; without it, you have no control over the air-exchange rate.

Interior moisture problems, such as excessive window condensation, mildew growth, or peeling paint, may indicate that you need a fresh-air ventilation system. (Photo © Mark Rosenbaum.)

"A house has to breathe…"

One of the wonderful qualities of the human respiratory system is that its level of activity adjusts to your needs. When you are active, you breathe quickly to increase the incoming oxygen flow; when you are at rest, your breathing slows. If a ventilation system acts as the lungs of a house,

Dehumidifiers

If you live in a region that has mild, rainy winters, such as the Pacific Northwest, or in a hot, humid climate, air exchange will not reduce the relative humidity in the house for much of the year. You should consider using a high-efficiency dehumidifier, either integrated with the supply airstream of your ventilation equipment or used as a stand-alone unit. The high-capacity, ultra-efficient dehumidifier shown here is available in a stand-alone model or a standard model that connects to a central ventilation system for automatic dehumidification. If you need a dehumidifier for indoor humidity control, choose one that's Energy Star rated.

(Photo courtesy Therma-Stor Products, Madison, WI.)

then it too needs to be capable of adjusting its airflow rate, depending on your family's ventilation needs. A good fresh-air ventilation system allows you to change the ventilation schedule, or vary the rate of airflow, so that you can add extra ventilation when the house is full of people or turn it off completely when nobody is home.

As for operating costs, in most climates a very tight home with mechanical ventilation is less expensive to operate than a leaky house. One big advantage of ventilation control is that you can set the air-exchange rate independent of outdoor conditions. If you leave ventilation to random air leaks, you get too much airflow when it's cold and windy outside (and fuel costs more) and not enough when the weather is mild. Of course, controlling moisture sources, such as a crawl space floor, or improperly vented combustion equipment should be dealt with first.

Ventilation systems typically provide better indoor air quality, while reducing the need for

A Home Ventilating Institute (HVI) sticker shows a fan's airflow rating in cubic feet per minute (cfm) and its sound level in sones. (Photo © Susan Kahn.)

building maintenance. Some of the indications that you may need ventilation include mold, mildew, or window condensation in your home. A stuffy-smelling house, cooking odors that linger for hours, and chronically peeling paint may also indicate high indoor humidity levels. If your house has any of these symptoms, fresh air ventilation is likely to help.

✔ According to Code

Code requirements for bathroom ventilation are usually satisfied by an operable window, but most people simply don't like to open bathroom windows in the winter. Every bathroom should have an exhaust fan of at least 50 cfm. Range hoods rated for at least 250 cfm are also highly recommended, but they are not usually required by code (though that may be changing). Bathroom and kitchen exhaust fans should always vent directly outdoors.

Kitchen exhaust hoods are more effective at a lower airflow than the popular downdraft exhausts are. Due to the grease and fire hazard, make sure the equipment and ductwork is rated for range applications. (Photo courtesy Viking.)

PRO TIP

To improve air quality, source reduction should always precede ventilation.

IN DETAIL

If you can vent an exhaust fan horizontally through a wall, a standard 4-in. or 6-in. exhaust hood with a flapper will work fine. However, to avoid long duct runs that drastically reduce airflow, it's sometimes necessary to vent it vertically through the roof. In that case, you'll need a roof jack as shown below. Be sure to follow the installation instructions carefully and make sure that the flashing tucks under the roofing shingles to avoid leaks.

Several manufacturers make bathroom fans that are quiet and long lasting and use very low power. This Panasonic WhisperCeiling is one of my favorites because it is so quiet (a 70-cfm model is 0.9 sones; a 50-cfm model is 0.5 sones). (Photo courtesy Panasonic.)

Types of ventilation systems

A background ventilation system is designed to provide a minimum amount of fresh outdoor air to the living space year-round. This type of system runs either full-time at an adjustable rate or on a schedule that you set according to your needs. Two simple, inexpensive background ventilation systems I have used successfully are the bath-fan ventilation system and the return-air ventilation system. The installation for these systems is covered on pp. 55–59. Types of whole-house ventilation systems include central exhaust systems and heat-recovery ventilation (HRV) systems, which are more complex, more effective, and more expensive.

Every house should also have spot ventilation: an exhaust fan in each bathroom and a range

+ SAFETY FIRST

Don't attempt to do the wiring for a new fan or controller unless you understand the safety and code requirements, and always turn off the appropriate circuit breakers before working on electrical circuits. This part of the job is best left to an electrician.

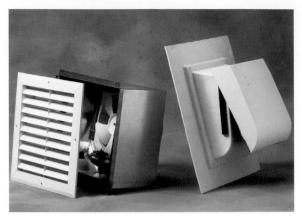

One advantage of a through-wall fan is that you don't need to install ductwork (with its associated drop in airflow). This model, the Preventilator from Tamarack Technologies, has a motorized cover that seals tightly when it's turned off. Both Fantech and Panasonic also make through-wall fans. (Photo © Kevin Kennefick.)

hood in the kitchen. The range hood is particularly important with a gas range or oven, which may produce carbon monoxide as well as water vapor. The warm, moist air exhausted from kitchens and bathrooms must be vented to the outside, not into an attic or back into the room.

Simple Ventilation Systems

The simplest type of background ventilation system is an exhaust-only, or supply-only, ventilation fan. An exhaust-only system draws outdoor air inside through small cracks and gaps that already exist, even in a tightly sealed house. I have seen it used successfully in hundreds of new homes—some of which are extremely tight—as well as retrofitted to solve moisture problems.

Bath-fan system

To set up a bath-fan background ventilation system, first choose a bathroom—the one that is either most used or most centrally located—in which to set up a controlled fan. If you need to replace an existing fan, choose a bathroom with an accessible attic area above. You may have an exhaust fan already, but it's unlikely that it will meet the requirements: it must be quiet, moderately powerful, and rated for continuous operation.

Most fans are rated for noise and airflow by the Home Ventilating Institute (HVI). Noise is rated in sones—the higher the sone rating, the more noise it makes. I think that fans with sone ratings of greater than 1.5 are too noisy for this applica-

tion; if you can, choose a fan rated at 1.0 or less. For most homes, choose a fan rated between 70 and 120 cubic feet per minute (cfm). In hot, humid climates, lower airflows of 50 cfm to 90 cfm may be adequate.

To do its job properly, a fan must be vented to the outside and have a duct run that is as short and direct as possible. If you can't reach an exterior wall or gable end within about 10 ft., you may be able to put in an elbow and vent it straight

Ventilation Ductwork

Small home ventilation fans are typically rated very optimistically for airflow. You may think that as long as a fan can blow air into a duct, air must come out at the other end. But if there's too much friction—caused by rough inner surfaces, too many elbows and bends, or a run that is too long—the fan can just spin in place, and virtually no air will come out.

What to do? First, stay away from flex duct. Whether it's inexpensive 4-in.-dia. vinyl dryer hose or 6-in.-dia. or larger insulated duct, flex duct is cheap, fast, and easy to use, and it fits easily in tight spaces. But there's a heavy price for convenience: All the coils and rough surfaces add resistance and slow the airflow. If you have a long run of flex duct and a few sharp bends, you can assume, at best, 50% of a fan's rated cfm—and you may get nothing at all!

Instead, use smooth, rigid-metal ducts whenever possible. Plan your ducts to keep the runs short, and keep the elbows and fittings to a minimum. With this approach, you can expect to get about 15% to 20% less than the fan's rated airflow. For a complex, central ventilation system, I recommend hiring an HVAC contractor who knows how to design ductwork for proper airflow, using the "equivalent length" method.

Flex duct, though easy to install, can seriously reduce airflow in residential ventilation equipment. (Photo by Scott Phillips, courtesy *Fine Homebuilding* magazine, © The Taunton Press.)

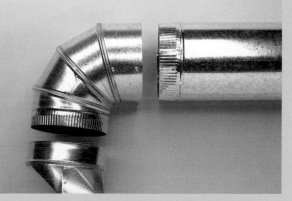

Rigid-metal ducts provide higher airflow with lower friction and give you the maximum performance from your fan. (Photo by Scott Phillips, courtesy *Fine Homebuilding* magazine, © The Taunton Press.)

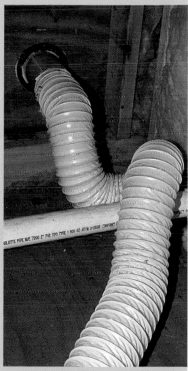

A contorted, vinyl flex hose is fairly typical. Not only do installations like this one fail to provide the required airflow, but low spots can trap water in cold weather or even fill with ice, which completely stops airflow. Flexible aluminum is not much better; fans should be ducted with smooth, rigid metal (or PVC pipe) whenever possible.

TRADE SECRET

Some ventilation experts have suggested the use of *fresh air inlets*, which are essentially intentional holes in the building envelope. However, research (and experience) has shown that these inlets often don't work as intended—air is just as likely to go out as to come in. Save your money: These inlets are really not necessary in any but the very tightest single-story house.

WHAT CAN GO WRONG

One drawback of the simple exhaust ventilation system is that there is no control over *where* the makeup air comes from. Although it is generally dispersed throughout a building, makeup air may derive from leaks in basements, garages, or other places with pollutant sources. Remember: Source reduction is the first step toward improving indoor air quality.

One common type of central exhaust fan is the in-line fan, made by Fantech and a number of other manufacturers. These fans can be sized to exhaust several bathrooms, and they may be mounted in the attic or basement for quiet operation and easy service. Note that the attic-mounted, rigid-metal ductwork and fan are fully insulated to prevent interior condensation.

+ SAFETY FIRST

Some people are concerned that exhaust fans may backdraft heating or hot water equipment. Typically, the fans that contribute to backdrafting are the large ones, including those for a dryer, central vacuum, or commercial kitchen exhaust hood or downdraft vent. Theoretically, a fan of 120 cfm could backdraft a water heater, but it is highly unlikely. A fan of 300 cfm is more likely to be dangerous, but only in a very tight house.

up to a roof jack. Always use rigid-metal duct (4-in. or 6-in. diameter); if the duct runs through an attic or other unheated space, be sure to insulate it with vinyl-covered duct wrap.

If you don't have access to add or replace a bathroom fan because there's no attic space or there is limited depth in the ceiling joists above, another option is to install a wall-mounted fan. Several models are available for through-wall mounting that are quiet and use very little power. Another less-desirable option is to place the fan in another area of the house that's more accessible. Keep in mind, though, that bathrooms are where the moisture is. I'd put an automatically controlled fan in another part of the house only if there are operating bath fans that are already vented to the outside. It will cost in the range of $175 to $325 for the necessary parts (including fan, ductwork, and controls).

Ventilation controls

To be considered a background ventilation system, the fan must be capable of running on a regular schedule or continuously, if necessary. There are several timers that can control fan speed, operating times, or both. When you're choosing a controller for your ventilation fan, check with your supplier to make sure that the controls are compatible with the equipment you are using. Regardless of the control you choose, I recommend first setting the fan to run about half the time, at least during the hours people are regularly home. Then you can adjust it to run more or less, as needed.

I usually install Airetrak or Aube controls in the bathroom, as they have a built-in boost override and the timing functions are hidden from view. You can put the 24-hour dial timer in the bathroom, but it's ugly and it shouldn't be used for day-to-day on/off overrides. I try to put that timer in a laundry area, utility room, or basement stairwell or near the electrical panel—somewhere convenient and accessible but not that visible.

Controls for Simple Ventilation Systems

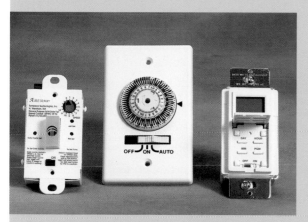

Left: The Airetrak is a special timer that can run the fan every hour, at any interval from 5 minutes to full-time; the push button overrides the program for on-demand ventilation. Center: A 24-hour dial timer fits in a single-gang box and allows on- and off-times in 20-minute increments. Right: This timer by Aube provides customized daily programs and a manual override button that lifts up to reveal the programming area. (Photo © Kevin Kennefick.)

A 24-hour timer (see the center object in the of photo above) provides flexibility and is easy to set and adjust. It controls the background air exchange—you need a separate switch to override the program, so that the fan can be turned on whenever it's needed. (Either of the switches shown in the photo at right is better than a regular switch, because it can run the fan for 20 or 30 minutes after you leave the bathroom and exhaust *all* the moisture after taking a shower.) This system does need more wiring; I recommend locating the dial timer where you can reach it easily but do not have to look at it every day.

The Airetrak (see the left object in the photo above) is a good alternative when you want to replace an existing wall switch but don't want to add a new electrical box for a timer. This unit can be set at varying fan speeds and/or hourly timed

settings. The button overrides the program and runs the fan for 20 minutes, then automatically goes back to the program. The speed control tends to make the fan noisier, so I recommend setting the Airetrak for full speed, using part-time operation every hour to obtain the desired air exchange. This unit runs the same program every hour, making it less flexible than the 24-hour timer.

A third control, made by Aube (see the right object in the photo at left), provides up to seven on/off cycles, each of which can be set daily or weekly. Although it can't provide short on-and-off cycles every hour, it is somewhat more flexible and less expensive than the Airetrak.

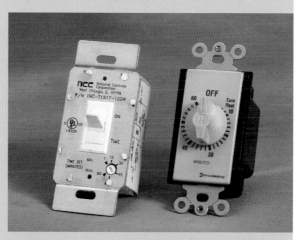

The fan delay timer switch at left turns on a bath fan when you switch it on, but when you switch it off, the fan runs for a preset time that can be adjusted from 1 to 60 minutes. It can also turn a light on and off without the shutoff delay. The windup timer at right is much simpler, allowing you to select the shutoff delay when you activate the fan. Both models allow you to run the fan for a period of time after you leave the bathroom, ensuring good moisture removal. If you use a 24-hour timer to program a ventilation system, either of these switches may be wired to override the program for on-demand bathroom ventilation. (Photo © Kevin Kennefick.)

WHAT CAN GO WRONG

I've tested a lot of ventilation systems—central exhaust only and HRV—that have low or poorly balanced airflows. If you install (or have installed) a central ventilation system, make sure the ducts are designed for adequate airflow from all registers. One critical element is an adjustable damper in every branch duct. After the system is in, it's a good idea to have it checked by a professional with a flow hood or an anemometer to make sure the ducts are adequate and the system is balanced.

This flow hood is one way to accurately measure the airflow at all the registers of your ventilation system. (Photo © Kevin Kennefick.)

Return-air system

If you have a ducted, central-air system for heating and/or cooling, another inexpensive (between $200 to $300 for parts) ventilation option is a supply-only system ducted through the furnace or air conditioner's air handler. This system pulls in fresh outdoor air whenever the air handler runs and distributes it throughout the house.

Although a simpler version of this system is common in some parts of the United States, most installations lack three important elements. First, a motorized damper is essential on the fresh-air-inlet duct—preferably where the duct enters the house. This prevents air from coming in through the duct when ventilation is not needed. Next, a timer is necessary to ensure that the air handler runs regularly, ventilating the house when there is no call for heating or cooling. This ensures a minimum ventilation rate year-round. There are a couple of timers that can handle this function. Finally, insect screening at the inlet hood is important, and it must be kept clean. With a return-air fresh air system, it is also very important to locate the outdoor-air inlet far from potential sources of pollution, such as a dryer, combustion appliance vent, the garage, or the driveway.

If your house has an existing forced-air system, a return-air system may offer better overall ventilation than a bath-fan system, though it may be less cost-efficient. For example, a 20-watt bath fan running 100% of the time may cost less than $20 per year in electricity; a furnace fan running a third of the time may cost between $30 and $120 per year. If you have an old furnace with a high-wattage blower motor, a return-air system is less desirable due to the higher cost of operating the blower motor. And if your central-air handler is noisy, your ventilation will be, too. However, this system has two major advantages: First, fresh air is drawn from a known place and can be filtered. Second, unlike a bath-fan system, it circulates fresh air throughout the house.

Central Ventilation Systems

In addition to the simple ventilation systems mentioned previously, central-fan ventilation systems can be set up either to provide fresh air to bedrooms and living areas or to exhaust stale air from bathrooms and the kitchen. These systems may be more effective than the single-point exhaust or supply-only air systems mentioned earlier, but, because they require quite a bit more ductwork, they are more expensive to install and more difficult to retrofit in an existing home.

Central-exhaust/ supply-only systems

Central-exhaust systems are more common than central supply-only systems. They use a central fan, typically located in a basement or an attic, to exhaust air from several points in the home at the same time. One major advantage of those systems is that the equipment is easy to service. For example, a single central fan located in a basement or an attic is easy to reach for repair or replacement. Those systems may also be quieter than the simple systems mentioned earlier, but that depends on the location of the fan and the care taken to install vibration dampers on the fan and ductwork. The cost in materials for central exhaust systems ranges from $250 to $400.

Ideally, a ventilation system should provide 10 to 15 cfm per person. I usually size a fan for a minimum of 15 cfm per bedroom, plus an extra 15 cfm for the master bedroom: a 3-bedroom house needs 60 cfm; a 5-bedroom house, 90 cfm. For flexibility, it's a good idea to size central systems for 50 cfm to 100 cfm more than the minimum requirement; you can always use a variable-speed control or timer to reduce the background ventilation rate. And, don't forget, airflow is generally lower than the fan's rating,

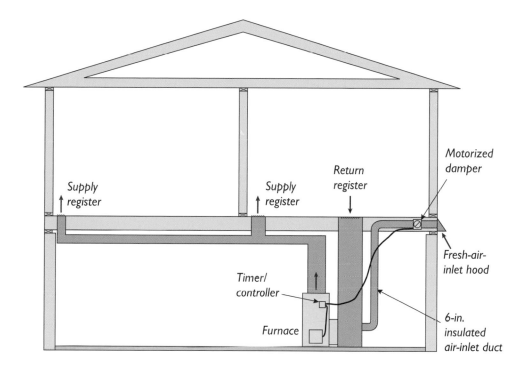

Supply register

Supply register

Return register

Motorized damper

Fresh-air-inlet hood

Timer/controller

Furnace

6-in. insulated air-inlet duct

Return-Air Ventilation System

This simple ventilation system draws outdoor air through a screened inlet, mixes it with house air, and sends it to the furnace, where it is distributed throughout the house. The motorized damper and the fan controller are essential for managing the ventilation rate. The inlet duct should be made of sheet metal and be as short and direct as possible. It should enter the return duct as close as possible to the furnace, but not between the furnace and the furnace filter.

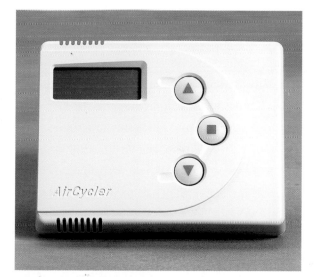

The AirCycler FR-V (see Resources on p. 194) can run a central air handler fan for ventilation, when it's not already being used for heating or cooling purposes, at any preset interval you wish. It can also control a 24-volt motorized damper (not shown). EFI sells a kit that includes the AirCycler timer, a Hoyme damper (Hoyme Model HAC 0610-0PO), and a 6-in. outdoor hood. (Photo © Kevin Kennefick.)

A motorized damper (right) by Duro Dyne (see Resources on p. 194) is an essential component of any return-air ventilation system. It can be controlled with Duro Dyne's AQC-1 Air Quality Control Center, provides 24-hour, 15-minute-interval control of air handler ventilation cycles, and also controls a 110-volt exhaust fan. This sturdy, well-built unit doesn't keep track of thermostat calls, as the AirCycler does (see the photo at left), but it can be set to ventilate differently at various times of day. (Photo © Kevin Kennefick.)

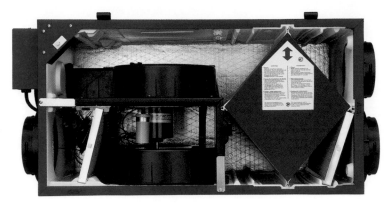

This view inside a heat-recovery system (HRV) shows the diamond-shaped heat-exchanger core. (Photo courtesy Venmar Ventilation, Inc.)

WHAT CAN GO WRONG

Although some installers claim that an HRV will solve all your ventilation needs, even a large unit may not adequately remove moisture from bathrooms, especially if the exhaust ducts vent to many locations. In my experience, it's better to use a smaller HRV unit that is sized for the background ventilation rate (100 cfm to 150 cfm for most homes), then install separate exhaust fans for removing steam in the bathrooms.

IN DETAIL

If you think you want a heat-recovery ventilation system, don't be too concerned about payback. After all, a ventilation system costs money to buy and operate. The value of that investment is priceless: It gives you control over air exchange and moisture, and it provides better indoor air quality for your family. The value of central systems and heat recovery for homes stems more from the added control of incoming and exhaust airstreams and filtration opportunities; the heat and/or energy recovery is an added bonus.

so add another 20% to 25% to the desired flow to achieve the appropriate cfm rating.

Central-exhaust systems typically are designed to draw air from bathrooms, the kitchen (but not from over the range), the laundry room, and other areas that have moisture or stale air. Usually, they are run at a low speed with a variable-speed control for continuous background ventilation. An override switch or windup timer is usually placed in bathrooms when a temporary full-speed boost is needed to provide maximum ventilation.

One disadvantage of a central-exhaust system is the greater electricity cost compared to that of a single high-efficiency bathroom fan. In addition, if it's ducted to too many locations, it doesn't always provide really good spot exhaust for bathrooms during boost mode.

Central supply systems use a fan and ductwork much like central-exhaust systems, but they bring fresh air from a known outdoor location and deliver it to the living space and bedrooms. This has a clear advantage, because incoming fresh air is

+ SAFETY FIRST

Don't install HRV exhaust ducts above a kitchen range. Instead, choose a separate range hood that is rated for the high temperatures and grease produced by cooking, which will help you avoid a fire hazard and a warranty problem.

filtered and delivered by ducts throughout the living space. However, in cold weather, the fresh air can create uncomfortable drafts, so the ducts must be placed very carefully. Also, separate spot-exhaust ventilation fans are still needed, increasing the cost of the entire system.

Heat-recovery systems

If you want a top-shelf ventilation system, you should consider one of the heat-recovery systems. These systems typically pull warm exhaust air from bathrooms and the kitchen and run it through a heat exchanger to preheat incoming fresh air. This warmed fresh air is then delivered to living areas and bedrooms. The stale and fresh airstreams don't mix but move in parallel through a series of flat plates that provide a lot of surface area for heat exchange. This way, the systems can recapture 65% to 80% of the heat from the outgoing airstream, which makes them real energy savers. And because they balance both supply and exhaust airflows, heat-recovery systems are the least likely to backdraft combustion equipment.

There are two kinds of heat-recovery systems: heat-recovery ventilation (HRV) and energy-recovery ventilation (ERV). HRVs are most efficient in cold weather. ERVs transfer not only heat but also humidity, using a special heat-exchanger wheel or core. This humidity exchange improves efficiency during the summer in humid climates, because it saves on the dehumidification load that

Heat-Recovery Ventilation

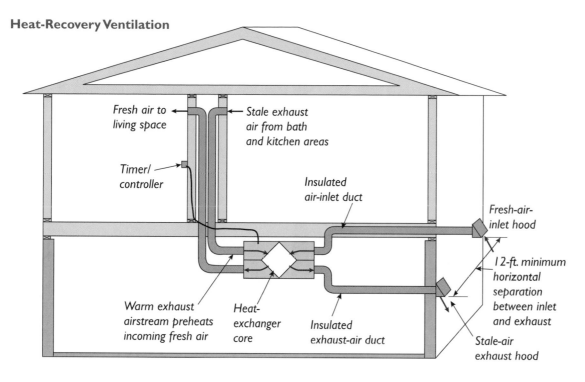

Fresh air to living space

Stale exhaust air from bath and kitchen areas

Timer/ controller

Insulated air-inlet duct

Fresh-air-inlet hood

12-ft. minimum horizontal separation between inlet and exhaust

Warm exhaust airstream preheats incoming fresh air

Heat-exchanger core

Insulated exhaust-air duct

Stale-air exhaust hood

A heat-recovery system uses the heat from the exhaust airstream to preheat incoming fresh air. The fresh air is ducted either directly to living areas or to the return plenum of a furnace air handler for distribution throughout the house. In hot weather, the exhaust airstream precools incoming fresh air.

air conditioners need to provide. This saves more energy and helps reduce moisture problems.

HRV and ERV systems are much more expensive than the simple systems outlined previously; they range from $1,500 to $4,000 installed (including labor). Installation of these systems is better left to a professional. There are some clear advantages for the price: The systems do a much better job at ensuring whole-house ventilation, and they are the system of choice for extremely tight homes and for people with respiratory sensitivities, because they filter incoming fresh air. They may even be cost-effective (meaning they will actually pay for themselves in energy savings) in some climates, but not unless you first make your house very tight. Depending on the unit, run time, climate, and fuel costs, HRV and ERV systems will probably save between $100 and $500 per year.

Insulating

CHAPTER FOUR
a House

1 Attic Insulation, p. 64

From the attic to the basement, insulation is like the down jacket around your house that keeps you warm in the winter (and cool in the summer). In many houses, it is probably easier to insulate than it is to seal air leaks, though it may be a bigger job if you need to insulate exterior walls. Attic and basement spaces are relatively easy to insulate, and most houses can benefit from some added insulation.

Regardless of the age of your house, don't be fooled just because there's some insulation in the attic. Some homes have a thin layer that does little good; others have insulation that was installed in only the areas that were easy to reach. Even brand new homes that have a lot of insulation can still have significant gaps and installation problems that are worth fixing—especially by someone who cares enough about the details to do it right.

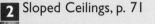
2 Sloped Ceilings, p. 71

3 Insulating Walls, p. 74

4 Insulating Floors, p. 81

5 Insulating Foundation Walls, p. 86

PRO TIP

Radiant barriers and reflective roof coatings are not enough to reduce cooling loads. Adequate roof insulation is important in both warm and cold climates.

WHAT CAN GO WRONG

Don't assume that attic insulation is optional just because you live in a warm climate. Attic and roof spaces heat up significantly in the sun and transfer heat to the living space below; insulation helps slow this heat transfer.

IN DETAIL

If you want to add attic venting (or your local building inspector requires it), here's how: Calculate the square footage of your attic or roof space, then divide it by 300 to get how much net-free vent area is required. For example, if your attic is 1,200 sq. ft., you need 4 sq. ft. of net-free vent area. Most manufacturers specify the net area for their vents, but if you can't find that information, assume that it's half of the overall vent area (because of the screen and louvers). Thus, a 12-in.-by-18-in. gable vent, which is 1.5 gross sq. ft., has about ¾ sq. ft. net-free vent area. Don't even bother with the small round "pop" vents—they aren't really effective.

Attic Insulation

Attics are typically insulated first, and they usually receive the most insulation. People usually assume that attics are insulated because "heat rises"—but, as I have pointed out (see p. 8), *heat* doesn't actually rise at all. The reason attics tend to get more insulation is much less glamorous: The attic is simply the cheapest and easiest place to add insulation, in both old and new houses. In fact, in a moderately insulated two-story house, there may be two to five times as much conductive heat loss (not including air leakage or windows) through the exterior walls as through the attic.

True to tradition, we'll start with attic insulation because it's the easiest job. Hopefully, you have already finished air-sealing up there. If not, do it now, because it is much more difficult to air-seal after you insulate. Also, if you intend to vent a bath fan, install a ventilation system, change any electrical wiring, or do any other work in the attic, now is the time.

How much insulation?

Insulation is measured in R-value; the higher the R-value, the less heat loss. To some extent, there is an effect of diminishing returns in that the first 6 in. of insulation will save you more money than the next 6 in. But it doesn't pay to skimp, either. Once you're up in the attic installing insulation, you may as well do it right. Generally, the minimum recommended R-value for an attic is R-38 (see the chart on the facing page). In cold northern climates, I aim for between R-50 and R-60.

Estimating how many fiberglass batts to buy for a job is pretty easy, because each roll or bundle is marked for the number of square feet it covers. Cellulose is a little trickier—you need to consult the tables found on the bags of material. Always go by the bag count, not the inches of thickness, to figure the amount of material and the actual R-value you're adding to your attic.

Prepping for insulation

Many building codes require attic venting. My experience has shown that, in most cases, attic vents are not critical, but they are good backup if you can't do a complete air-sealing job. If your attic doesn't have any ventilation, try to put 50% to 80% of the total required ventilation area up high—in the ridge, gable, or roof vents. The remainder should be down low, usually in the soffit.

✔ According to Code

Most codes require passive attic venting to reduce condensation, but building scientists have found that a combination of air-sealing and indoor humidity control is the most important measure for preventing moisture damage. Attic ventilation *is* good: It helps the roof dry out when it gets wet. However, I would rather have a good air-sealing job and a mechanical ventilation system in the house, without attic vents, than a well-vented attic without a good air barrier. So, install roof ventilation if you can, but always concentrate on air-sealing the attic first.

If there's no access into the attic, you can cut an opening for a roof vent. Climb in and insulate, then install the vent to cover the hole.

R-Values of Insulation Materials

Different materials have different R-values per inch. To find out how much R-value your insulation materials have, multiply the values in the table by the average number of inches of material. Notice that fiberglass batt performance degrades significantly with the gaps and compression found in a typical installation. To obtain fiberglass's high-density value, it must be installed perfectly, or "by the book."

Category	Insulation Type	Description (typical)	Approximate R-values per in. thickness
Loose-Fill Insulation	Loose, chopped fiberglass or rock wool	Yellow, white, pink, or green clumps of chopped fibers	1.8
	Vermiculite*	Gray or brown metallic granules	2.4
	Cellulose	Gray or tan shredded newspaper; fluffy and/or dusty	3.3
Fiberglass Batts	Typical installation	Pink, yellow, or green blanket; installed with gaps and compression	1.8
	Installation "by the book"	Pink, yellow, or green blanket; installed perfectly	3.2
	High-density batts	Stiffer, denser batts; installed perfectly	3.8–4.3
Rigid Foam Board	Expanded polystyrene	White bead board	4
	Extruded polystyrene	Uniform blue, green, or pink board insulation	5
	Isocyanurate hi-R board	Yellow or tan stiff foam with foil facing	7
Spray-in-Place Foams	Urea-formaldehyde*	Yellow or gray-white, brittle, dusty foam; breaks easily	3–4
	Modern low-density	Yellow, green, or white soft foam (Icynene® or similar)	3.4
	Modern urethane foams	Yellow, green, or other color tough foam	6

*Potential safety concerns; see Hazards of Insulation Material on p. 67 for more details.

In general, I avoid adding ridge vents and 16-in. aluminum soffit louvers because they are ugly; continuous ridge or soffit vents that are installed during a reroofing or soffit replacement job tend to look much better. Roof vents placed near the peak on the rear of the house are inconspicuous, and they can even provide access to attics that have no scuttle.

Whether or not you install attic ventilation, take some time baffling the eaves area before installing insulation. The idea is to allow an airspace between the insulation and the roof sheathing. The most common approach is to use standard foam or plastic ventilation chutes held in place with a wad of fiberglass. Make sure the fiberglass extends to the outside edge of the top plate so that you can get as much insulation as possible in that vulnerable area. Cardboard baffles also work well. The top of the baffle should be several inches above the height of the planned insulation, at a minimum.

At some point, 3½-in.-thick R-11 batts were added to the original insulation, unfortunately with the vapor barrier facing the wrong way. Blowing at least 14 in. of cellulose on top will add adequate insulation, ensuring that the vapor barrier stays warm enough so that it won't need to be flipped upside down.

WHAT CAN GO WRONG

Poorly installed fiberglass batts, like the ones shown above (and on p. 170), can lead to serious performance problems. Research and experience have shown that gaps between batts may eat up anywhere from 25% to 75% of the rated R-value, depending on the thickness of the batt, the size and number of the gaps, and the difference in temperature between indoors and out.

Estimating Cellulose

To determine how much insulation you need, measure the approximate thickness of any existing insulation, then multiply that by its R-value per inch (see the chart on p. 65). For example, if you already have 4 in. of blown-in fiberglass, you have an existing R-value of about 7. To reach R-50, you need to add R-43; 43 ÷ 3.3 = approximately 13 in. of cellulose.

Cellulose is usually packaged in bags of 12 or 25 lb. After determining your target R-value, measure the square footage of the area you wish to cover. Each manufacturer provides information on the bag describing how much insulation to use for a desired R-value. In some cases, that information may be indicated by the number of square feet that a bag covers at a given R-value, in which case you just need to divide your total square feet by that number to purchase the correct number of bags.

Don't worry about cellulose losing R-value over time as it settles. For one thing, settled material is denser and has a higher R-value per inch, so settling generally does not decrease the insulation's performance. Second, most settling tends to occur in the first year or two after installation, and—unlike corn flakes in a box—once the material has reached its settled density, it cannot settle further unless it's physically compressed. The amount of air running through the hose with the material does have a big effect on its initial thickness, so pay more attention to the bag count than the depth of the installed cellulose, whether you are doing the job yourself or hiring a contractor.

The chart printed on this cellulose bag shows how many bags of material are needed per 1000 sq. ft. for a range of desired R-values.

Standard foam vent chutes can be held in place with fiberglass batts and pushed in tightly to cut down on wind washing.

In addition to the eaves area prep, flag each electrical junction box with a piece of ribbon or caution tape stapled to a rafter above and hanging down to identify it once it's buried. Make sure that every electrical box has a proper cover on it and that the wires are properly clamped.

You will need to find a way to keep blown insulation at least 3 in. away from chimneys (I typically use fiberglass batts; see the bottom left photo on p. 69); and don't cover combustion air intakes or recessed light fixtures that are not IC rated. And whatever you do, don't insulate over old-fashioned live knob-and-tube wiring. In some cases, that kind of wiring will already be deacti-

If you have an older house with knob-and-tube wiring that looks like this, the wiring *must* be replaced before you insulate the attic or wall areas. To make sure there's no active knob-and-tube wiring hidden in wall cavities, you may want to hire an electrician to verify that it's inactive. (Photo © Kevin Kennefick.)

Hazards of Insulation Materials

Some older insulation materials are hazardous, but few pose significant danger if they are isolated from the living space—another argument for thorough air-sealing. Asbestos is clearly a hazardous material; even moderate levels of exposure can cause lung cancer and other diseases, and it should never be moved or disturbed except by a properly licensed asbestos-remediation contractor. Commonly found as insulation on pipes and ducts, asbestos is rare in attics. Some types of vermiculite, added as insulation in attics and walls in the '60s, '70s, and '80s, contain traces of asbestos. When I find vermiculite, I leave it in place. Insulating over it is fine, but definitely wear a HEPA respirator, which I recommend for anyone working in any attic.

Vermiculite insulation is grainy, not fluffy or fibrous. Although some vermiculite contains asbestos, don't try to remove it—it is more dangerous when disturbed than left in place. (Photo by Tom O'Brien, courtesy *Fine Homebuilding* magazine, © The Taunton Press.)

Urea-formaldehyde foam insulation (UFFI) is a spray foam that was retrofitted in houses prior to 1980. This material was banned because of potentially toxic formaldehyde gas emissions, but gas emissions fade with time, so any UFFI that is still around is unlikely to be hazardous. If you find UFFI, be cautious, because it is likely to be fragile and may turn to a powdery dust if disturbed.

Modern insulation materials, including spray foams, fiberglass, and cellulose, are much safer but still involve some risk. Although fiberglass fibers are definitely an irritant to the skin, no increased risk of cancer has been found even at occupational exposures. Cellulose is a respiratory irritant, due to the fire-retardant chemical treatments, and produces lots of dust during installation, but it is not dangerous once it has been installed.

vated; if you're not sure, you'll need to hire an electrician to check it for you.

Fiberglass attic insulation

I generally prefer to use cellulose insulation wherever possible, but if you have trouble finding a machine, or if you have only a small area to insulate, fiberglass may be the best choice. If there is little or no insulation between the ceiling joists, start by installing a batt that will come up at least to the top of the joists. Use unfaced batts in the attic and make sure you buy batts that are the same width as the spacing of the ceiling joists.

There are three important things to be aware of when installing fiberglass. First, a new bundle or roll of fiberglass is highly compressed, and it *must* be fluffed to the full thickness listed on the package. Second, it must be fit neatly between the joists and come in full contact with the ceiling, with no compression, binding, or rounding of the corners. Finally, it must be cut neatly to fit around any obstructions, such as wiring, plumbing, blocking in between the joists, or other objects. Anything that compromises the installa-

tion can have a serious effect on the insulation's performance.

Choose the first layer of batts so the top of the insulation is up to—or slightly above—joist level. Then install a second layer on top, at right angles to the first layer. Buy 24-in.-wide batts for that layer, regardless of the joist spacing. Again, make

TRADE SECRET

No matter which type of machine you use to blow cellulose, it's important to break up the material as much as possible when pulling it out of the bag. This helps prevent clogging in the hose, which is frustrating and time-consuming. And for safety's sake, *never* reach down into the hopper while the machine is running. The person handling the machine should always unplug the power line if it's necessary to clear a clog.

Fiberglass Batts

Fiberglass batts are typically the insulation of choice for do-it-yourselfers. The material is easy to transport and install by yourself. It's ideal for an attic where you may want to add living space later (or make other changes), because it is easy to remove and replace. But there is a price to pay for convenience. In my experience, no matter how carefully you detail fiberglass batts, they never work as well as the factory ratings suggest. After three winters in the house I built, I pulled out the fiberglass insulation that I had carefully installed in the attic and replaced it with cellulose; the dramatic improvement surprised even me.

Because of the annoying, itchy quality of fiberglass, and the possible danger from inhaling glass fibers, several manufacturers market encapsulated batts that have plastic or other material surrounding the fiberglass. Steer clear of these products; they are more of a marketing gimmick than a worthwhile innovation. Encapsulated batts are more expensive and harder to install properly. Although the coverings may make the material more comfortable to work with, they also increase the difficulty of detailing the batts properly.

sure each batt is fluffed to its full thickness, and lay each one snugly against the next.

Don't be satisfied with 12-in.-thick batts laid in a single layer in between the joists—the gaps that are left between the batts will really hurt the overall performance of your attic's insulation. You may need to notch the batts at the edges near the rafters, or tuck in short pieces, to bring the insulation to its full thickness as close as possible to the roof sheathing and still leave a 1-in. space between the insulation and the sheathing.

Blowing attic insulation

If your roof is made with trusses, or the attic has flooring with little or no insulation under it, you'll never get great results with fiberglass. In those cases, your best bet is to use a loose-fill material, such as cellulose. One big advantage of blown cellulose (besides the fact that it works better) is that it is fast and easy to install. You don't have to worry about cutting, fitting, fluffing, or most of the other details that concern fiberglass batts. You can also cover the top of existing fiber-

To cut a fiberglass batt to length, compress it with a ruler and cut it with a sharp utility knife. It's best to cut it about 1/2 in. longer than you need, so that it will fit snugly.

The second layer of insulation should be fluffed to its full thickness, laid across all the joists at right angles, and be installed neatly and completely.

glass batts with cellulose, which will settle into all the gaps and defects between the batts. This improves what's already there and adds R-value.

The biggest drawback with blown insulation is that you need a machine and a helper to install it. Many building-material suppliers that sell bagged cellulose will lend or rent a machine to anyone who buys the insulation from them. A local rental yard, or even a friendly local insulation contractor, may rent out a cellulose machine (you'll have to find the helper yourself).

When installing cellulose, you must do the same prep work as for fiberglass (see pp. 64–66). In addition, get enough fiberglass batts to make a dam around chimneys and recessed lights to keep the cellulose away from them. Even with IC-rated recessed lights, I prefer to surround and cover them with fiberglass before installing the cellulose. Keep the batts at least 3 in. away from non-IC-rated fixtures. Also, make a dam around the attic hatch so cellulose doesn't fall out when you open the door.

Set up the blowing machine in a convenient place, and snake the flexible hose and control cable into the attic. You may want to run them through a second-story window or an attic window, or temporarily remove an attic gable vent. Have

Keep the end of the hose low and pointed slightly down to reduce dust levels and keep the cellulose density high, especially near the eaves.

It's important to keep cellulose away from chimneys, recessed lights, and attic hatches. The easiest way is to make a dam with fiberglass batts. (Photo © Kevin Kennefick.)

Cellulose Blowing Machines

Cellulose machines range in size from a box slightly bigger than a milk crate with a hopper to a large truck-mounted rig. All of them have some type of agitator to break up the material and a blower to separate the fibers, mix them with air, and send them through a hose. Most machines have a cable with an on/off switch, allowing them to be controlled remotely, where the work is being done. Most machines also allow you to control the fiber-and-air mixture, either by adjusting a gate to control the rate of material fed through the hose or by adjusting an air inlet to introduce a variable amount of air. For open-attic blowing, set it for more material and less air.

This medium-sized cellulose blower is typical of the type of machine that you might rent or borrow from an insulation supplier.

The job will go faster, and the material won't settle as much after you're done.

Of course, not all cellulose machines are created equal. The smaller machines are perfectly good for open attics, though they are slower. But they lack the air pressure to dense-pack closed cavities. The key for doing that is to select a machine that can supply adequate air pressure, but the easiest thing to look for is a machine that requires at least two separate electrical circuits (or a single 220-volt circuit) to run. If you plan to dense-pack cellulose, stay away from a machine that can run off a single 15- or 20-amp, 110-volt circuit.

IN DETAIL

If your attic is floored, you must fill the space under the flooring, unless that space has already been well insulated. With a plank floor, it's much easier to rip up a row or two of boards along the length of the attic than to blow insulation under the floor with a fill tube. A plywood floor is more difficult. You can either rip up an entire row of plywood sheets or, if that's too much trouble, use a hole saw to drill a 3-in.-dia. hole in each joist bay, then insulate with a fill tube. Once the cavities are full, apply more cellulose on top until you have the R-value you want.

(Photo by Andrew Engel, courtesy *Fine Homebuilding* magazine, © The Taunton Press.)

an assistant ready, put on protective gear, and position yourself in one corner of the attic area. Turn on the switch, and the material should start to flow within a few seconds. Start in one corner, allow the material to build to the thickness you want, then pull back the hose as you start to fill in the area.

The object is to get the insulation fairly even and avoid spraying too much into the air. You can turn off the switch occasionally to take a break, then move yourself and the hose to another area. Use a tape measure occasionally to check the thickness of the insulation, and aim for about 2 in. more total depth than the actual depth you want to end up with (to allow for settling).

When you are blowing near the eaves, push the end of the hose nearly all the way into the baffle, and fill the space between the rafters to the desired thickness. Pushing the hose deep inside helps ensure that the cellulose will be packed tightly in those critical areas. Slowly pull back the hose from the roof, being careful not to cover the upper end of the vent chute.

Start with five or six rafter bays at a time, then work your way across the attic toward the opposite eave, leaving space for yourself to get into the eaves area on the other side. Work your way back toward the attic hatch or access door, then start at the other end of the attic and work your way back toward the hatch. Make sure you don't "paint" yourself into a corner—it's not fun crawling through 12 in. to 18 in. of this stuff after it's installed.

Storage areas

People often use attics for storage. My first advice is to eliminate attic storage, if possible. There are plenty of good reasons to get rid of stuff (both thermal and psychological). Still, many homes lack storage space, and the attic is a natural place for those boxes of holiday decorations. If you have a

Raising a floor deck above the existing framing is the best way to create storage space in the attic without compromising insulation levels. (Photo © Kevin Kennefick.)

partially or fully floored attic, you can set aside an area near the access hatch or stairs by making a dam out of 12-in.-thick fiberglass batts. Insulate the rest of the attic, making sure there is insulation under the floorboards as well. Once the dust has settled, you should be able to move stuff in and out without disturbing the insulation.

Even better, you can create storage with the full insulation thickness by building a raised floor deck. Run 2×6 or 2×8 joists perpendicular to the ceiling joists at 16 in. o.c. Nail a header joist across each end to hold them vertically, insulate the cavities, and cover them with planks of ½-in. plywood. You will lose some headroom, but this way you can reserve as large an area as you like for storage without compromising the insulation job.

With either approach, be cautious about the amount of weight the ceiling joists are able to hold. A built-up floor adds dead load and storage adds live load to the existing framing—too much weight can create a structural problem. If you're uncertain, consult a structural engineer before proceeding.

Sloped Ceilings

Many homes have sloped ceiling areas—places where plaster or drywall is applied directly to the underside of the roof rafters. Examples include Cape-style houses, which usually have sloped ceilings between the kneewall and the flat ceiling above (see the drawing on p. 35) or rooms with partial or full cathedral ceilings. Some homes just have a narrow sloped area for a few feet near the eaves.

These enclosed cavities present more of a challenge than an open attic. Some, like the typical Cape, have fairly easy access from an attic space either above or below. Others, like a full cathedral ceiling, are more difficult. The basic techniques shown in this section for dense-packing cellulose are referred to in many other parts of the book. The biggest distinction between dense-packed and open-blown cellulose is that dense-pack is installed in an enclosed cavity. But it's not enough just to be enclosed—to dense-pack, by definition, means using enough air pressure to compress the material more densely than it could ever compress from settling.

Prepping for the job

When filling in a rafter bay with cellulose, you must prevent the insulation from pouring out of the cavity on the other end. If the rafter bay is accessible from only one end—for example, from the attic above—this may be easy enough, but you will need to plan for extra material because the eaves may become filled. If you can reach both the top and the bottom, choose the end that is more awkward to reach and stuff a piece of fiberglass into each bay; then blow in the insulation from the other end.

Make sure the ceiling is sound before starting. In particular, acoustical tiles pose a real potential for blowout, as well as air leakage. They should be dealt with before dense-packing. And make sure the roof is in decent shape before insulating closed cavities; any water that leaks in after insulating will make a bigger mess—and be more difficult to locate—than it would otherwise.

Another preparation issue, which is the same for flat attic areas, relates to venting a cathedral-ceiling space. Good air-sealing (which dense-packing helps) and indoor humidity control via mechanical ventilation best address most of the concerns around condensation and moisture buildup.

Roof-shingle warranties are another concern. Unvented cathedral ceilings experience hotter roof temperatures—typically by 2% to 4%—than vented roofs. Because those higher temperatures may accelerate degradation (venting is assumed to reduce roof temperatures), many roofing manu-

Stuff pieces of fiberglass batts into rafter bays so that cellulose won't blow through when you fill them from the other end. Stuff the batts into the empty cellulose bags, as shown here, or just stuff the fiberglass alone. (Photo by Andrew Wormer, courtesy *Fine Homebuilding* magazine, © The Taunton Press.)

PRO TIP

Low-e™ coatings on glass do cut heat loss substantially, but Low-e paint is a different matter. Save your money and invest in insulation instead.

TRADE SECRET

Don't waste your money on "energy saving" Low-e paint. The claims of potential savings at a level comparable to insulating a wall or roof are purely theoretical. It would be nice if an inexpensive, noninvasive product could make such a big impact, but here's the truth: Adding insulation is a proven strategy that really makes a difference. And if your house is already insulated, Low-e paint won't make a significant impact.

IN DETAIL

From a building science perspective, venting in sloped ceilings is essentially a backup strategy; indoor humidity control and air-sealing are more important. In general, attic ventilation is a good thing because it helps the roof deck dry out, but you needn't be fanatic about it. Enclosed cavities can be difficult or impossible to vent properly, and it's more important to insulate them well.

On this machine, you increase the air-to-cellulose mix for dense-packing by closing a gate in the hopper, which reduces the material feed. Other machines have air-inlet ports that open to increase the air pressure; either type will increase the air-to-material ratio.

A 1¼-in.-dia. vinyl fill tube attached to the end of a larger-diameter hose makes it easy to snake into confined spaces for dense-packing cellulose. The marker line near the end warns you that the end is near as you pull the tube out.

facturers won't honor warranty claims on unvented, or hot, roofs. But research has shown that shingle color actually has a much larger impact (about 10%) on roof temperature than venting does, and several manufacturers do provide warranty service for unvented roofs. Choose one of those, or ventilate if shingle-warranty service is important to you.

I've insulated many roofs (including my own), and I know a number of contractors who collectively have done hundreds of hot roofs with cellulose—very few have reported problems. But the decision is yours, and it depends on the climate, building inspector, shingle warranty, and condition of the roof, as well as your confidence in the success of air-sealing and indoor humidity control.

Filling rafter bays— dense-packing cellulose

To dense-pack cellulose, you'll first need to set up the blowing machine. Depending on the machine, this means setting it for either *less* material or *more* air. If you have a large, open ceiling cavity, use 3-in. flex hose. For cavities less than 5 in. deep, or

for those that already contain some insulation, use a smaller vinyl fill tube. Starting at one end of the house, insert the hose into the first cavity. Try to insert it so that the end is within 1 ft. to 2 ft. of the far end of the cavity, and cover the end of the bay with a loose piece of fiberglass to keep the cellulose from blowing back out. It helps if you keep the fill tube or hose in one corner of the opening. Make sure the switch is handy, turn on the machine, and let the fun begin!

The tricky part of any dense-pack operation is making sure that you pack in as much material as possible, without clogging the hose or blowing out the drywall or plaster. As the material fills near the end of the tube, the flow through the hose will start to back up. When it does, pull back the tube 6 in. to 8 in. to relieve the pressure and allow more packing of the cavity. It may take a while before you have to back up the first time, but then you may have to pull back every 5 to 10 seconds until the cavity is full (depending on the size of the fill tube and the pressure of the machine). When the cavity is full, turn off the blower and let the pressure drop before pulling out the hose. You

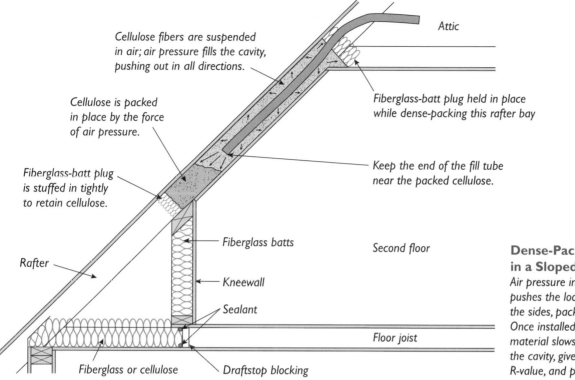

Cellulose fibers are suspended in air; air pressure fills the cavity, pushing out in all directions.

Cellulose is packed in place by the force of air pressure.

Fiberglass-batt plug is stuffed in tightly to retain cellulose.

Rafter

Fiberglass or cellulose

Attic

Fiberglass-batt plug held in place while dense-packing this rafter bay

Keep the end of the fill tube near the packed cellulose.

Fiberglass batts

Kneewall

Sealant

Draftstop blocking

Second floor

Floor joist

Dense-Packing Cellulose in a Sloped Ceiling
Air pressure in the enclosed cavity pushes the loose fibers tightly against the sides, packing them into place. Once installed, the high-density material slows air movement through the cavity, gives the insulation a higher R-value, and prevents future settling.

will know that you have reached the proper density when you remove the covering batt and press the insulation. The material should be firm, and it should be difficult to force your hand through the insulation.

If your sloped or cathedral ceilings aren't accessible from an attic space, you have several options for dense-packing cellulose. You can get at the

When insulating a closed cavity, such as this rafter bay, hold a piece of fiberglass batt across the opening. Wear a dust mask and safety glasses in case the cellulose blows back at your face. (Photo © Bruce Harley.)

Dense-Packing

It's not difficult to notice the changes that happen just before your blowing machine starts to bog down. The sound changes, the material feed slows, and the added pressure may make the hose wiggle. If you wait too long to pull the tube back, the cellulose can back up and dense-pack the hose instead of the wall. On the other hand, pull the tube out too quickly, and the density will suffer.

Clogs are most likely to occur at a reducer or other restriction. Usually, opening up the hose at the restriction will do the trick. If not, a long stick or a heavy-duty tape measure and a lot of thwacking on the side of the hose can loosen it. If you find that you are getting a lot of clogs, try reducing on the material feed or increasing the amount of air. If you are lucky enough to have a machine with separate switches for the agitator and the blower, you can maintain the air pressure and reduce clogging by turning off the agitator for short periods of time. That allows the air pressure to build without feeding any material, and it is a handy technique to use when you are almost finished with each cavity or bay.

Clogs occur where hoses reduce in size. To clear the blockage, disassemble the joint. (Photo by Andrew Engel, courtesy *Fine Homebuilding* magazine, ©The Taunton Press.)

PRO TIP

Whether you drill from inside or outside to blow in cellulose, it's important to make a hole (or a pair of holes) in each stud bay.

TRADE SECRET

If you're insulating a cathedral ceiling, stay away from non-IC-rated recessed light fixtures and chimneys. Blowing cellulose in these areas could create a fire hazard.

TRADE SECRET

I make a probe out of a piece of insulated wire, stripping the jacket off a piece of electric cable and pulling out one wire with the insulation still on it. I use it to explore stud bays after drilling them, probing sideways to find the next stud, as well as up and down to find any blocking or diagonal bracing that may be in the wall. Now I can aim for the center of the next stud bay to drill the next hole.

Before you try insulating blind roof cavities, make sure the rafters aren't already full of insulation. If so, you'll have trouble getting a fill tube—or much cellulose—into the space. (Photo by Steve Culpepper, courtesy *Fine Homebuilding* magazine, © The Taunton Press.)

rafter bays by opening up the soffit and/or fascia, or by removing the cap layer of shingles and cutting back the sheathing a few inches. Either method allows you to run a fill tube into the rafter cavity to fill it with insulation. Another option is to drill and patch cathedral ceilings from the inside, similar to filling walls from indoors. Of course, be extra careful whenever you work on a roof or on a ladder.

Insulating Walls

If you have little or no insulation in your walls, you will definitely benefit from installing some. Conductive heat loss through uninsulated walls represents a significant heating and cooling load, and it's usually cost-effective to add insulation.

Exterior walls are fairly difficult to insulate, unless you are remodeling, installing new drywall, or re-siding the house. Retrofitting insulation almost always means blowing in insulation, usually cellulose; the process is very much like that of the sloped-ceiling dense-pack outlined above. The type of siding has a big impact on how easy it is to get into the wall, and it may help you decide whether to tackle the job yourself or hire an insulation contractor.

What's in there now?

How do you know what's in the walls already? If you have done any remodeling, you probably already know. If not, there are a several ways to find out. It's important to know what is in there, because that will have a big impact on how easy—or useful—it will be to insulate the walls.

Remember that there may be different types of insulation (or none at all) in different parts of the house. If parts of the house have been remodeled (for example, the kitchen) or built at a different time, they will likely be insulated differently. And sometimes people start to insulate a house and don't finish, so look in at least five or six places to be fairly certain of what there is.

Insulating from outdoors

If you have wooden clapboard, shingles, or vinyl siding, it probably makes sense to insulate from outdoors. First, you'll need to remove a row of siding and drill a hole in each stud bay. If you are using a fill tube (my preferred method), plan for a row of holes one-third to halfway up the wall on each story. If you have a nozzle, you will need one row of holes about 3 ft. from the bottom and another one within 1 ft. of the top on each story.

Whether you are using a tube or a nozzle, you'll also need to drill a hole in each stud bay below windows. I make those holes about 12 in. down from the bottom of the window. In addition, there are usually some odd cavities formed by diagonal bracing, bridging, fire-stopping, and other blocking. The more thoroughly you can find and access those cavities, the better your insulation job will be.

To drill the holes, first strip off a layer of siding for each horizontal row of holes. Shingles or clapboards can be removed by cutting just at the line of the next overlapping layer. Carefully insert a small prybar from the bottom to lift out any nails (in clapboards) and help snap the wood at the cut. Set the siding pieces aside carefully—you may want to label the backs with a marking pen, using letters or numbers to match their locations. Asbestos-cement siding must be treated with care—use a small cat's paw or diagonal cutters to

Insulation in Older Homes

Most homes built before the 1930s had no insulation at all, so if your home is from that era, you will be looking for insulation that was added later. It may be blown-in cellulose or urea-formaldehyde foam. If the walls were already insulated, it is rarely worth adding more, unless you find large areas that were never done at all. One thing to be careful of in older homes is back-plastering. Although unusual, back-plastered walls were built with an extra layer of lath and plaster in the middle of the stud space—this added an extra airspace and reduced heat loss through the wall. Those walls are difficult to insulate due to the narrow space, and it's probably better to leave them alone unless you do major remodeling.

Homes that were built more recently may have minimal insulation—some have insulation that looks like layers of wrinkled paper that may be sandwiched between layers of black paper. Or you may find thin, 1-in. to 2-in.-thick batts made of glass fiber or rock wool. It is possible to add cellulose insulation to walls with those thin layers of insulation, but it is definitely advisable to use a fill tube. If the wall has thicker batts, it will probably be almost impossible to get the fill tube into the wall cavity without bunching the insulation; in that case, it won't be worth trying to add more.

Vinyl and Aluminum Siding

Vinyl siding can usually be unlocked one course at a time (two clapboards in height) with a Zip tool, which is simply an insulation push rod with a hook at one end and a handle at the other. Unlock the top of the course where you want to drill holes, then reach in with a prybar and remove the nails holding the siding strip. Short pieces of siding may not flex enough to pull out safely; you can slide them down between the trim channels to expose the sheathing. When working with vinyl, make sure your hands are clean, or you could permanently stain the plastic. Aluminum siding can also be removed with a Zip tool, but watch out—it dents easily. On a windy day, the material can easily bend and, once damaged, both vinyl and aluminum siding may be difficult to match.

The unlocking tool for vinyl or aluminum siding is just an insulation push rod, with a bent hook at one end and a round handle at the other. Be very gentle, especially near the corners and around window trim. You can also use a prybar to help open the siding, but be careful not to mar, bend, or break the lower piece.

PRO TIP

When preparing to insulate walls from the outside, be sure to remove pictures from walls and breakable objects from shelves.

Before drilling holes for blown-in insulation, remove the siding, so that you're only drilling through the sheathing. That makes it easier to find stud bays and patch the holes once you're done blowing the cellulose.

WHAT CAN GO WRONG

Beware of loose plaster or drywall, which can be a problem in older homes with plaster on wood lath and in newer homes with poorly installed drywall. If there are any loose or spongy areas, secure them by driving drywall screws into studs before blowing cellulose; they can be patched later. And always keep an eye on the plaster and drywall while filling wall cavities. If there is any sign of bulging or nail pops, cut back on the air pressure or increase the material feed to reduce the density. If you are working from the outside, periodically look indoors or station a helper inside to warn you of any trouble.

To remove a wooden shingle or clapboard, first cut into it with a sharp utility knife, tilting the blade upward so the joint will shed water when you put it back together.

Once the top edge is scored with a knife, pry up from the bottom to snap off the shingle.

Estimating Cellulose Wall Insulation

To figure the amount of cellulose needed to insulate walls, multiply the height and width of the walls to obtain the square footage. Subtract areas that are already insulated, as well as any large window or door areas. Divide the area by 3 (assuming a 4-in.-thick wall cavity) to get the total cubic feet you are insulating. Then multiply the cubic feet by 2.5 (if you are using a nozzle) or 3 (if you have a fill tube) to get the approximate weight of material needed (in pounds). This method will probably overestimate, but it's easier to bring back some unopened bales than to have to run out and buy more when you are in the middle of a project.

When working with asbestos-cement siding, rule number one is never damage the shingles! Drilling, cutting, or sanding them can release harmful asbestos fibers.

Start filling each wall bay by pushing the fill tube *up* from the center of the bay. Keep the control switch close at hand, so that you can find it in a hurry when you need to shut off the flow of cellulose.

pull the nail heads and gently ease out the shingles. If necessary, take off two courses to expose the exterior sheathing.

If the house is sided with vertical tongue-and-groove or board-and-batten, or some type of plywood siding, you'll have to make a decision. One option is to drill right through the siding and try to patch it seamlessly (good luck with that!). Another option is to try to remove a substantial amount of siding. A third (and maybe the best) option is to drill and blow the wall cavities from the interior. If you have brick veneer, stucco, or other masonry cladding, you really don't have much choice but to insulate from the inside.

Filling walls with a tube

Once you've drilled the holes, you're ready to begin. Whether the holes are on the inside or the outside, the basic technique is the same. If you have a fill tube, start by inserting the tube up into the wall bay, pushing it in so the end is close to the top. It's not a bad idea to cover the hole around the tube with a small piece of fiberglass

Once you have dense-packed the upper half of the wall cavity, continue by inserting the tube down at the bottom.

PRO TIP

If one wall bay seems to take a long time to fill, check the basement or nearby closet for a pile of cellulose.

WHAT CAN GO WRONG

Wall cavities that open into a basement, chimney chase, built-in cabinet, or other open area can turn into bottomless pits for insulation. Before you start blowing cellulose, check for any of these potential cavities against exterior walls. Also, check the subfloor in the basement just above the sill. If you find any openings, you must block them to avoid filling the basement with a pile of cellulose!

In some cases, walls are framed so that the bays open into the basement. The bottoms of the wall bays must be stuffed with fiberglass before the wall cavities can be blown with cellulose.

Be sure to plug any holes cut in the sheathing, even if the siding will cover them later. Precut tapered plugs are generally available from a cellulose supplier.

Once the hole is plugged, set the shingle or siding in place and attach with siding nails.

or a rag; this helps control dust and keep cellulose from blowing back out of the hole.

Start the machine, let it fill the wall cavity until the material flow starts to back up, then pull back the tube 6 in. to 8 in. (this process is described in more detail on p. 73). Continue until you have filled the upper half of the cavity, then fill the lower half of the cavity in the same way. The lower part will fill up quickly, since it will already have a fair amount of material in it.

Cavities under windows are filled in the same way, except there's no upper half to do. When you finish each hole, make sure that it is tightly packed; it should be difficult to push a finger through the cellulose.

When you are finished, plug the holes and refinish the surface. From the outside, tap in wooden plugs, then neatly replace the siding. You will probably need to apply some touch-up primer and paint as well, depending on the finish.

Some walls in older houses open into attic areas. Before you start drilling, check for this situation—you'll save yourself a lot of drilling if you can just insulate the wall cavities from the attic. (Photo © Bruce Harley)

Whether you're drilling from the interior or the exterior, a self-feeding bit makes it easy to drill the large holes needed for blowing cellulose into walls.

After filling each stud bay with cellulose, the nozzle holes in the wall are patched with slightly inset Styrofoam® plugs and ready-mixed patching compound.

Drilling and patching from indoors

If you have siding that you don't want to deal with, or if you are planning to substantially remodel, paint, or paper the interior, it may be easier to drill and insulate from indoors. Of course, this will be much more disruptive and dusty, but it may be a lot faster and easier, especially if you are doing significant refinishing anyway.

The preparation is basically the same as insulating from the outside, except there's no siding to remove. If you have a fill tube, make a row of holes about halfway up the wall, with one or two holes in each stud bay (don't forget the bays under windows). If you are using a nozzle, drill one row about 3 ft. from the floor, fill the holes with material, then do another set 12 in. to 18 in. from the ceiling.

There are two options after you've finished blowing cellulose into the wall. One is to insert

PRO TIP

If you are insulating an overhang that is covered with a vinyl or aluminum soffit material, you will first have to remove it carefully—don't try to drill through it.

WHAT CAN GO WRONG

One common mistake when installing kraft-faced fiberglass batts is to staple the facing tabs to the bottom of the floor joists. In most climates, this is incorrect for two reasons. First, the vapor barrier is on the cold side; more important, the insulation is typically not in contact with the subfloor. I've never seen problems resulting from vapor diffusion into a floor, but unfaced batts are better than improperly installed faced batts. And the insulation should be in contact with the subfloor.

While stapling a faced batt to the floor joists is common practice, this is the wrong way to install fiberglass insulation in floors—unless you live in a hot climate. A vapor barrier belongs on the warm side of the insulation. (Photo © Kevin Kennefick.)

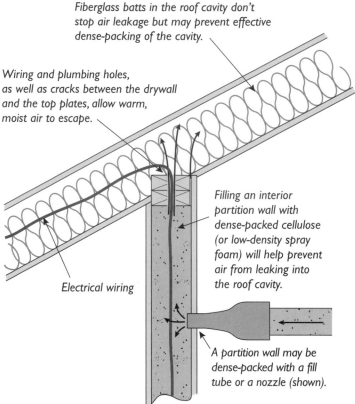

Fiberglass batts in the roof cavity don't stop air leakage but may prevent effective dense-packing of the cavity.

Wiring and plumbing holes, as well as cracks between the drywall and the top plates, allow warm, moist air to escape.

Electrical wiring

Filling an interior partition wall with dense-packed cellulose (or low-density spray foam) will help prevent air from leaking into the roof cavity.

A partition wall may be dense-packed with a fill tube or a nozzle (shown).

Strategic Dense-Packed Cellulose
If you have cathedral ceilings that are already insulated with fiberglass batts, or for some other reason are unable to dense-pack the roof cavities, dense-packing partition walls with cellulose is about the only way to reduce air leakage without demolishing the interior walls.

premade styrene foam plugs (they're usually available from a cellulose supplier), slightly inset from the existing wall surface. The holes can then be conventionally patched with a good-quality Spackle or setting-type joint compound. If you

+ SAFETY FIRST

Before working on a ladder, always make sure it's stable. Keep your body weight in the middle—don't overreach. Ladder jacks and staging can help. They are well worth the trouble of setting up, because you can strip siding and insulate a large area before having to move the staging. Follow the safety instructions carefully, use common sense, and be especially careful while drilling. The torque developed by a 1½-in. or 2-in. self-feed drill bit can be quite dramatic. If the bit binds in the wall sheathing, the handle can kick back violently, knocking you right off your perch.

are doing substantial refinishing, or if you want a more solid patch, it may be worth making drywall patches instead; they are more time-consuming but less likely to crack or pop over time.

Strategic dense-packing

You can also use dense-packing to seal air leaks between interior partition walls and cathedral-ceiling or flat-roof cavities. The technique is the same as that of filling exterior wall cavities from the interior. Use it for plumbing walls, duct chases, and other places that are likely to have big leaks into the ceiling cavity (avoid doing this around a chimney chase!). This is a messy job, but if you have significant ice damming or cathedral-ceiling dripping, it may be the cheapest and best fix. In that case, try to do all the interior partitions as well. Be extra careful when drilling into walls that contain plumbing and other services.

Insulating Floors

There are several types of floors that need insulation: those over a basement or crawl space (if you choose not to insulate the foundation walls); those that extend past the house in cantilevers, on stilts, or on piers; and slab-on-grade floors that surround heated spaces. Slab-on-grade floors include the open side of a walkout basement, if it is conditioned space.

Insulating an open floor with batts (over a basement or crawl space)

If your floor is open—that is, with exposed joists to which you have access from below—the easiest way to insulate it is with unfaced fiberglass batts. Be sure to buy batts that match the size of the joist spacing (usually 16 in. o.c.) and hold them in place with insulation push rods spaced every 2 ft. or so.

Don't depend on friction to hold fiberglass batts in place, or they will soon fall down. And don't use faced batts, thinking that the flanges can be stapled to the joists, because the vapor barrier will end up on the wrong side of the insulation. The batts should be in full contact with the floor and not compressed too much by the push rods. Be sure to cut and fit the batts neatly around any cross-bridging, plumbing pipes, and other obstructions in the floor system. If you want a finished appearance, cover the bottom of the joists with a vapor-permeable housewrap or, better yet, drywall.

I recommend the following R-values for floor insulation: In mild climates, R-19 will meet or exceed energy codes; in cold climates, R-30 or R-38 will do. Plan to fill the floor framing close to its full depth. If you have only 6-in.- or 8-in.-deep joists and want more insulation, attach extruded-polystyrene (XPS) foam to the underside of the floor for a higher R-value. Use screws and 1-in.-dia. fender washers to make

Push rods are used to hold unfaced fiberglass insulation batts in place in the floor joists. It's important not to compress the fiberglass too much with the push rods.

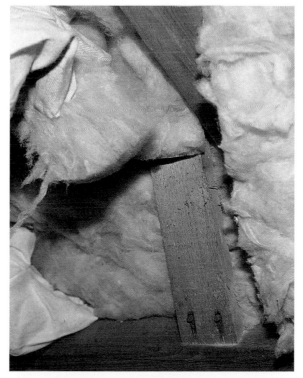

Fiberglass batts must be carefully cut and woven around any bridging, blocking, or other obstructions in the floor framing.

PRO TIP

Be extra careful when drilling holes in floors, walls, and ceilings; you may run into pipes or wires.

WHAT CAN GO WRONG

When insulating a cantilevered overhang, drill into the soffit at the bottom and use a nozzle. But be careful: Some floor cavities open into a basement or other part of the house. If you have access, stuff the bays from inside with a big hunk of fiberglass. If there is no access, set the machine for more material (or less air pressure), to reduce the density, and to avoid overfilling the cavities.

This overhang was hidden by a porch ceiling made of perforated vinyl soffit. The only solution was to remove the soffit and insulate the overhang before installing a drywall ceiling. Note the patches below the overhang that resulted from drilling and blowing the exterior house wall.

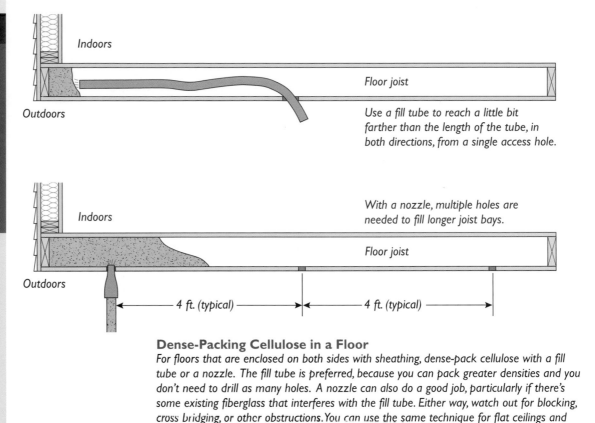

Indoors

Outdoors

Floor joist

Use a fill tube to reach a little bit farther than the length of the tube, in both directions, from a single access hole.

With a nozzle, multiple holes are needed to fill longer joist bays.

Indoors

Outdoors

Floor joist

|← 4 ft. (typical) →|← 4 ft. (typical) →|

Dense-Packing Cellulose in a Floor
For floors that are enclosed on both sides with sheathing, dense-pack cellulose with a fill tube or a nozzle. The fill tube is preferred, because you can pack greater densities and you don't need to drill as many holes. A nozzle can also do a good job, particularly if there's some existing fiberglass that interferes with the fill tube. Either way, watch out for blocking, cross bridging, or other obstructions. You can use the same technique for flat ceilings and attics with subflooring (drill from above, or remove a floorboard).

sure the foam stays in place. Check your local building code; foam insulation may need to be covered with ½-in. drywall or plywood for fire safety.

+ SAFETY FIRST

Be extra careful when drilling holes in any building cavities, including floors, walls, and ceilings. You may run into pipes or wires. Before you start, make a note of the general location of plumbing fixtures and pipe runs that may be nearby; wiring will be more difficult to assess. Go slowly, avoid pushing the drill or saw past the sheathing or drywall, and use the holes you have already opened to probe or look with a flashlight to find out what's there. And make sure there is no active knob-and-tube wiring before installing any insulation.

Insulating an enclosed-cavity floor with cellulose

Any floor that is exposed to outdoor conditions or unconditioned space and has solid sheathing on the underside can be insulated with blown-in cellulose. Examples include garage ceilings, exposed heated porches, cantilevered overhangs, and sheathed floors built on piers. The process is the same as that of filling cavities in cathedral ceilings or walls (see pp. 71–74). You must drill holes in each bay, then patch the holes when you are done.

First, determine whether you will use a fill tube or a nozzle to fill the spaces. A fill tube requires fewer holes and does a better job, but it takes longer to install the material, and the tube may be difficult to find. You can also use a 2-in.-dia. nozzle, which requires many more holes if you are doing a large area. If the floor is already partially insulated with batts, a nozzle may be preferable, because a fill tube can easily get caught in fiberglass. Some contractors use 1-in.-dia. nozzles, but it's impossible to get a truly dense application with a smaller nozzle.

You will need a heavy-duty hole saw or rotary drill bit large enough to fit the fill tube or nozzle—generally 2 in. or 2½ in. Drill one hole between the joists in the middle of each floor bay. Use a stud finder to locate the first joist bay, or drill a hole and probe the space with an insulated wire to find the nearest joist and the direction in which it runs.

If you are using a fill tube, drill a line of holes, one in each bay, across the space. The row of holes should not end more than 2 ft. past the length of the fill tube (see the drawing on the facing page), because the tube cannot blow material farther than 2 ft. If the length of each bay is much greater than twice the length of the fill tube, drill an additional row of holes farther down, so that you can reach the entire floor. You will also need extra rows if you find solid blocking between the joists.

Blow in the insulation in the manner described for attic slopes (see pp. 72–74). If you have a fill tube, push it in as far as it will go, turn on the machine, and keep pulling out the tube slowly as

Using a piece of fiberglass to contain the air pressure and help control dust, the cellulose is blown into a floor bay. (Photo © Bruce Harley.)

Protecting Foam Insulation

If you insulate a slab or foundation wall from the exterior, you must protect the insulation above grade to prevent damage from sunlight; typically, this is done with some type of stucco. Other materials that protect foam board include pressure-treated plywood and bendable vinyl coil stock. Several companies also make a preformed insulating panel with a tough UV-resistant surface, or a layer of solid cement.

One problem with applying rigid or spray-on (shown here) foam insulation to the exterior wall of a foundation is that it is difficult to finish reliably. (Photo © Bruce Harley.)

PRO TIP

Avoid installing carpeting on uninsulated slab floors. Moisture may condense on the cool concrete, creating a mold problem.

WHAT CAN GO WRONG

In termite-prone areas, exterior foam board is not recommended, because insects can hide behind the insulation on their way into the house. However, some manufacturers have begun to make insect-resistant polystyrene-foam products. Typically, those products do not have insect-repelling qualities that will protect your home; they only prevent critters from nesting in the material. Check your local building code to see whether those products are acceptable for such applications in your area.

TRADE SECRET

If your floor already has some insulation, but it does not fill the cavity, dense-packing with cellulose can dramatically improve the performance of the existing insulation—particularly if it is not fully in contact with the floor above. Dense-packing also significantly helps reduce cold drafts in the area.

the material backs up. If you need to, hold a small piece of fiberglass over the hole so the dust doesn't blow in your face (always wear a dust mask and safety glasses). When the end of the tube nears the hole, turn off the machine, push the tube into the joist space in the other direction, and repeat the process. When you are done with that hole, you should have a tightly packed fill that is difficult to push a finger through.

If you are using a nozzle, drill a hole in each joist bay about 2 ft. from one wall. Fill each hole until the material backs up, then go on to the next hole. Drill another set of holes about 4 ft. from the first, then fill them; work your way across until you've filled the entire floor.

When you are done, put a plywood plug in each hole so the surface is just shy of the drywall or sheathing material, and patch it with a good-quality instant patching compound or a nonshrinking wood filler. Prime and paint to match.

A finished floor can be installed over an uninsulated concrete slab. First, cover the slab with a layer of 6-mil polyethylene sheeting, followed by a continuous layer of rigid foam, then 1×3 sleepers at 16 in. o.c., and a plywood subfloor.

Insulating an open floor with cellulose

If you want to do a better job insulating an exposed floor, consider installing some sheathing and using cellulose. This method is more expensive and takes longer than using fiberglass batts, but the results are worth it. The basic idea is to install sheet material, such as plywood, oriented strand board (OSB), or drywall, on the bottom of the joists to hold the insulation in place. Nail or screw ½-in.-thick sheathing to the bottom of the joists. If you use drywall, set your screws 8 in. o.c. and make sure the heads don't tear the paper. Don't use drywall in an area that is prone to moisture, such as outdoors or in a crawl space.

The cellulose can be blown in through holes drilled in the sheathing, as discussed above, or, if you have a fill tube, you can leave a 6-in. gap between rows of sheathing across the joist bays in the middle of the floor. Fill in the bays with cellulose, and then fill in the gap with a 6-in.-wide strip of sheathing to match.

Insulating a slab floor

An uninsulated slab floor can cause a lot of heat loss, especially if the edges are at or above grade level. It can be cold and uncomfortable in the winter, and cool and damp in the summer. If the floor is unfinished, or you are planning to remodel anyway, a layer of extruded polyethylene, with

+ SAFETY FIRST

Insulating hides both structural and water-leakage problems in your foundation walls—at least temporarily, until the wall caves in or the space floods. Make sure the foundation is both well drained and structurally sound *before* installing insulation. If you can't be certain, it is probably better to insulate the floor above.

FOUNDATION MOISTURE CONTROL

New foundations for any substantial addition or renovation project should be built so that they are warm, dry, and mold-free. Here are some important details that can help with those objectives. Of course, check local codes regarding additional requirements, including structural requirements.

Even when footing drains successfully carry water away from foundation walls, they usually don't draw groundwater below the level of the footing. This means that even a "properly" drained footing can be sitting in water, and wick water up and into the foundation wall. Capillary action between footings and foundation walls can be stopped by a layer of cementitious waterproofing, such as Thoroseal™, applied to the tops of footings before pouring the walls. Because large pores can also stop capillary action, footings can be poured on top of several inches of washed, uniform, graded stone (between ½ in. and 1½ in. dia.), as shown in the drawing below. The drain pipe should not be below the level of the footing unless the footing is poured on top of washed stone, as shown!

Note the 4-in.-dia. PVC pipe, which ends at an open tee fitting, embedded in the washed stone just under the slab. For less than $200, you can simply run the pipe through the roof to provide passive ventilation. In the event that radon is found later, all that would need to be added is an in-line fan (in the attic) to actively vent the subslab area. Capping the pipe just above the slab saves money up front; later, if radon is found, an in-line exhaust fan can be added with an exhaust pipe venting to the outside, but it's more expensive to add that once the building is finished.

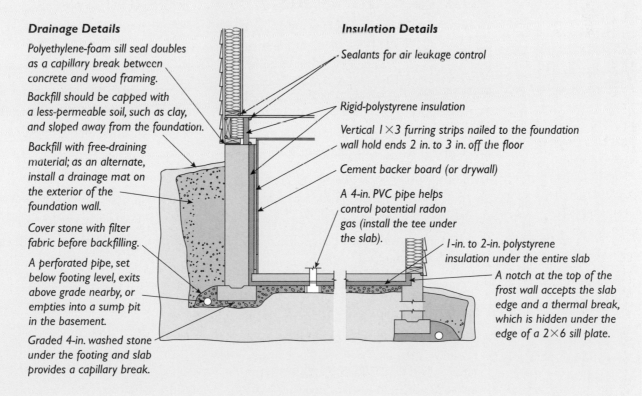

Drainage Details

Polyethylene-foam sill seal doubles as a capillary break between concrete and wood framing.

Backfill should be capped with a less-permeable soil, such as clay, and sloped away from the foundation.

Backfill with free-draining material; as an alternate, install a drainage mat on the exterior of the foundation wall.

Cover stone with filter fabric before backfilling.

A perforated pipe, set below footing level, exits above grade nearby, or empties into a sump pit in the basement.

Graded 4-in. washed stone under the footing and slab provides a capillary break.

Insulation Details

Sealants for air leakage control

Rigid-polystyrene insulation

Vertical 1×3 furring strips nailed to the foundation wall hold ends 2 in. to 3 in. off the floor

Cement backer board (or drywall)

A 4-in. PVC pipe helps control potential radon gas (install the tee under the slab).

1-in. to 2-in. polystyrene insulation under the entire slab

A notch at the top of the frost wall accepts the slab edge and a thermal break, which is hidden under the edge of a 2×6 sill plate.

PRO TIP

Most of the heat loss in a foundation occurs near the top of the wall, which is exposed to outdoor temperatures, but I recommend insulating the entire wall.

TRADE SECRET

Slab floors that are more than a few feet below grade don't cause much heat loss but, because they stay cool in the summer, they may trigger moisture condensation in humid weather. If it has carpeting on it, a slab floor has the potential to be a mold factory. For this reason alone, a slab floor may well be worth insulating for health concerns.

The surface of this uninsulated slab floor stays damp from condensation for most of the summer. (Photo © Bruce Harley.)

IN DETAIL

Insulate foundation walls with polystyrene foam to provide substantial contact between the insulation and foundation wall, which prevents air circulation. To meet code, the foam may still have to be covered with a fire barrier (½-in. drywall or cement tile backer board on wood studs).

1×3 furring as a nail base, makes a good foundation for a plywood subfloor. First put down a layer of 6-mil polyethylene sheet to act as a moisture barrier. Attach the sleepers to the slab with powder-actuated fasteners or concrete screws (if recommended by the manufacturer of the finished flooring you plan to install). You will lose a couple of inches of headroom with this approach, but it may be well worth it in greater energy efficiency, comfort, and moisture control.

Because most of the heat loss from a slab-on-grade floor is at the edges, you can install rigid-foam insulation (polystyrene) vertically on the outside of the slab instead. The insulation must descend vertically at least 2 ft. from the top of the slab. The technique is not worth doing unless you are excavating around the perimeter of the house for some other reason.

Insulating Foundation Walls

If you have a basement or a crawl space, chances are pretty good that the walls are not insulated. If you have heating equipment in the space, it is probably not very cold in the winter, either—the thermal boundary is ambiguous. If you use it for anything besides storage, or if you are planning to finish all or part of the basement later, I recommend insulating the foundation walls rather than the floor above. I also recommend insulating the crawl space walls instead of the floor joists (see the top right photo on p. 46). Remember that if you do insulate the floor, you will also need to insulate the furnace ducts or the heating pipes in the basement (see pp. 110–115 and the sidebar on p. 125).

Foam insulation with drywall

If you insulate the walls, I recommend using rigid foam board, or rigid foam with a stud wall. It's common to build a stud wall and put fiberglass in

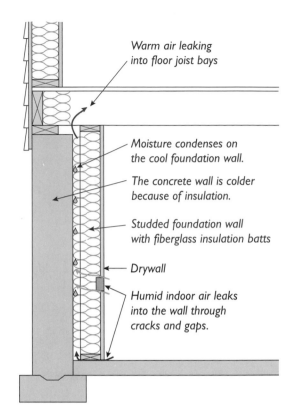

Warm air leaking into floor joist bays

Moisture condenses on the cool foundation wall.

The concrete wall is colder because of insulation.

Studded foundation wall with fiberglass insulation batts

Drywall

Humid indoor air leaks into the wall through cracks and gaps.

Basement Condensation
Foundation walls are often cool, and they get cooler when they are insulated. If indoor air can circulate past the insulation, it is more likely to cause condensation on the foundation wall. The resulting damp conditions can contribute to smelly and unhealthy mold growth.

the wall cavities, but this may result in mold or moisture problems, regardless of the climate (see the drawing above). Extruded polystyrene (which is typically blue, yellow, or green) is, for several reasons, the best material to put against a foundation or crawl space wall. It doesn't deteriorate when exposed to moisture and is vapor-permeable enough to allow walls to dry in either direction—an important quality for foundations.

Most of the heat loss in a foundation wall occurs near the top of the wall, where it's exposed to outdoor temperatures, but I recommend insulating the entire wall. The cost to insulate the entire wall is not much more than doing just the upper half. Also, if you insulate and finish the entire wall, you will have a much nicer finished space in the basement.

I recommend a minimum insulation value of R-10 (2 in. of XPS). In cold climates with full basements, you can double that with a 2×4 wall built inside the foam and insulated with fiberglass batts. Either way, set the foam board against the wall, then build a 2×4 stud wall just inside to hold the drywall in place. Code requires that the drywall not depend on adhesives for its attachment to the foam board.

As an alternative to building an entire stud wall, you can install 1×3 vertical furring strips to hold the foam in place and provide a base for attaching the drywall. The wood furring must be mechanically attached to the foundation wall with powder-actuated nails or concrete screws. Make sure the fasteners are long enough to pass through the foam board and furring and attach reliably to the foundation wall. Then the drywall can be screwed directly to the furring strips.

Basement Finish Materials

If you are trimming finished basement walls with baseboard, consider installing molded vinyl or a fiber-cement product to help protect them against moisture and mold. If the basement is damp, consider using cement tile backer board instead of drywall. It's more expensive, but it won't break down with moisture. Most important, cement board lacks the paper facing that makes drywall a very mold-friendly material. A compromise: Install cement board for the bottom 1 ft. to 2 ft. and moisture-resistant drywall for the rest. I use skim-coat (veneer) plaster for a nice finish on cement-board wall surfaces.

A recipe for mold and rot: Wood studs and fiberglass against an uninsulated concrete foundation wall can harbor mold. Humid indoor air leaking through gaps around the plate, electrical boxes, or elsewhere can condense on the cool concrete and damage the wall.

Instead, insulate behind the studs with 1-in. to 2-in. polystyrene insulation. The wall is then insulated with fiberglass batts.

To avoid moisture problems, hold the bottom end of the drywall at least ½ in. above the floor to prevent wicking of water. Note that this wall needs no vapor barrier.

✓ According to Code

Building codes require that foam board be covered with a minimum of ½-in. drywall or plywood as a fire barrier. In a crawl space, the floor *may* be considered adequate separation between the foam board and the living space—but check with your local building inspector to make sure.

CHAPTER FIVE

1 Window and Energy Basics, p. 90

2 Replacing Windows, p. 92

3 Improving Existing Windows, p. 99

Over the past decade, updated energy codes, increasing energy prices, and improved technologies have given us much better windows at affordable prices. The question is, should you replace the old windows in your house with new, more energy-efficient windows? The short answer is, probably not. Air-sealing, insulation, duct-sealing, and other thermal measures almost always save more energy for less investment.

However, if you do choose to replace your windows, don't spend your money on relatively cheap replacement windows that probably won't significantly reduce your energy costs. In this chapter, I'll show you how to select the right windows. You will also see that one size does not fit all: The right window specifications vary according to climate. Finally, I'll show you how to improve the thermal performance of your existing windows.

IN DETAIL

Replacement windows usually don't pay for themselves in energy savings. But once a house has had air-sealing, insulation, and duct-sealing, the energy costs associated with windows make up a proportionately larger percentage of the total energy dollars. At that point, window improvements may make more economic sense, and when you do replace windows for any other reason, the added cost of high-performance windows is usually easy to justify based on the energy savings they offer.

WHAT CAN GO WRONG

Don't waste time weather-stripping windows and doors unless you've first air-sealed your attic and basement. Otherwise, you'll just build a chimney, with nice, tight sides of weatherproofed doors and windows and insulated walls. Air will leak in from the basement, flow up through the house, and out from the attic.

Where Your Heating Dollars Go
As this chart shows, the windows in a typical New England house—most of which are single-pane wooden windows with storms—only represent 19% of its annual heating bill. Replacing them with vinyl-insulated glass windows would save less than 3% on the heating bill. Vinyl, low-e argon-gas windows would save quite a bit more, about 11%, at very little extra cost. A set of high-performance replacement windows may save 15% to 17%, but expect to pay a premium. Windows are rarely a cost-effective improvement based solely on energy savings.

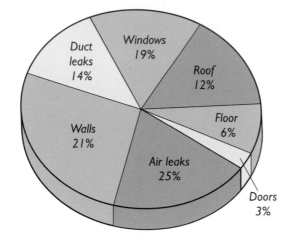

Some replacement windows can be installed without your having to replace the interior or exterior trim. Although these new windows may look and function better than the old ones, don't be lured by a promise of big energy savings.

Window and Energy Basics

Of all the materials we use in our homes, we probably expect the most of windows. They are constantly forced into compromise: We want them to let light in, then we add shades to keep light out. We require that they seal tightly against air and rain, but we want to open them to let in air, then we cover them with screens to keep insects out. We want them to keep heat in during winter and out during summer; we want them to keep water out all the time. It's no wonder that windows end up being expensive to buy and maintain.

The lure of replacement windows

Replacement window manufacturers and installers often sell their products with the promise that new windows will reduce your heating

and cooling bills. In certain cases, big savings may theoretically be possible, but it is rare to find a situation where that is realistic. In fact, in a typical New England house, windows account for less than 20% of annual energy costs. Even if you shuttered all of them with 4 in. of high-R insulation, you still couldn't save any more than that.

I have seen homes in which the owners replaced their old, single-pane and storm combination windows with cheap double-pane units, and their energy bills (and street noise) actually increased. Even if you buy replacement windows at a good price and install them yourself, the payback is unlikely to be within 20 years. If you pay someone to install inexpensive replacement windows, it's more likely to be 40 years or more, far longer than the expected service life of the windows themselves. In short, the benefits of replacement windows are often overstated. If you're buying replacement windows, you need to do your homework: Windows are expensive, and buying the wrong ones can be a costly mistake.

Types of windows

Up until the 1960s, standard windows in the United States were built with a single layer of glass. In cold climates, they were often accompanied by storm windows. Since then, standard fare has been a sealed double layer of clear glass, commonly called *insulated glass*. Now, homes with single-pane glass are relatively rare in the cold- and mixed-climate zones of the United States.

Typically, the insulated glass used in most residential windows is composed of two layers of glass separated by a metal spacer and sealed to keep out moisture. But not all insulated glass windows are the same—most of the improvements in window technology over the past two decades are practically invisible, but the energy performance from window to window can vary a lot.

Most significant energy features fall into three categories: improvements in the glass, or glazing; improvements in the spacers at the edge of the glazing; and improvements in the sash and frame materials. Glazing improvements can be further divided into two categories: reductions in conductive heat loss and control of solar heat gain.

Energy-efficient features, such as Low-e coatings, warm-edge spacers, and thermal-improved frames, can improve window performance significantly, but they can also be confusing. The frame material does matter—aluminum frames, which are inexpensive and durable, perform poorly in cold climates but don't have as much effect in warm climates. Wood, vinyl, and wood-clad frames and sashes conduct less heat, so they help you keep it in (or out).

Low-e coatings and gas fills

Two window technologies that are fully commercialized and readily available are Low-e coatings and gas fills. Low-e coatings help improve the thermal performance of windows by controlling the amount of solar energy that passes through

them and decreasing the amount of radiated heat transfer. The coating is virtually invisible and is applied to one of the inner surfaces of the sealed double-glazed unit. Low-e windows also have warmer indoor surface temperatures in winter (and cooler in summer), making indoors more comfortable year-round.

Gas fills—typically argon or krypton—replace the air that would normally be between the layers

In cold or mixed climates, most homes with older single-pane windows probably have some variation of this triple-track aluminum-frame storm window.

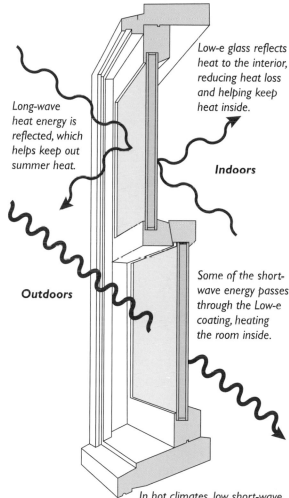

Low-e glass reflects heat to the interior, reducing heat loss and helping keep heat inside.

Long-wave heat energy is reflected, which helps keep out summer heat.

Indoors

Outdoors

Some of the short-wave energy passes through the Low-e coating, heating the room inside.

In hot climates, low short-wave transmission is best for reducing cooling loads. In winter, higher transmission is better for increasing solar gains.

Low-e Glass Reflects Heat, Saving Heating and Cooling Energy
A Low-e coating on glass reflects heat, reducing conductive heat transfer. The amount of short-wave energy the glass should transmit depends on your climate. Low-e coatings also reduce ultraviolet (UV) rays, which fade furnishings.

Most new windows are made with sealed, double-glass units. The edge spacer separates the two layers of glass and provides an insulating airspace that keeps out moisture. However, aluminum spacers conduct heat and are a thermal weak link in the design of a window. (Photo by Jefferson Kolle, courtesy *Fine Homebuilding* magazine, © The Taunton Press.)

WHAT CAN GO WRONG

One thing to consider when buying new windows is the quality of the edge seals. Pay attention to the manufacturer's warranty, which should give you some idea as to how long the seals will last. Well-designed and -constructed edge seals should last 20 years or more. When the seals fail, moisture can condense between the panes of glass, giving them a cloudy appearance.

The death knell of any sealed glazing unit is the failure of the edge seal, which allows moisture to migrate into the space between the glass, resulting in condensation.

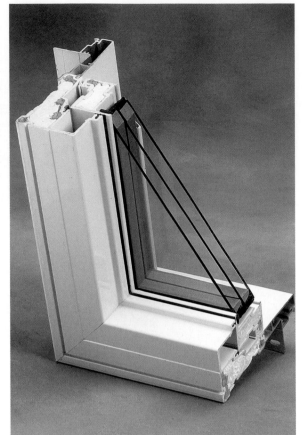

This fiberglass frame conducts much less heat than vinyl and wooden frames do, and it is more dimensionally stable, too. This Canadian-made sample has a third layer of glass, instead of plastic film. (Photo © Kevin Kennefick.)

of glass. Usually added to Low-e windows, these nontoxic, inert gases further decrease the amount of conducted heat, primarily a heating-season benefit. Low-e coatings and gas fills cost a little more, but at $20 to $50 per window (assuming the same frame and sash), the upgrade from ordinary insulating glass to Low-e with argon is well worth it, because their extra cost can be quickly recovered in energy savings.

Advanced windows

A number of other window features that are relatively new to the market are gaining a foothold in the industry. Some of them, such as warm-edge spacers, are finding applications in a wide variety of products. Others, including multiple layers

Anatomy of a High-Efficiency Window

Heat mirror glazing systems usually contain one or two layers of plastic film suspended between two layers of glass. The plastic film has an additional low-e coating embedded in it, but the film is much lighter and thinner than additional glass layers would be. These windows usually have warm-edge spacers, an alternative to the standard heat-conducting metal spacers.

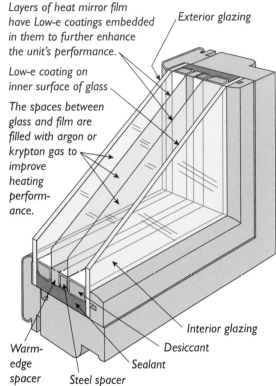

Layers of heat mirror film have Low-e coatings embedded in them to further enhance the unit's performance.

Low-e coating on inner surface of glass

The spaces between glass and film are filled with argon or krypton gas to improve heating performance.

Exterior glazing

Interior glazing

Desiccant

Warm-edge spacer

Steel spacer

Sealant

heat mirror film and insulated fiberglass frames, are found in premium products that cost considerably more. In general, depending upon the climate in which you live and the climate-specific features of the windows, my advice is to buy the best windows that you can afford.

Replacing Windows

Window replacement rarely makes sense from purely an energy perspective. If you have already improved your insulation, performed air- and duct-sealing, and have moderately to highly efficient heating and cooling equipment—all of which are typically more cost-effective upgrades—windows would be the last weak link in the thermal performance of a house.

Of course, there are many other reasons to replace windows. Ease of cleaning and maintenance, aesthetics, damage or rot on the existing windows, and general remodeling are all non-energy-related factors that contribute to the value of window replacement. However, here I'll specifically address the energy features and performance values you should consider when assessing the cost and benefits of new or replacement windows.

Choosing windows

Determining the right combination of window features and price is a complex undertaking, which is further complicated by climate differences. Broadly speaking, when you choose windows, you need to consider function (daylight, glare, egress, ventilation, and maintenance); aesthetics; energy performance (heat loss, UV transmission, condensation control, comfort, and solar gain); and warranty.

I will not say much about the functional qualities of windows, other than to point out that investments in maintenance features—such as vinyl or aluminum cladding on wood windows or tilt-out sash for easy cleaning—can easily pay for themselves with saved hassle and expense. The values of aesthetics and manufacturers' warranties

☑ According to Code

Many energy codes apply not only to new construction and additions, but also contain energy requirements for remodeling and replacement windows. Recent model codes, for example, require a maximum NFRC-rated U-factor of 0.4, or 0.35 for all replacement windows in most cold climates. If you choose Energy Star–rated windows for your house, they will probably meet or exceed local code requirements, but it's always a good idea to check with your local building official to make sure.

Climate Matters!

For a resident of Orlando, Florida, living in a house with typical single-pane aluminum windows, more than half of the cooling bill may be due to the windows. However, changing to insulated glass (yet keeping aluminum frames) will save less than 5% on annual cooling costs. On the other hand, replacing them with vinyl windows with Low-e insulated glass and gas fill may save 24% or more on the cooling bill.

If you are considering upgrading your air-conditioning system, you may first want to upgrade your windows. Window performance has a large impact on cooling loads and can affect an air conditioner's operating efficiency (see chapter 7). If you size a new or replacement air conditioner based on regular glass and later change to insulated Low-e glazing, you will actually hurt the air conditioner's efficiency by decreasing the cooling load. If, on the other hand, you change the glass first, you can save money by installing a smaller air-conditioning unit.

speak for themselves. For all those criteria, as with most products, you get what you pay for—with windows, at least as much as with other products, it is worth buying the best you can afford.

As for energy performance, I consider double-pane, Low-e glass an absolute *minimum* requirement for all climates. Next, avoid aluminum frames. Although still popular in some areas because of their low profile and durability, aluminum frames have a much higher degree of conductivity and are more prone to condensation, which promotes mold growth. Wood, vinyl, and fiberglass frames generally have lower U-factors (an indicator of conductive heat loss) and lower solar heat gain coefficient (SHGC) ratings than those of aluminum frames (with similarly glazed windows). Those are generally beneficial qualities in any climate.

Beyond those basic guidelines, the two primary characteristics to consider are a window's U-factor and SHGC. In cold climates, you should generally buy the lowest U-factor you can afford—that will save you the most on heating costs. In those cases, gas fills are generally desirable, and extra layers

PRO TIP

In northern and mixed climates, south-facing windows can provide free heat gain in winter, while adding little to the cooling load in summer.

WHAT CAN GO WRONG

South-facing windows are a great benefit in cold climates, providing free heat and ample light in winter, but some houses have far too much. Glass area to the south should not exceed 7% of the floor area of the house, unless you have properly designed thermal mass to absorb the excess energy. If there is too much south-facing glass, the space will overheat when the sun shines, and the excess glazing will add to heat loss at night and on cold, cloudy days. Very low U-factors with low SHGC can compensate, but it's better (and cheaper) to replace excess glazing with insulated walls.

This south-facing overhead glass provides free passive solar heat, but it overheats the room when the sun shines and loses too much heat when the sun doesn't. (Photo © Conservation Services Group.)

A tilt-out sash is one useful feature found in replacement windows. (Photo © Kevin Kennefick.)

of heat mirror film are great, if you can afford them. Don't buy a product with a U-factor above 0.35; the best products on the market are rated at about 0.15.

In hot climates, the U-factor is secondary to SHGC—in those case, buy the lowest SHGC available to reduce air-conditioning loads. Tinted glass or spectrally selective Low-e coatings help reduce unwanted heat gain without impacting visibility. Choose a product with a visible transmittance (VT) that is higher than the SHGC

NFRC Window Label

The National Fenestration Rating Council (NFRC) is a non-profit, public/private organization created by the window, door, and skylight industry. The NFRC has established a voluntary national energy-performance rating and labeling system for fenestration products, which is typically the best way to compare true energy performance of windows. This label can be found on most new window products—many states mandate NFRC listing for energy code compliance, and virtually all major manufacturers have their products rated. (The information on the label is typically also available in manufacturers' catalogs; the NFRC product directory is also available online at www.nfrc.org). Note that the numerical values shown are for the entire window unit, including the glass, sash, and frame, and they make it easy to do energy calculations for any window of known dimensions.

Residential size: Use this row for the "average" residential window. The exact sizes of Res and Non-Res vary by window type.

Commercial size: Only use this row if you're buying a really big window.

The "U-factor" (U = 1/R) represents conductive heat loss—smaller is better. Double Low-e windows typically range from 0.3 to 0.4; clear double glass is typically 0.5 to 0.55; and aluminum-frame, single-glazed windows can be over 1.

Solar heat gain coefficient—SHGC— is the amount of direct solar radiant heat that gets in through the window. Lower SHGC reduces summer cooling loads, but higher SHGC increases solar heat gain in winter. Most windows fall between 0.3 and 0.6 on this 0-to-1 scale.

Visible Transmittance—VT—is a measure of how much visible light gets through. Lower VT means reduced glare, but also less night-time visibility. Most windows fall between 0.4 and 0.6 on this 0-to-1 scale.

World's Best Window Co.

Millennium 2000⁺ Casement
CPD#000-x-000

Vinyl-Clad Wood Frame • Double Glaze
Argon Fill • Low E + Solar Control Coatings

National Fenestration Rating Council

CERTIFIED

ENERGY Performance

- Energy savings will depend on your specific climate, house and lifestyle
- For more information, call 11-800-123-4567 or visit NFRC's web site at www.nfrc.org

Technical Information

	U-Factor	Solar Heat Gain Coefficient	Visible Transmittance
Res	.32	.45	.58
Non-Res	.31	.45	.60

Manufacturer stipulates that these ratings conform to applicable NFRC procedures for determining whole product energy performance. NFRC ratings are determined for a fixed set of enviormental conditions and specific product sizes.

rating. Try to select products with SHGC ratings below 0.4; the lowest rated products have an SHGC of about 0.2. Another specification for glass is the light-to-solar gain (LSG) ratio. In hot climates, high LSG means good heat rejection with minimal impact on view and daylight. Look for the highest LSG products, and never buy windows with an LSG less than 1.0.

In a mixed climate, you'll want to compromise between the U-factor and the SHGC. Generally, a low U-factor combined with a low SHGC is desirable. One complication in northern and mixed climates is solar gain. South-facing windows provide free heat gain in winter and add little to the cooling load in summer.

In cold or mixed climates, varying SHGC ratings in a house can really maximize energy efficiency. High-SHGC for south-facing windows maximizes free solar heating in winter. Low-SHGC for east- and west-facing windows, which produce most summer heat gain, minimizes air-conditioning loads. Some manufacturers sell products aimed at northern or southern climates, and you can order matching windows with different glass for different orientations. As long as the low-SHGC glass is not tinted, you'll never see the difference. Mixing window specifications takes some careful planning and a special order, but it can usually be done at little or no extra cost.

If you are comfortable with a computer and really want to optimize your window choices, get some help calculating the benefits of different specifications with free window-energy software called RESFEN (available free on the Internet for Windows™ 98, 2000, NT, or ME users at windows.lbl.gov/software/resfen/). The detailed calculations are a little slow, but the inputs are fairly simple. RESFEN provides results in annual heating and cooling dollars attributed to your windows, so you can compare the differences between product costs and likely annual savings

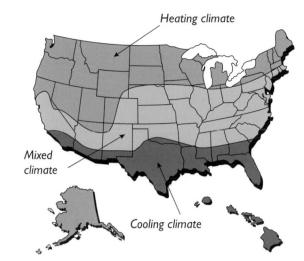

Heating climate

Mixed climate

Cooling climate

EPA's Energy Star Window Regions
The U.S. Environmental Protection Agency (EPA) rates numerous household appliances and other energy-using products in its Energy Star labeling program. Here, windows are rated for better-than-average performance in three climates. The requirements for Energy Star windows include: double, low-e glass in all areas; in the northern U.S., a U-factor of 0.35 or less and nonmetal frames; in the central U.S., a U-factor of 0.4 or less, an SHGC of 0.55 or less, and metal or nonmetal frames; in the southern U.S., a U-factor of 0.75 or less, an SHGC of 0.4 or less, and metal or nonmetal frames. For more information, check out the Energy Star Web site at www.energystar.gov; click on "find products."

and calculate your payback period. Be careful to accurately input your electric and gas utility rates if they are different from the defaults supplied.

Alternatively, you can hire a Home Energy Rater or other building-performance consultant to help you calculate the cost-effectiveness of various options. Those professionals are more likely to understand the nuances of U-factor and SHGC (and are less likely to be biased) than the average window-replacement salesperson.

Replacement sash

When you do decide to replace your windows, there are two basic approaches: replacing the entire window, including the frame, or replacing

Windows Sell

In an admittedly unscientific survey of two *Yellow Pages* directories in my area, one listed seven times as many replacement-window contractors and dealers as it did insulation contractors (the other listed three times as many window dealers). Neither one had a listing for "Air-sealing" or "Building performance," but both had a small handful of businesses listed under "Energy Management and Consulting," which would probably be a good place to look for someone who can give whole-house recommendations.

PRO TIP

If you decide to replace your windows, there are two basic approaches—replacing the entire window (including the frame) or replacing just the sash.

WHAT CAN GO WRONG

Don't try to second-guess the downsizing adjustment between the inside dimensions of an existing window frame and the frame dimensions of the replacement sash or pocket. Buy window kits from a reputable dealer who is experienced in the replacement business and let him or her do the figuring. Otherwise, you may end up with gaps that are too big to be covered by the trim...and lots of headaches.

TRADE SECRET

Some people are concerned about argon gas leaking through glass and wasting their investment, but this is largely a myth. Studies have shown that the vast majority of gas loss is due to poor design or assembly of the edge seals. In well-built units, gas loss results in just a few-percent change in the window's performance over a 20-year lifetime. By the time the seals fail and fill the unit with moisture, no one will care about the performance of the gas fill.

just the sash. Sash replacement is usually accomplished with a unit that includes a new frame to carry the replacement sash. The frame fits in the pocket between the old stops. This approach is less expensive and involves a lot less trim work, but most products are limited to double-hung styles. If you choose that approach, keep in mind that the added frame thickness will slightly reduce the glass area and view. Some kits include only the sash, jamb liners, and hardware, without the integral frames. They are trickier to install well, though they tend to look more like original windows.

You must accurately measure the dimensions of the existing frames, then order replacement units that will fit properly. Check both the height and the width in several places, in case the jambs are not parallel, and use the shortest distance for ordering purposes. If your existing window frames are badly out of square, replacement-sash or pocket kits will never fit properly. If the side frames are bowed inward, it may indicate that the window frame is carrying loads from above due to inadequate header support. Either of these conditions requires replacing the entire window. In the latter case, you may need to make significant structural repairs as well. Check the old frame carefully for moisture damage, and remember that a damaged sill can indicate that water has leaked into the wall beyond the window frame.

If you are replacing old double-hung windows that have rope-and-pulley sashes, be sure to remove the old steel weights and insulate the pockets before installing the new windows. One

Many replacement windows can be set into the existing window frame, minimizing disruption to the interior and exterior trim. If you are replacing only the sash, you can use a short length of rope and snake a strip of fiberglass batt into the weight pocket.

Tucking in a strip of fiberglass helps ensure a good fit, but the gap must still be caulked afterward to make an airtight seal.

Before attaching the stops, caulk the frame of a new window to the old frame to ensure a good, airtight seal.

Drafty Windows

Most people assume that their windows leak through the spaces around and between the sash. And some windows do leak pretty badly; old, rattling double-hung or aluminum horizontal sliders tend to be the worst. But often it's the space *between* the window and the rough opening that needs to be sealed. This space is normally covered by casings on the interior and the exterior, and, depending on how tight the casings are, a lot of air may leak through that area. If you aren't otherwise removing the trim, the easiest way to seal those leaks is to caulk the casings where they meet the wall and the jamb—use paintable, siliconized acrylic caulk here. If you are replacing windows or removing the trim for any other reason (or if it's easy to remove), use low-expansion foam.

Another misconception is that insulation R-value is important here. I have seen instructions that suggest how important it is to tuck little tufts of fiberglass gently into the jamb space; that will do nothing to stop air movement. The conductive heat loss through an entire window is probably 10 times greater than that through a small plug of foam around it, as long as you stop the air from leaking. Use low-expansion foam and make sure it bridges the gap completely. Don't use too much foam; if the gap is large, first fill most of the space with a piece of rigid-foam insulation.

When foaming around a new window, be sure to use a light touch (left), or you'll end up with problems. The window opening shown above was sealed with low-expanding foam, but the space was so large that the foam distorted the window frame as it cured. This window probably won't open without some remedial work.

way to do this is by pulling a length of fiberglass batt into the pocket. If you are removing the old trim, seal the pockets with low-expansion foam. Be careful not to fill too much, because it may distort the frames.

As you insert the frames, carefully follow the manufacturer's instructions for shimming and supporting them, and be sure to carefully caulk any gaps between the new frame and the old before installing the trim. Don't use foam between the frames, unless the new frames are very sturdy and well supported. If the gaps are large, tuck in backer rod to fill the spaces, then caulk.

PRO TIP

Replacing an entire window frame offers you the opportunity to inspect the framing, correct water damage, and air-seal the new window.

TRADE SECRET

Before installing adhesive vinyl v-seal weatherstripping on your windows, make sure the surfaces are as clean as possible. Don't depend on the adhesive to hold it in place. It's a good idea to drive a few light-gauge staples every 12 in. or so (through only the back half). The upper sash may already be painted shut; if you don't need to use it, you may want to caulk around the edge to seal it.

Don't depend on the adhesive to hold this weatherstripping in place. Peel it back and staple the backing to the frame at least every 12 in.

This spongy foam rope, called backer rod, can be used to fill large gaps between a window frame and the rough opening. It is available in various diameters and should be caulked in place so it seals well. Backer rod is available at home centers; from masonry-supply dealers; and through energy efficiency suppliers, such as EFI. (Photo © Kevin Kennefick.)

One detail that is especially important is the flashing of any new window frame, which keeps any wind-driven rain that gets past the siding or leaks in the window frame from seeping into the wall cavity. You can only flash if you replace the entire window (see p. 179). Also, pay attention to the instructions for trim installation and exterior caulking details. For example, the gap where a new sill sits on top of the old one is generally left unsealed to allow any water that penetrates to drain freely.

In old, double-hung windows, the spaces in which the counterweights run are potential voids in the wall insulation, and they tend to be drafty. If you are removing the interior trim or plaster, the pockets can easily be sealed with spray foam.

Installing new windows

Replacing the entire unit, jamb and all, offers some advantages over sash replacement. Foremost, new units often let in more light, because they don't have the extra frame thickness that's common with replacement units. Although replacing the frame requires a lot more trimwork, it's also an opportunity to get a good look at the house's framing to see whether there is any damage from leaking water. It is also much easier to seal weight pockets when the interior casing has been completely removed. Of course, adding new trim is significantly less trouble if you are also doing major renovation work on the interior or exterior.

If your existing windows are horizontal sliders, casements, or awning units, replacing the entire

+ SAFETY FIRST

When setting a replacement window in place, have a helper on hand. Replacement units that don't have nailing flanges or trim attached can accidentally push right through the opening and fall out the other side. As always, use caution when working on ladders. To get a window to an upper story (if you can't set it from inside), set up two ladders and have another helper carry the window up with you.

window will likely be your only option. However, existing double-hung windows can be replaced with a different-style unit to change the feel of the house or increase or decrease the view opening (for information on installing new and replacement windows, see *Windows and Doors,* by Scott McBride, a companion volume in the Taunton's Build Like a Pro™ series).

Improving Existing Windows

Short of replacing windows, you may be able to improve their performance significantly—and for a lot less than it would cost to replace them. On one end of the spectrum are the plastic interior storms that you can shrink-wrap onto the window with a hair dryer, as well as the reusable types with a plastic zip strip. Those "renter's" storm windows cost very little and are moderately effective for old, rattling single-pane windows, but they are not very practical or aesthetically pleasing. In many cases, older windows can be successfully weatherstripped, and adding storm windows can be a cost-effective improvement if your budget rules out replacement windows.

Improving old double-hung windows

The classic rope-and-pulley double-hung wood window is a very elegant design that is simple, functional, and repairable. In a drafty, uninsulated wood frame house, they provide light, views, and ventilation without appreciably affecting the house's energy performance. But as the years pass, the wood sash loosens and layers of paint disrupt their fit and operation. Once you effectively insulate and air-seal the building, they become a potentially large energy liability.

If you aren't ready to replace them, rattling window sashes can be tightened with leaf-type or v-seal weatherstripping and pulley seals. In many cases, simply removing excess paint so that the sashes meet properly and the sash locks work can make a big difference in their performance.

Storm windows

Adding storm windows to single-pane glass will reduce the heat loss through the windows by about 50%, in addition to reducing interior condensation and frost, so this project may be worth it. However, storm windows are generally not as attractive as replacement windows, they don't add as much to the resale value of a house, and they

Adhesive vinyl v-seal weatherstripping can be applied to a window frame to reduce air leakage. Cut the weatherstripping to fit, press it in place between the sash and the frame, and peel the paper off the adhesive backing around the edge of the window.

Interior plastic storm windows may save some energy, but they don't do anything for a house's value or appearance. This one has a reusable plastic zip strip to hold it in place.

Installing a pulley seal over the rope and pulley of old double-hung windows is one way to save a little bit of energy, and it is inexpensive and easy to do.

PRO TIP

New storm windows won't save as much energy as new, airtight, Low-e replacement windows, but their cost is relatively low.

IN DETAIL

For years, passive solar and energy-efficiency guides have advocated the use of movable insulation to reduce nighttime heat loss. Effective when used properly, movable insulation saves energy—but at the price of human energy. Insulation also cools the glass, so it must fit snugly; if indoor air touches the cold glass, condensation can result. Panels must be stored during the day; insulating shades on roller tracks are finicky and often fail.

(Photo © Bruce Harley.)

increase the hassle of window cleaning and maintenance. They will not save as much energy as new, airtight, Low-e replacement windows, but they are relatively inexpensive.

Storm windows have been around since the 19th century. Typically, they were fixed panels that were installed seasonally on the exterior of windows. That approach is still an option; a skilled do-it-yourselfer with a decent shop can probably make them for less than the cost of triple-track aluminum storm windows, and they will look much better. If they are carefully made, they will fit much more tightly and not have leaky, movable sashes that allow air through. However, they aren't as flexible—you can't just decide to open them on a mild day. They must be installed and removed every winter and stored somewhere during the summer. If you do decide to make storm panels, try to get hard-coat Low-e glass for better perform-

ance. It's a special order from a glass shop, but the better performance is worth the trouble.

Large picture windows and other fixed-sash glass may also be treated with permanent, fixed storm sashes. In very large openings, Plexiglas®, acrylic, or polycarbonate may be more affordable than glass, which must be tempered for safety. And the only way to add storm panels to casement or awning windows is with clip-on panels that open and close with the sash.

Today, most people who install storm windows choose triple-track aluminum combination units, with movable sashes and screens all in one package. If you do invest in those windows, be sure to get ones with low-leakage ratings (less than 0.3 cfm per ft.), and try to find Low-e glass. Regular Low-e coatings used in sealed, double-glass windows are soft and can't be exposed to weather or handling, but there are special hard-

An exterior storm sash (left) is still a viable option, particularly for a traditional home. The holes at the bottom are vents to let moisture escape, and they are mostly covered by an adjustable stop. Clip-on storm panels (above) with aluminum- or vinyl-edge trim can be permanently installed over fixed picture windows and casement windows. (Left photo by Steve Culpepper, courtesy *Fine Homebuilding* magazine, © The Taunton Press.)

coat Low-e products that hold up well. When installing storm windows, follow the manufacturer's instructions carefully, and don't use any glues or sealants until the frame is screwed firmly in place and you can verify that all the sashes and screens operate smoothly.

With any storm window application, make sure that any moisture that gets between the primary window and the storm can escape, or you may get condensation on the inside surface of a cold storm window. In practice, this means that the storm window must be at least a bit leakier than the primary window. Therefore, if your primary window is very leaky, you will need to improve the weatherstripping, or the storm won't help very much. Controlling indoor relative humidity during the winter can also help, because that reduces the amount of moisture in indoor air.

Other strategies to improve window performance

A number of other strategies can improve window performance without changing or treating the windows or glass directly. In cold climates, drapes or movable insulation can reduce heat loss in winter. If you are diligent, night insulation can be very effective, but few people want to move insulation panels twice a day.

Also, be aware of the effect of shading on south-facing windows. The branches of deciduous trees, often touted as providing beneficial shade in summer while allowing solar gain in winter, actually diminish solar radiation by about half and should be avoided near the south side of a house. Even insect screens on the south side should be removed in winter, because they also cut solar gain significantly.

Be sure to caulk around the frames of new storm windows to maximize their benefit. Remember: It's important to leave the weep holes at the sill open, so any moisture that collects there can drain freely.

On the cooling side, even more can be done to decrease air-conditioning loads. Although shades and blinds on the inside significantly reduce solar gains, external shading is even more effective, because the sun's rays never even hit the glass. Shading that is built onto the house—overhangs, awnings, or porches—or nearby, such as trellises, arbors, and other structures, can prevent or reduce solar heat gain.

Landscaping choices, such as trees and other plantings, can also shade windows. You can shade east- and west-facing windows in any climate to reduce cooling loads, and overhangs can be as deep as you like. It is a little more complicated on the south side of a house. In a hot climate, shading south-facing windows will also help cut cooling loads. In a mixed or cold climate, shading the south side reduces cooling loads, but at the expense of also reducing free solar energy in winter. Moderate overhangs attached to the building right above the windows are the best choice. If they are properly sized, they will admit solar rays in winter, when the sun's angle is low in the sky, and still shade windows in summer, when the sun is overhead.

Heating Systems

CHAPTER SIX

W hat's the best kind of heating system? A good building envelope. A comfortable, draft-free house with high levels of insulation is economical and easy to heat with any type of heating system. Insulate and air-seal first; you'll get the most for your heating dollars. In fact, a new home can be designed in just about any climate with heating loads so low that a conventional heating system will be too big— and thus an unnecessary expense.

While you're improving your home's thermal envelope, basic maintenance of the heating equipment, relatively simple mechanical upgrades, duct-sealing and insulation, and even clock thermostats can all can help save energy. New high-efficiency heating systems and controls can be very cost-effective compared to standard systems, but, of course, the energy savings potential is greater in colder climates, and the cost to replace an entire system is rarely justified by energy savings alone.

PRO TIP

Turning down a thermostat overnight or when people are out does not mean using more energy to bring the house back up to temperature.

IN DETAIL

One problem with setting back the thermostat at night (or while you're away) is that the house is cold when you get up (or come home). If you have a fairly regular schedule, an automatic clock-thermostat can help. Program it to turn down the heat 30 minutes after bedtime and turn up the heat just before you get up. Once it's set, you don't have to do anything. Most clock-thermostats can handle two or more setback periods during the day, and many have 7-day programs for weekends. Some have battery backup to retain the settings in case the power goes out. If you don't like to program your VCR, try to avoid the fancy electronic models.

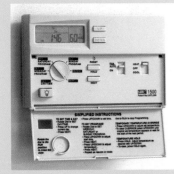

Automatic clock-thermostats can help save energy. (Photo © Kevin Kennefick.)

Simple Conservation

In colder parts of the United States, heating is the biggest single energy expense in most homes. In that case, saving on heating can make a big difference. Aside from the building envelope, your heating system is probably the next biggest factor in your energy use, so anything you can do to improve its operation has the potential to save a lot of energy.

There are many kinds of heating systems (which will be covered later in this chapter), but they all have three common elements: a heating plant, which converts fuel into heat; a distribution system, which delivers heat around the house; and controls, which regulate the system's operation. All have an impact on the efficiency of the system, and all can typically be improved to save energy.

Thermostats

A thermostat is one control that is common to virtually every heating system. Thermostats sense the room temperature and turn the heating plant on when the temperature drops below the set point. The simplest thing you can do to save energy is to turn down the thermostat. Depending on the climate, you can save between 1% and 3% for every degree (Fahrenheit) colder that you keep the house.

Turning down a thermostat saves energy, but only if you're consistent. If one person is always turning down the set point, and another is always turning it back up, you can actually use more energy, because the heating system cycles more than it would otherwise—particularly if the person who gets chilly sets the thermostat even higher than he or she otherwise would. This "dueling manager" syndrome is particularly bad if you have a heat pump. Find the lowest setting that *everyone* in the family is consistently comfortable with, and then leave it alone (other than for long-term setbacks of several hours or more).

Turning down your thermostat can save significant energy, but don't turn it down to the point of discomfort.

Keep in mind that saving energy doesn't mean shivering in the dark. Deprivation is not the best route to efficiency. On the other hand, once you have insulated and air-sealed a house, and perhaps installed high-performance windows, you may find that you are perfectly comfortable at a lower thermostat setting. For example, one of my construction consulting clients built a new house just up the hill from the old Victorian farmhouse he and his wife owned. "One of the most amazing things," he told me, "is the change in our thermostat setting. The old house was so drafty that we had to set the thermostat at 72°F or more to stay comfortable. In this one, we get too warm if we set it above 64°F!"

Another way to save energy with your thermostat is by using a regular setback. Turning down the house temperature for 6 or 8 hours while everyone is asleep, or away during the day, can save a lot—close to 10% for an 8-hour, 10-degree setback. Contrary to popular belief, it does not take more energy to bring the house back up to temperature. Remember, your heating system's only function is to replace heat that the house loses; if the indoor temperature is lower for a period of time, the house loses less heat during

Furnaces or heat pumps that have a ducted distribution system should have manual balancing dampers, like this one, near the takeoffs from the main trunk duct to the branch runs. It is better to adjust the airflow here than at the supply register (shown with duct disconnected for clarity).

that period. When the thermostat goes back up, the long cycle while the heating system catches up is actually more efficient than the more typical, shorter cycles.

Comfort and energy use

Another fairly simple factor that affects heating-system performance is system balancing. *Balancing* refers to the temperature consistency from one room to the next. If one or more rooms are consistently too cold, people tend to set the thermostat high enough to be comfortable in those rooms. The rest of the house will then overheat, using more energy.

Balancing problems can be caused by thermal defects in the building, by problems in the heating distribution system, or by the thermostat location. Rooms that have air leaks, drafts, or missing insulation may lose heat faster than neighboring rooms, or they may just be uncomfortable. Thermal problems should be fixed before addressing the heating system. Once the building envelope is properly treated, the distribution system can usually be adjusted for better balance.

Efficiency Losses in a Furnace

Not all the heat contained in the fuel you buy contributes to keeping your house warm. *Furnace efficiency* is the percentage of the heat that you buy (100%) that does useful work for you; anything less than 100% represents a wasted expense, or loss in efficiency. There are three kinds of furnace efficiency losses: combustion efficiency, off-cycle losses, and distribution losses.

Combustion efficiency is the percentage of the heat bought at the meter that is delivered by the furnace; it varies from 50% to 95%. Of the 5% to 50% of heat that's lost, most is simply heat that goes up the chimney; other combustion losses include incomplete combustion (caused by burners that are dirty or out of tune) and heat that escapes through the cabinet.

A standing pilot flame in a furnace uses gas constantly, even during the summer. That can be a waste of energy.

Off-cycle losses occur when the furnace starts and stops. Each time the furnace shuts off, some heat remains in the furnace; most of that heat goes up the chimney. If you have a standing gas pilot, most of the heat produced by the pilot is lost, particularly if the pilot is left burning all summer long.

Distribution losses occur when heat that is generated by the furnace can't get to where it's needed. Distribution losses include duct air leaks, conductive losses through uninsulated ducts, and airflow problems. Other heating systems (boilers and heat pumps) have similar efficiency losses.

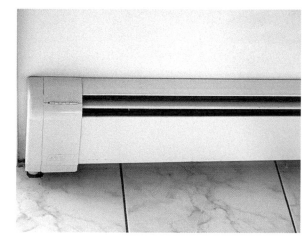

This is a typical hot water radiator, or fin-tube baseboard. Like most fin-tube units, it has a hinged damper to close the slot at the top of the unit and reduce heat output.

PRO TIP

Regular furnace maintenance—including filter replacements, burner tune-ups, and cleanings—is important for safe, efficient operation.

WHAT CAN GO WRONG

Once in a while, I run into a homeowner who tells me, "I never need to change the filter, because it never gets dirty." This typically happens when the filter is installed in a filter grille. If the filter isn't trapping any dirt, it's because there's no air going through it—all (or most) of the return air reaching the furnace is being pulled in through leaks in the return duct, or through some other unintentional pathway between the filter and the furnace.

Filter grilles make changing the filter more convenient, but any air leaks in the duct between the grille and the furnace can pull dust and dirt into the furnace. This filter obviously works and should have been changed months ago.

Gas-fired Hot-air Furnace

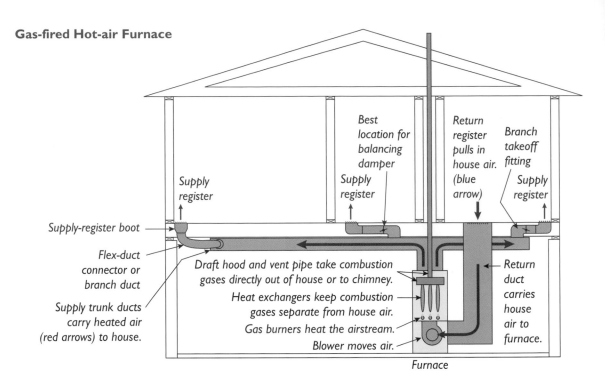

Best location for balancing damper

Return register pulls in house air. (blue arrow)

Branch takeoff fitting

Supply register

Supply register

Supply register

Supply-register boot

Flex-duct connector or branch duct

Supply trunk ducts carry heated air (red arrows) to house.

Draft hood and vent pipe take combustion gases directly out of house or to chimney.

Heat exchangers keep combustion gases separate from house air.

Gas burners heat the airstream.

Blower moves air.

Return duct carries house air to furnace.

Furnace

A furnace directly heats air by burning fossil fuel, such as natural gas, oil, or propane (liquefied petroleum, or LP) gas. The air-handler fan creates air pressure to push house air through the ducts and into the house. Trunk ducts may be made of sheet metal, fiberglass duct board, or flexible round ducts. Branch ducts are typically made of round or rectangular sheet metal or flex duct. Return ducts may be a single central return, as shown here (some bigger homes have two or three), or may run to every room like the supply-duct system. The furnace may be located in a basement (as shown), an attic, a closet, or a garage, depending on the style of house and region of the country.

Air filters should be replaced regularly for best furnace performance. This pleated filter is more efficient than the standard throwaway fiberglass filter, and it doesn't cost much more.

Furnaces

The furnace is by far the most common type of heating system in the country. In fact, it's so common that many people use the word *furnace* to describe any type of heating equipment.

Furnaces create heat by burning fuel, usually natural gas. Oil and propane are also used in areas where piped gas is unavailable. By contrast, heat pumps and electric furnaces use electricity to heat the air; they also use a duct system to deliver heat, but they are not furnaces and do not have a fuel supply, chimney, or vent pipe. Boilers burn gas or oil but create hot water or steam instead of warm air. Furnace efficiency can be improved by performing regular maintenance, improving airflow, adjusting control settings, and sealing leaky ductwork.

Keep furniture away from furnace air registers, and generally leave the dampers open for highest furnace efficiency.

Regular maintenance

The first thing you should do to keep a furnace running efficiently is replace the filter. Airflow is important, and a dirty filter cuts airflow. In most cases, changing the filter is pretty easy, but sometimes access can be difficult. During the heating season, the filters should be replaced every month. Stay away from the washable electrostatic filters or other permanent air filters; most of them provide a lot of resistance to air movement, cutting furnace efficiency. Also, keep the air registers clean and free of obstructions—don't put furniture over them. Close the dampers on registers only in rooms you do not wish to heat, and even then only if there is no hand damper near the trunk duct.

The next important thing is regular burner maintenance. If you have a gas or propane furnace, you should have it cleaned and tuned every two to three years. An oil-fired furnace should be tuned every year. A hint: Don't wait until cold weather hits—that's when the service companies are busy. You may get a better price if you get the tune-up in the spring, just before the heating season is over. Depending on the age of your furnace, you may want to consider a service contract for regular tune-ups and emergency service calls.

Furnace Tune-Up

A good professional tune-up for a gas or propane furnace includes cleaning the burner and heat exchanger, checking the adjustment of air and fuel flow, cleaning and checking heat exchanger integrity, and testing draft pressure and carbon monoxide levels. The air handler fan should be cleaned and lubricated as needed. In addition, internal controls may be checked and adjusted. A combustion efficiency test before and after the tune-up will give you an idea of how much difference the tune up made, but it won't account for the benefits of all the improvements.

Oil burners are more finicky than gas burners. Most oil furnaces benefit from annual professional service; the burner nozzles, electrodes, combustion chamber, heat exchanger, and flue pipe all need regular cleaning and adjustment. It is common practice to replace oil nozzles and fuel filters regularly. In addition, cleaning and checking heat exchanger integrity, cleaning and lubricating the blower, testing the flame sensor, and testing combustion efficiency are all important. Try to find a technician who is knowledgeable, methodical, and thorough.

If you have an oil furnace, the service technician can also install a smaller oil nozzle. This effectively derates, or reduces, the heat output rating of the furnace, better matching it to the house and increasing operating efficiency (see p. 129 for more about the importance of equipment sizing). Some gas furnaces can also be derated, but usually by only 10% to 15%. That won't improve the efficiency as much as it can for oil-fired equipment, and it must be done carefully.

It's surprising how much dirt and grime can accumulate on the furnace blower; cleaning the fan blades can make a significant difference in the airflow.

PRO TIP

Low airflow—which can be caused by dirty filters, undersized ducts, or poorly maintained equipment—is a common cause of furnace inefficiency.

IN DETAIL

If your return-duct system is restricting airflow, installing a grille can significantly increase airflow. But you can't install a return just anywhere; there must be a clear path for the air supplied to the house to get back to it. The return may suck combustion byproducts from the furnace or water heater down through the chimney. If it is located in an attic, a garage, or a crawl space, the new return will bring cold air into the furnace, lowering its efficiency. You may need to add a duct (well sealed, of course) to a new grille in the house.

A probe thermometer can be used to check the temperature rise in a furnace. Be careful locating holes, so that you don't penetrate the A/C coils.

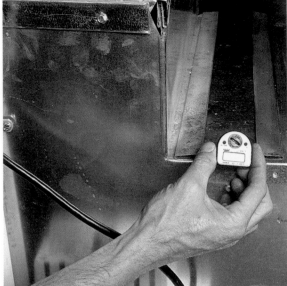

Check the return temperature through a filter slot or a hole drilled in the duct near the air handler.

Low airflow

One of the biggest furnace efficiency problems is low airflow, which has several common causes, including clogged or dirty furnace filters, dirty fan blades, dirty air-conditioning coils, low fan speed settings, loose fan drive belts, undersized duct-work, and duct obstructions.

Diagnosing low airflow is complex, but, once identified, the fixes are usually fairly easy and inexpensive. Other than routine cleaning, most of the fixes need to be performed only once. Most improvements are probably better left to a professional, but it's good to be informed, because many technicians don't bother looking for those problems. If a service person is unable to explain in sensible terms what is happening in your system, you may want to get an opinion from another technician.

Before testing airflow, do the obvious things: Replace the filter and clean the blower fan blades, heat exchanger, and air-conditioning coils. Open all the registers in the house that may be closed. Also, check for cycling caused by the *high-limit control*, a safety switch that protects your furnace and house by turning off the burner if the air gets dangerously

hot (for example, if the blower motor suddenly stopped). To do that, set the thermostat high enough to run the furnace for 15 or 20 minutes. The burner should fire immediately; after a brief delay, the blower should turn on. Once the blower starts, the burner should stay on until the thermostat is satisfied (or turned back down). If the high-limit control thinks that the air is getting too hot, the burner will cycle off and on periodically while the blower runs. That could mean the control is broken or set incorrectly or that the airflow is extremely low.

If the high limit is working properly, the next airflow test is to measure the temperature rise between the return and the supply airstreams. That can be done by using a probe type of thermometer (a wire thermocouple is better if you can find one) to measure the temperature in the supply and return ducts. The supply temperature must be measured in a main supply trunk duct close to the furnace. Drill a small hole on the supply side, close to the middle of the duct but around the first corner or bend in the main supply trunk from the furnace. Be careful not to drill into air-conditioning coils that may be located in the ductwork just above the furnace.

For the return temperature, insert the thermometer into the filter slot or a small hole drilled in the middle of the return duct near the furnace. It's okay to measure the return temperature at the nearest return grille to the furnace, if that's your only option; insert the probe past the grille.

Again, set the thermostat so the furnace will run continuously for 15 or 20 minutes. After the blower starts, let it run for at least 5 minutes before you measure the temperatures. Hold the thermometer in the return airstream, and then in the supply airstream, long enough for the temperature to stabilize, so you can get an accurate reading. The supply minus the return temperature is the temperature rise; it should be between 40°F and 75°F. Try to get a manufacturer's specifications for acceptable range of temperature rise. A temperature rise greater than 75°F indicates low airflow, which should be increased to improve efficiency. A temperature rise less than 40°F may result in condensation and rust in the heat exchanger. In that case, the airflow should be reduced.

Many furnace fans have several speed settings; often, a lower speed is used for heating and a higher one for cooling. Airflow can often be increased simply by changing the heating fan speed setting and/or adjusting the belt drive pulleys.

Undersized or restrictive return ductwork, which can severely reduce airflow, is also common but relatively easily diagnosed. Take the cover off the blower compartment door, and repeat the temperature-rise test. If there is a safety interlock switch at the cabinet door, hold it down temporarily with a piece of tape (remember to keep your fingers away from the fan). Now measure the return air temperature at the opening to the cabinet. If the temperature rise drops below 75°F, the low airflow is caused by a restricted return duct. If the temperature rise doesn't change much, the trouble is in the furnace fan or supply ducts.

Sealed Combustion

One feature that is common in high-efficiency gas furnaces and boilers is sealed combustion. Sealed-combustion appliances draw all their combustion air directly from the outside, usually through a PVC pipe. That makes it virtually impossible to backdraft combustion gases from the appliance (see the sidebar on p. 111). Most oil-fired equipment is not available in a true sealed-combustion configuration, but most burners accept retrofit kits that bring outdoor air through a duct directly to the burner. Both oil and gas systems are also available with induced draft, or power vent, configurations that use a small fan to send combustion products reliably outside.

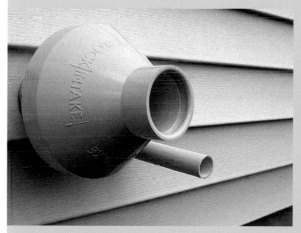

A sealed-combustion condensing furnace or boiler is vented through a sidewall with a compact unit similar to a dryer vent. If your chimney is old, the savings from not having to improve the chimney may pay for upgrading to a sealed-combustion heating system.

Sealed-combustion appliances not only eliminate backdrafting but also reduce heating loads by eliminating the draw of outdoor air into the house to supply the combustion process.

IN DETAIL

Another control setting that affects furnace efficiency is the anticipator, which is located inside the thermostat. The anticipator does just what its name implies: It anticipates the fact that the room will heat up, then keeps the furnace from running too long and overshooting. The dial should point to the number representing the electric current (in amperes) drawn by the gas-valve circuit. A technician can check the current with an ammeter. A lower anticipator setting can shorten run-time and improve efficiency.

The anticipator is a sort of timer that prevents the furnace from firing too long as the house heats up. Setting the pointer correctly can improve the furnace's efficiency and your comfort.

The blower control turns on the fan when it senses heat from the burner. The fan's on and off temperatures (the tabs at the bottom of the dial) must be set properly for maximum efficiency. This one also has a built-in adjustable peak limit (the tab on the right side of the dial).

Undersized return ducts can be relatively easy to fix; sometimes just adding a return grille can make a big difference. Often, though, you'll need to add extra ductwork with extra supply or return registers. Sometimes, entire sections of ductwork will need to be replaced. Duct upgrades may range from a few hundred to a few thousand dollars, depending on the house.

Furnace control settings

The furnace control can also have a significant impact on efficiency. The blower control, located above the heat exchanger, turns on the blower when it senses heat from the burner. It may be right next to the high-limit control or in the same device. The fan-on temperature should be set so the blower comes on between 90°F and 105°F; if it's set too high, the burner will fire for a long time before the fan comes on, letting excess heat go up the chimney. If it's set too low, the circulating air may feel uncomfortably cool. Attic-

mounted furnaces may need higher fan-on settings so the blower doesn't turn on in the summer. As an alternative, an extra relay may be installed to turn on the fan as soon as the burner fires; that will provide maximum efficiency, if you don't mind the cooler air at the beginning of the cycle.

The fan-off temperature must be slightly lower than the fan-on temperature: between 85°F and 100°F. The lower it is set, the longer the fan will run at the end of the cycle when the thermostat turns off the burners, taking residual heat from the heat exchanger. If your fan-on and fan-off temperatures are fixed (rather than adjustable) and set too high, the control should be replaced. Note that the temperature markings on adjustable controls are often poorly calibrated. Verify the actual fan-on and -off temperatures with a thermometer in the supply duct.

Duct-sealing

Air leaks in a ducted distribution system can have an enormous effect on furnace efficiency, health and safety, comfort, and moisture dynamics in a house. The impact of small duct leaks located in fairly tight basements or between interior walls

It's amazing how often I find ducts that are actually disconnected in attics and basements. Once in a while I even see sections of ductwork that were never installed! (Photo by Bruce Harley, © Conservation Services Group.)

COMBUSTION AIR

Any atmospheric-vented heating appliance needs adequate air supply for safe and efficient combustion. Codes generally allow one of either two strategies to provide that air. One strategy is to provide a minimum volume of air-space around the appliance; it must be unobstructed by partitions, unless there is a louvered door. The other strategy is to supply inlet openings for outdoor air. Both systems are calculated based on the input rating (firing rate in btus per hour) of the equipment. A higher input requires more volume or larger openings. Following building code guidelines for combustion air helps but doesn't guarantee that equipment will work properly. Negative pressures caused by leaky returns, large exhaust fans, or other combustion equipment can still suck potentially deadly combustion byproducts back down a chimney.

Research has shown that passive combustion air inlet openings on the leeward side of a house can become outlets when the wind blows, even causing backdrafts themselves!

One improvement is to build a tightly sealed and insulated mechanical room around the equipment and provide combustion air to just that room, preferably with a motorized damper that opens the air inlet when the burner fires. Fan-powered makeup air kits actively bring in combustion air when the furnace runs, but they can add to the heating load of the building. The best guarantee is to install sealed-combustion equipment (see the sidebar on p. 109). You can also have a building-performance professional or trained HVAC contractor do a combustion safety test under worst-case conditions to make sure your equipment has adequate draft and produces no carbon monoxide.

Every home that has combustion equipment, a gas range, or an attached garage should have one or more carbon monoxide detectors. (Photo courtesy Kidde.)

Platform Return

High combustion air inlet:
DO NOT SEAL or insulate over

Top plate cutout for low combustion air inlet:
DO NOT SEAL or insulate this stud bay

Line the platform area with drywall or duct board to prevent the return from drawing in attic or combustion air.

Drywalled furnace closet

Low combustion air inlet in wall:
DO NOT SEAL

Furnace/
air conditioner

Seal the top plates in the attic to prevent the return from drawing in attic air.

Supply air register

Heated
(or cooled)
air to house

Block wall bays with drywall or duct board, sealed at the edges, to prevent the return from drawing in attic air.

A return grille cut through the wall carries house air to the furnace.

House air returns to the system.

Dotted arrows = Unintentional airflows

Blue arrows = High and low air inlets, which supply combustion air, are required by code for a furnace in an enclosed space.

Platform returns can be serious energy and safety hazards. The dotted lines show potential unintended airflows, which pull in attic, garage, or outdoor air and also cause combustion problems by allowing the return suction to interfere with the combustion air supply.

The platform should be lined with drywall or duct board and all edges sealed thoroughly with duct mastic. Be sure to identify combustion air paths and intentional return air paths, and avoid sealing those.

Some closet furnaces may have a louvered door instead (bringing in combustion air from inside the living space) or grilles that open out through the wall and into the garage or outdoors.

PRO TIP

If your furnace is in the garage, pay extra attention to sealing return ductwork, so garage air isn't pulled into the house.

WHAT CAN GO WRONG

One of the biggest risks in sealing leaky ducts is that you may decrease the airflow, reducing efficiency or even causing damage. If a duct system is undersized, much of the air flowing through the furnace may travel through those leaks, so sealing them has the potential to seriously choke off the air supply to the furnace. Be sure to check the airflow with the temperature-rise test before and after sealing the ductwork.

IN DETAIL

Gas furnaces that have standing ignition pilots may benefit from an electronic pilot, or intermittent ignition device. An electronic pilot uses a spark or hot surface to light the gas burner but uses no fuel when the furnace is off. That may save 2% to 5% of your heating fuel consumption and costs $150 to $250 installed.

Duct-Sealing Supplies

The most important duct-sealing supplies are a good-quality latex-based mastic and a box of vinyl gloves. Fiberglass mesh tape is helpful for reinforcing large gaps and doing structural repairs. A clamp stapler is invaluable for reattaching duct insulation. Sheet-metal screws are handy in many places; I prefer the ones with really sharp points, commonly called Zip screws.

Although sealing ducts is a messy and dirty job, it can be done with a few inexpensive supplies and potentially save a lot of money.

may be fairly small, but poorly designed and installed ducts with major leaks can rob up to 40% or more of your home's heating energy! In fact, sealing a leaky duct system can be the single most effective way to save energy in a home.

Leaky ducts do more than waste energy. Research has shown that they also increase the air exchange in a house by 30% to 300% whenever the air handler is running. That is why furnaces have the reputation for drying out houses in winter. Return leaks in mechanical rooms can backdraft nearby water heaters or even the furnace itself. If the furnace is located in a basement or crawl space, return leaks can also draw in radon gas, water vapor, subsoil pesticide treatments, or airborne molds, distributing them throughout the house. Supply air leaking into an attic or enclosed cathedral ceiling cavity can shoot moisture into those areas at an accelerated rate.

If you can reach them, sealing duct leaks is a relatively easy job. Most of the effort involves getting to the leaks; this can mean some difficult crawling around in attics and crawl spaces or peeling back duct insulation to get to them. Duct leaks can happen almost anywhere in the system. In addition to connections between duct sections,

Duct mastic is a nontoxic, latex-based compound that is used to seal holes, cracks, and seams in ductwork.

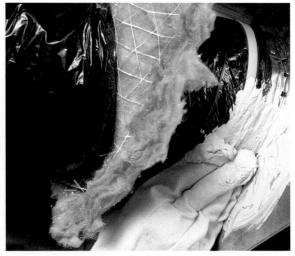

Cotton work gloves protect your hands from cuts while applying mastic; a vinyl glove on the inside keeps the mastic from soaking into your skin.

Floor, ceiling, or wall registers exposed to attics, basements, or other unconditioned spaces may have large gaps that are a big source of lost energy. Use mastic or caulking to seal the gaps.

Often, return ducts are constructed from floor-joist bays with sheet metal panning. Large gaps between the panning sections or at the end caps are common—I've even seen entire pieces missing. (Photo courtesy Certain Teed.)

Theoretically, systems made of duct board (a high-density fiberglass with a foil-scrim kraft facing) can be very airtight but, in practice, are typically very leaky. Taped joints often fall apart, and the thin foil surface is fragile and easily damaged during installation or work by other tradespeople. (Photo by Scott Phillips, courtesy *Fine Homebuilding* magazine, © The Taunton Press.)

All joints in both supply- and return-duct systems should be sealed with mastic, including those in duct systems constructed in building cavities (such as this panned joist bay).

many sheet-metal fittings have built-in holes and cracks, which should be sealed with duct mastic.

The simplest and most effective way to apply duct mastic is to put on some vinyl gloves, reach into the bucket for a small handful of mastic, and smear it onto the leaky areas. It's a good idea to wear two or three layers of gloves to protect your fingers from sharp metal edges. If the duct is insulated, be sure to seal the duct itself, not the vinyl or foil facing on the outside of the insulation.

In addition to sealing the joist panning, you must seal the panned joist bay to the trunk duct. Note the mesh tape embedded in the mastic for a strong joint.

Many HVAC installers don't understand the importance of tightly sealed return ducts.

IN DETAIL

Leaky ducts waste energy in four ways. The most obvious one is that heated air never reaches its destination when it leaks out of supply ducts in attics, basements, crawl spaces, and garages. You paid to heat that air, and now it's gone forever. Second, leaks on the return side suck in cold air, reducing the supply-air temperature and the furnace's efficiency. Third, leaks in the ductwork allow cold air to seep into the house and warm air to escape, just as other leaks in the thermal envelope do (this is true even when the furnace isn't running). Finally, pressure imbalances caused by duct leaks push air through other leaks in the building.

This variation on a platform return is not as leaky as a plywood platform, but it still leaks badly to the exterior closet in which it's located.

An HVAC contractor, building-performance professional, or home-energy rater uses a duct tester like this one to measure duct leakage. (Photo © The Energy Conservatory.)

On the supply side of the system, it is usually fairly easy to follow the duct runs and identify the leakage areas. Places to focus include connections between the main trunk, the duct sections, the end caps on main ducts, and register boots. Swivel elbows and branch-duct takeoffs tend to be particularly leaky. Each register boot must be sealed where the branch duct connects to it, at its corners and folds, and where the boot meets the drywall or subfloor. Sometimes, it is easier to seal the boot area from inside the house—just remove the register grille and reach inside to seal the leaks.

Return ducts can be a bigger challenge. Many return systems are patched together using a combination of plywood, sheet metal, building cavities (including joist bays and wall bays), and a lot of wishful thinking.

In some regions, platform returns—furnaces in a closet or a garage that are mounted on a framed platform on a plywood base with a cutout for the return air—are common (see the drawing on p. 111). A return grille is cut into the drywall to allow house air to return to the furnace. Unfortunately, the platforms are rarely sealed and are typically framed in such a way that wall or floor cavities carry return air sucked in from attics, basements, crawl spaces, and garages. It is critical to seal off these platforms from the inside so return air is pulled from only the house.

Many HVAC installers don't pay much attention to return ducts, thinking they aren't required to get the air where it's supposed to go. What they don't understand is the importance of tightly sealed returns for furnace efficiency, occupant health and safety, and building durability. You must pay attention to where the return air is supposed to come from, then get in and seal all the cracks and gaps between return-duct materials. If your furnace is in the garage, pay extra attention to carefully sealing any ducts, especially return air ducts. You don't want garage air being pulled into the house.

Two places to pay close attention to are the large duct sections connected directly to the supply side and the return side of the furnace (called *plenums*). The air pressures are highest there because of the proximity to the blower. Any openings in the corners or connections of the supply and return plenums, at the flanges where the plenums connect to the furnace cabinet, at the filter rack, or at the filter cover panel leak the most air because of the high pressure. Use mastic to carefully seal the supply and return plenums, especially any gaps between the filter and the air handler, where dust and dirt can be drawn in past the filter. (Don't seal the access to the filter, however!) If access is limited, you may need to cut access openings in the duct-work or remove sections of ductwork in order to reach the leaky areas.

Depending on how easy the access is to your duct system, you may want to hire a professional to test and seal your ducts. Building-performance or HVAC contractors use a duct tester, which is like a miniature blower door (see the bottom photo on the facing page), to pressurize the duct system and measure leakage. If a majority of the ductwork is hidden in walls, cathedral ceilings, or restricted attic areas, hiring someone with an aerosol duct-sealing machine is another option. See www.aeroseal.com for a list of contractors who can provide that service.

Duct insulation

Ductwork that runs through unconditioned space should be insulated, if it is not already. Typically, supply ducts are insulated but often have weak spots at register boots and other major connections. Often, return ductwork is left uninsulated.

Ducts should be insulated with vinyl-faced fiberglass wrap; R-6 is the minimum allowed by most residential codes. However, ducts in attic areas should have higher R-values. Think about it: In winter, attic temperatures are nearly as cold as outdoors; in summer, they are often much hotter than outdoors (if you have air-conditioning). If the ducts are close enough to the attic floor, cover them completely with loose-fill insulation. If that is not possible, try to find an R-10 or higher duct wrap. Of course, all the duct connections must be tightly sealed before insulating.

All supply ducts in unconditioned spaces should be insulated with a minimum of R-6 duct wrap. The wrap should be installed neatly and snugly, with plastic washers and screws to hold it in place. A clamp stapler is handy to close the seams.

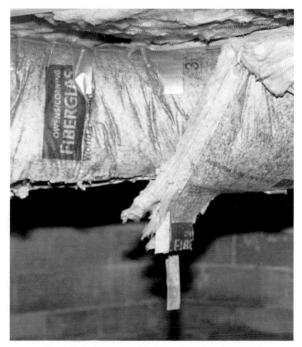

Wrong: Don't insulate ductwork with material intended for wall insulation.

TRADE SECRET

One way to increase a heat pump's efficiency is to adjust the defrost-cycle timer. In cold weather, the heat pump runs periodically in reverse, sending some heat to the outside coil to prevent frost formation. Frost cuts airflow through the outside coil, which is very bad. Often, defrost timers can be set for longer cycles (90 minutes is recommended) and/or controls can be installed to prevent defrost cycles when outdoor temperatures are mild. If you make that adjustment, keep an eye on the outdoor unit to make sure that frost does not form.

In cold weather, heat pump operation is usually supplemented by an electric-resistance strip heater, like this one. It is essentially a giant toaster located in the main supply duct. (Photo © Kevin Kennefick.)

If you have a source of fuel-fired hot water, such as a gas water heater, a hydro coil like this one can be used to replace electric-resistance backup heat. (Photo © Lin Wagner.)

Heat Pumps

Air-source heat pumps, popular in some parts of the country, are basically air conditioners that can work in reverse to deliver heat into the house in winter. Heat pumps provide heating and cooling in one machine, with one duct system and no combustion. Heat pumps are not subject to back-drafting, combustion air requirements, and some of the off-cycle losses to which furnaces are prone.

Because they use ducts to deliver warm air to the house, heat pumps have the same problems with duct leakage and insulation, and heat-pump ducts must be sealed thoroughly and insulated. Heat pumps are more prone to airflow problems—both indoor and outdoor—than furnaces are, and improper refrigerant charging and electric-resistance backup heating can have a negative impact on heating efficiency (see the drawing on the facing page).

Operating efficiency and resistance heating

Heat pumps are typically rated at efficiencies between 200% to 300%, which is expressed as a coefficient of performance, or COP, rating of 2 to 3. A COP of 2 means that for every kilowatt-hour of electricity you buy, you get two kilowatt-hours of heat delivered to your house. Newer heat pumps use a different rating system, called Heating System Performance Factor, or HSPF. An HSPF of 6.8 corresponds to a COP of 2. How can the system generate more energy than it consumes? The difference is made up by heat energy absorbed from the outdoor air. That energy goes into the system; it just happens to be free.

Heat pumps, by themselves, operate at reasonable efficiencies until outside air temperatures drop to about 35°F to 40°F. As the outdoor air gets colder, less heat is available, and the heat pump output drops off just as the house needs more heat. So cold-weather performance is typically supplemented with electric-resistance backup heaters.

This auxiliary heat costs two to three times more per unit of heat than the compressor heating cycle. That may be fine in regions with long summers, mild winters, and relatively low electric rates, but it's not in the Northeast, where electricity is expensive and winters are cold. One fairly inexpensive way to reduce the use of electric-resistance heating is to install an outdoor cutout thermostat. For about $100 to $150 installed, this device locks out the supplemental electric heat when the outdoor air temperature is above 30°F or 35°F.

One way to eliminate electric-resistance heating altogether is to remove or disable the electric coils and install a hydro-air coil. This coil is like a radiator installed in the supply plenum (about $500 to $1,000 installed) and is heated by a gas-, oil-, or propane-fired (not electric) domestic hot water heater. One potential pitfall of a hydro-air coil is that the installation may significantly cut the airflow through the heat pump. Hydro coils have much more resistance to airflow than electric-resistance coils do, so installers must be careful to select the right model. Depending on the heat pump's existing airflow, additional duct modifications may also be necessary.

Airflow

Heat pumps are even more sensitive to airflow than furnaces are. Heat pumps need to move a much larger volume of air, but installers who are used to working with furnaces often skimp on duct sizing, leading to low-airflow problems. Unfortunately, checking the airflow of a heat pump is not as easy as checking that of a furnace.

It can be done with special instruments or with the temperature-rise method used for electric-resistance backup heat.

HVAC technicians may use an anemometer or pitot tube to measure the air velocity in one of the main trunk ducts; the total cfm equals velocity (in feet per minute) times duct area (in square feet). Total airflow can't be measured with a flow hood or anemometer at the registers, because duct leakage will be missed. If you have electric-resistance backup heat, the airflow can be calculated by measuring the temperature rise (as described on pp. 108–109). Set the thermostat to "emergency heat," so that the compressor doesn't run; turn up the thermostat and let the heat run for 10 minutes. The total cfm equals the strip heat power (in

Air-Source Heat Pump

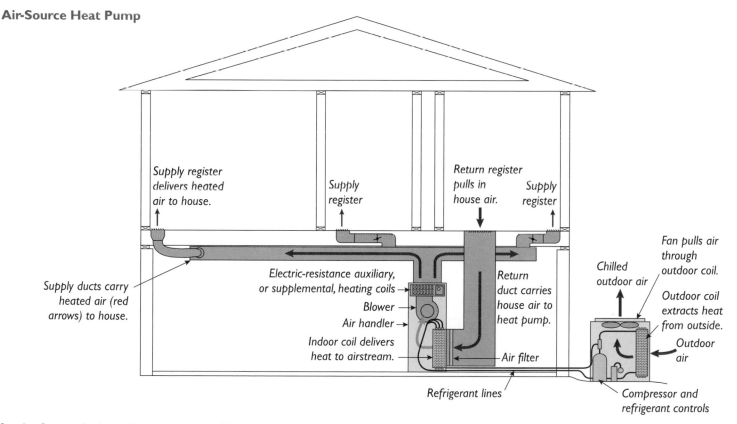

Supply register delivers heated air to house.

Supply register

Return register pulls in house air.

Supply register

Supply ducts carry heated air (red arrows) to house.

Electric-resistance auxiliary, or supplemental, heating coils

Blower

Air handler

Indoor coil delivers heat to airstream.

Return duct carries house air to heat pump.

Air filter

Refrigerant lines

Chilled outdoor air

Fan pulls air through outdoor coil.

Outdoor coil extracts heat from outside.

Outdoor air

Compressor and refrigerant controls

People often wonder how a heat pump can push heat energy "uphill" from cold outdoor air to warm indoor air. It's not magic; it's physics. The secret is in the compressor and refrigerant cycle. Liquid refrigerant flows through the outdoor coil at about 20°F, picking up heat from the outside air. Remember that heat always flows from hot to cold, so when the air temperature is higher than the refrigerant temperature, the refrigerant absorbs heat. The compressor concentrates the heat in the vaporized refrigerant, and its temperature rises to about 100°F as it goes through the indoor coil, making it warm enough to heat the indoor air.

PRO TIP

Heat pumps are finicky about refrigerant charge. Many systems, even when serviced regularly, are either overcharged or undercharged.

WHAT CAN GO WRONG

Why is the refrigerant charge so often incorrect? Often, the manufacturers' instructions are not followed during the initial installation, resulting in the wrong charge. Then, some technicians automatically connect their refrigerant gauges at every service call, even when there is no evidence of refrigerant leakage. Some refrigerant escapes each time a gauge is used. To make matters worse, many service technicians add a little refrigerant each time "for good measure." The end result is an unknown quantity of refrigerant. Even if they don't do those things, many technicians do not first test for adequate indoor coil airflow or properly measure superheating or subcooling.

A coil and a blower are the main components of a heat pump's indoor unit.

Always keep material and debris away from the outdoor unit of a heat pump. Proper efficiency depends on good air circulation, so never cover up or build a deck over the unit.

watts) multiplied by 3.1 and divided by the temperature rise. Watts (amps × volts) are measured with an amp clamp and voltmeter at the service disconnect or breaker box. Don't attempt to take this measurement unless you understand exactly what you are doing—get a service technician to do it for you if you aren't sure.

For best efficiency, heat-pump airflow should be 375 to 425 cfm per *ton* of heating capacity. It should never be below 300 cfm/ton. With 1 ton equalling 12,000 btu/hour, equipment is typically rated in increments of ½ ton, such as 24 (2 tons), 30 (2½ tons), 36 (3 tons), etc.

Refrigerant charge

Heat pumps are also finicky about refrigerant charge. Many systems, even when serviced regularly, are either over- or undercharged. Both cases have a negative impact on efficiency. Unfortunately, many service technicians have a limited ability to diagnose or correct those problems. For one thing, airflow must be in the recommended range *before* refrigerant charge can be correctly diagnosed, and very few technicians test airflow as a matter of course.

There are very specific ways to measure refrigerant charge during unit operation. Depending on the type of unit, the superheat or subcooling must be measured carefully, as it is for an air conditioner (see pp. 140–141). As an alternative, refrigerant may be removed with a vacuum pump, and the correct amount for the system may be weighed on a scale as it's installed. The latter method is time-consuming but accurate.

Heat-pump service

Like furnaces, heat pumps should be serviced regularly. Basic service can be done by anyone. Air filters should be replaced monthly during the heating season, and the outdoor coil should be kept free of snow and debris. Because of the

Geothermal Heat Pump

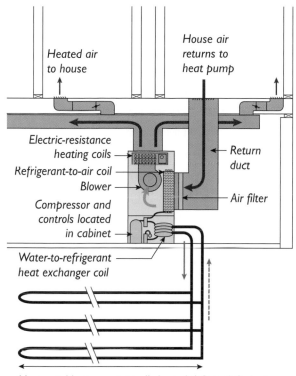

Heated air to house

House air returns to heat pump

Electric-resistance heating coils

Refrigerant-to-air coil

Blower

Return duct

Compressor and controls located in cabinet

Air filter

Water-to-refrigerant heat exchanger coil

Horizontal loops are typically buried 4 ft. to 6 ft. deep. The length and configuration of loops vary depending on the system's size and design.

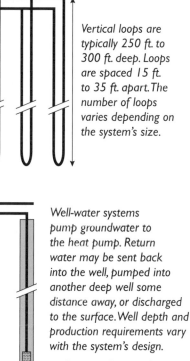

Vertical loops are typically 250 ft. to 300 ft. deep. Loops are spaced 15 ft. to 35 ft. apart. The number of loops varies depending on the system's size.

Well-water systems pump groundwater to the heat pump. Return water may be sent back into the well, pumped into another deep well some distance away, or discharged to the surface. Well depth and production requirements vary with the system's design.

Deep well pump (typical)

Geothermal, or ground source, heat pumps use a refrigerant cycle to absorb heat from underground. The heating source is typically a series of sealed underground pipes; very cold water or antifreeze is pumped through the loops, where it picks up heat from underground at fairly cold temperatures (typically 30°F to 50°F). Sometimes, the heat comes from a source of clean underground water, such as a deep well. The compressor concentrates the heat and sends hot refrigerant to the coil, which heats the airstream to a much higher temperature. Some geothermal systems have electric-resistance heaters, but they are often not needed.

importance of indoor airflow, keep all registers open. Regular service calls—typically every two to three years—should include testing the controls, cleaning the blower, cleaning both the indoor and the outdoor coils, and checking the insulation on the refrigerant lines.

An initial service appointment should include testing and fixing airflow problems, and then carefully measuring and correcting refrigerant charge. Once that has been done, service technicians should *not* attach refrigerant gauges to the system unless the system performance drops off or there is other evidence that something is wrong. Refrigerant does not escape unless there is a leak or a technician attaches gauges.

Geothermal heat pumps

Geothermal heat pumps (also called *ground source heat pumps*) extract heat from the earth or from underground water, rather than from outdoor air.

Because temperatures are much more stable underground, geothermal systems can have much higher heating efficiencies than air-source heat pumps; COPs range from about 2.8 to 4.8.

There are two basic types of geothermal heat pumps. Closed-loop (ground-coupled) systems are more efficient but much more expensive to

Except for the ground loop, this geothermal system is entirely self-contained. Note the ground-loop circulating pumps mounted on the small white box to the right. The large, sweeping return plenum helps ensure good airflow. (Photo © John O'Connell.)

WHAT CAN GO WRONG

A typical humidifier is basically a large sponge sitting in water. Some air from the furnace supply duct is shunted through the sponge, then sent back into the return. This air recirculation reduces efficiency, and the humidifier may contribute to health problems. A high humidity level is not healthy for your family or your home. The last thing you want is to send the air you breathe through a damp sponge. Some new humidifiers are safer, but remember: Once the house is tightened, it is much less likely to dry out in winter. My recommendation for built-in humidifiers is to shut off the water supply, remove them, and permanently seal the holes in the ductwork.

Polyethylene pipe, used for most geothermal ground loops, is joined with heat-fusion techniques that are stronger than the pipe itself. Pipe failure is relatively rare and most new installations are warranted for 20 to 50 years. (Photo by Scott Gibson, courtesy *Fine Homebuilding* magazine, © The Taunton Press.)

install. Open-loop (groundwater or water source) systems have a lower initial cost but are more expensive to run. Dealers may claim otherwise, but the power consumption of the large well pump that's typically required for open-loop systems means that the higher operating cost often more than offsets any up-front savings. A third type of geothermal heat pump, called *direct exchange*, or *DX*, uses a copper pipe ground loop to circulate refrigerant underground. Those systems promise to be the most efficient, but long-term reliability is less clear than that of closed-loop water-based systems.

Like air-source heat pumps, geothermal heat pumps can be very cost-effective in regions with mild or hot climates and moderate electric rates.

However, in regions with cold climates and high electric rates, geothermal heat pumps do not provide enough savings to justify the high installation cost, particularly in a retrofit.

Geothermal heat pumps can also have very high cooling efficiencies. The efficiency and maintenance issues are the same as those for air-source heat pumps, except that there is no outdoor coil. Low airflow, refrigerant charge, and electric-resistance heat can all impact the operating efficiency. The heating capacity of geothermal heat pumps is much better in cold weather than that of air-source heat pumps, so there is typically less need for supplemental electric heat. In many cases, the resistance heat can be shut off completely. Closed-loop systems need little or no maintenance, but open-loop systems may have water-quality issues, filters that need replacing, and well pumps with shortened life expectancies.

Electric-Resistance Heat

Most electric-resistance heating systems are simple electric baseboard heaters. There are also various types of radiant-heat systems (usually panels mounted on ceiling or walls, built into valances, or built into ceiling or wall-finish systems). Occasionally, you'll even find an electric-resistance boiler or furnace.

Cheap to install but expensive to operate, electric-resistance baseboard heaters operate on the same principle as that of a toaster, hot plate, or electric space heater. An electric current passes through a wire element, heating it. Air passes through and is heated by fins in the baseboard. Electric-resistance heat is 100% efficient; every kilowatt-hour of electricity that you pay for is converted to heat.

The reason electric baseboards are expensive to operate is that electricity costs more than fossil fuels per unit of heat—typically two to three times more. One advantage of electric heat (besides the low installation cost) is the ease with which rooms can be zoned (see the sidebar on p. 126). But with the high fuel cost, it's difficult to justify except in special situations, such as isolated rooms, extremely mild climates (southern Florida or Hawaii, for instance), or superinsulated, passive solar houses.

Because these systems are so simple, there is very little that can be done to improve their efficiency. Short of completely replacing them, the best approach (as always) is to insulate and thoroughly seal the building envelope to reduce heating loads.

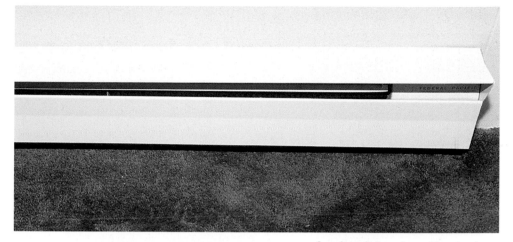

An electric baseboard heater is its own distribution system and is usually precisely in the area where heat is desired, so there are no distribution losses like those found in ductwork.

Individual-room thermostats have often been a selling point for electric heat. Don't always believe your eyes, though; a poorly calibrated thermostat can fool you into thinking that you've set the room temperature lower than you really have.

+ SAFETY FIRST

Never use an unvented propane or kerosene heater indoors. And *never* install a "vent-free" fireplace like this one, which dumps significant amounts of potentially toxic combustion byproducts and water vapor into the air while burning. For about $200 more, you can get a unit with a vent system or, better yet, a sealed combustion system.

Avoid "vent-free" fireplaces; despite manufacturers' claims, the devices dump combustion byproducts and water vapor into the air when they're burning. (Photo courtesy Buck Taylor, Connecticut Light and Power.)

Thermal Storage Heaters

Electric thermal storage heaters promise economical operation, but they work only if your electric company offers a cheaper time-of-use rate, which is a discounted price for electricity during periods of low demand. These well-insulated wall heaters use electric-resistance elements to heat a large mass of ceramic bricks to a high temperature during off-peak hours, when electricity is cheap. Then, during the expensive time periods, heat is distributed into the room as needed with a small fan. Although they don't save energy, they can save money, but their value depends heavily on long-term availability of a utility rate structure. In my experience, that may not be something on which you can depend.

TRADE SECRET

Hydronic systems are more efficient when the circulating water is only as hot as necessary to keep the house comfortable. Most boilers run at about 180°F. Because boilers—and radiators—are typically sized larger than necessary, even on the coldest day of the year, the Aquastat® setting can often be reduced to as low as 130°F. This is particularly true if the thermal envelope has been improved. More sophisticated controls, called *outdoor reset* ($400 to $1,500 installed), modulate the boiler temperature based on outdoor sensors, so water circulates at exactly the right temperature. Either one of these options should be installed only by a qualified service person. Low water temperatures must be carefully controlled to prevent condensation in the appliance's vent pipe.

Supplemental Heat

A great way to offset a significant portion of electric heat, for a fraction of the cost of a new central-heating system, is with the installation of a gas- or propane-fired wall-mounted space heater. The best types of fuel-fired wall-mounted space heaters are direct-vent, or sealed-combustion, units. They pull all their combustion air directly from outdoors, and the combustion process is completely separate from the house air. The systems may cost $1,000 to $2,500 installed.

Most of the units are mounted on an exterior wall and use a single combination inlet/outlet for venting both fresh combustion air and combustion byproducts.

Don't try to supplement built-in electric heat with portable electric space heaters. Despite some manufacturers' marketing claims, those heaters all run on electric resistance and are exactly the same as the baseboard heaters on the wall.

This wall-mounted gas or propane heater by Monitor has electronic controls and high efficiency. Similar units are made by several manufacturers (Monitor, Rinnai, Toyostove) and are available in many sizes. (Photo © Kevin Kennefick.)

Replacing electric heating systems

Because of the high operating cost of electric-resistance heat, many people are interested in replacing such systems with another type. This is the only situation in which installing a new heating-distribution system may be cost-effective. Take, for example, a moderately sized house that uses 15,000 kilowatt-hours (kWh) for heating every year. At 10¢ per kilowatt-hour, the annual heating usage is about $1,500. Let's say you get a bid to install a propane-fired gas boiler for $4,500. At a propane cost of $1.20 per gallon and a boiler efficiency of 85%, this house will cost a little less than $800 a year to heat. At a savings of $700 per year, this system has a simple payback of about six years.

Propane tends to be more expensive per unit of heat than fuel oil or natural gas, so one of those alternatives would be even more cost-effective. If you use this opportunity to replace an electric hot water heater with an indirect-fired tank off a boiler (see p. 161), the payback would probably improve. On the other hand, lower electric rates would reduce the potential savings.

Hot Water and Steam Boilers

Boilers, an old standby in the Northeast, are becoming more popular around the country with the advent of radiant, hydro-air, and hybrid systems. Instead of heating air, a boiler heats water.

The classic boiler system uses hydronic distribution. Water is heated by the boiler and pumped through pipes to hot water radiators or baseboard fin-tube convectors to heat the house. Some older systems use a boiler to make steam, which expands to fill steam radiators without the need for a circulator pump.

Basic maintenance

Boiler maintenance is similar to that of a gas or oil furnace (see the sidebar on p. 107), but there is no blower fan to clean. Oil boilers should be serviced once a year, while gas boilers should be serviced every two to three years.

Any swishing or gurgling sounds that you hear in the radiators indicate air trapped in the system, which reduces heat-exchange efficiency. A service technician can bleed out the air and show you how to do it if it is needed frequently.

Occasionally, bleed valves may need to be installed or replaced. The technician should check the hydronic system pressure and expansion tank; the smallest leak anywhere in the system should be repaired immediately to prevent corrosion-causing oxygen from being brought in via makeup water connections.

Boiler controls and upgrades

A typical hot water boiler operates throughout the winter with a water temperature determined by the Aquastat®, or low limit, setting (an *Aquastat*

Radiant Floor Heating

In the past decade, built-in radiant floor hydronic systems have become quite popular. Quiet and out of sight, they employ specialized flexible tubing embedded in concrete slabs or framed flooring systems, turning the entire floor surface into a cozy, low-temperature radiator. When properly designed and installed, radiant floor systems provide reliable, even heat with unsurpassed comfort. Radiant heating is commonly touted as an energy saver, because people are comfortable at a lower thermostat set point. However, recent research has shown no significant difference in thermostat settings between radiant floor houses and others, suggesting that energy savings are largely theoretical.

Staple-up radiant floor systems, such as this one, provide the benefits of a cozy, warm floor in wood-frame structures. Other systems embed the tubing in a lightweight gypsum slab poured over a framed floor or concrete slab. Radiant floor systems must be insulated very carefully so the heat goes only where it's wanted. (Photo © Lin Wagner.)

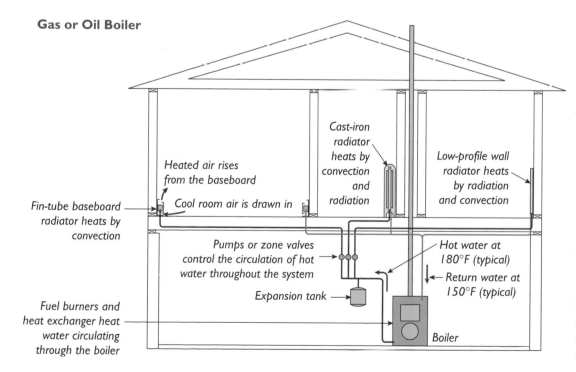

Gas or Oil Boiler

Heated air rises from the baseboard

Cool room air is drawn in

Fin-tube baseboard radiator heats by convection

Fuel burners and heat exchanger heat water circulating through the boiler

Cast-iron radiator heats by convection and radiation

Pumps or zone valves control the circulation of hot water throughout the system

Expansion tank

Low-profile wall radiator heats by radiation and convection

Hot water at 180°F (typical)

Return water at 150°F (typical)

Boiler

Boilers heat water, which is circulated throughout the house to deliver heat. Valves or individual pumps may control the flow to separate zones in the building. Occasionally, European-style hardware is used for continuous circulation and individual thermostats mounted on each baseboard. In the popular fin-tube baseboard, a copper pipe runs through the middle of an array of aluminum fins; the large surface area of the fins provides heat transfer to the air. The air moves through the baseboard by natural convection: Cool air is drawn in from the bottom and the heated air rises and escapes from the top. Older houses may have cast-iron hot water radiators; recently, European-style wall radiators have become popular. All three are shown here, though they are not usually mixed in the same house.

PRO TIP

When air-venting doesn't work properly on a steam-heating system, it can lead to uneven heating, large temperature fluctuations, and discomfort.

WHAT CAN GO WRONG

A common problem with steam systems is too much pressure. The boiler pressure controls should be set just high enough so that the boiler shuts down just as each radiator fills with steam. Too much steam pressure increases the boiler's cycling losses and leads to overheating. That can particularly be a problem if the building envelope's efficiency is improved dramatically and/or some radiators are removed during remodeling. Timed-cycle controllers vary the boiler cycle length to match the outdoor temperature, further improving the system's efficiency.

TRADE SECRET

If you have an oil-fired boiler or a furnace with a standard, inefficient oil burner, have a technician replace the burner with a flame-retention burner. Those units, which cost about $400 to $500, do a better job of mixing the oil with the combustion air, which better controls the fire. They also reduce the amount of heat lost up the chimney, bringing the overall efficiency improvement to between 10% and 20%.

A new oil boiler may have an efficiency rating of 84% or higher.

Every hydronic radiator should have a bleed valve, which can be opened slightly with a screwdriver or a special key to let trapped air escape. (Photo © Kevin Kennefick.)

is like a thermostat that senses the water temperature inside the boiler and shuts off the burner when the water is hot enough). Boiler controls may maintain full boiler temperature throughout the year, which is very inefficient but necessary if a tankless coil water heater heats the domestic hot water (see In Detail on p. 154). In the absence of a tankless coil, typical boiler controls may be set either to maintain constant boiler temperature all winter or to shut down and let the boiler cool off when not in use. Clearly, the latter is more efficient and is the preferred configuration.

This vent damper automatically opens when the boiler fires, then closes when the burner shuts down, reducing the amount of heat lost through the chimney.

Electronic pilot ignition may be installed on gas boilers and furnaces (see In Detail on p. 112). Another improvement that can save boiler energy is installing a mechanical vent damper. This device closes off the flue pipe after the burner shuts off, stopping the flow of heat through the heat exchanger and up the chimney. It costs $125 to $350 installed. I don't recommend gravity-actuated vent dampers that depend on the heat from the burner to stay open; they are much more likely to contribute to backdrafting. (Vent dampers are not much benefit to a furnace; a low fan-off temperature setting allows the fan to carry most of the residual heat into the house after the burner stops.)

Steam boilers

Steam boilers are very different from hot water boilers. Steam systems were popular in the early 20th century, and many of them are still in service in older homes. Instead of relying on pumps to circulate hot water, steam boilers boil water to create steam. The steam naturally expands to fill all the pipes and radiators in the system, distributing heat throughout the house. Although steam-heat distribution is simple and reliable, steam boilers have a number of unique maintenance and efficiency issues.

Most residential steam systems are one-pipe systems. When the thermostat calls for heat, the boiler fires and steam begins expanding to fill the system. As the steam expands, it displaces air contained in the pipes and radiators, and that air must be allowed to escape through air vents typically located at the top of each steam radiator. Once the steam reaches the radiator, the air vent senses the heat and closes, keeping the steam inside. As the steam emits heat through the radiator, it condenses to water and flows back via gravity through the same pipes to the boiler.

Pipe Insulation

Both hydronic and steam-boiler systems can benefit from insulating distribution pipes, particularly in unconditioned basements and crawl spaces. Be sure to install insulation neatly, and miter the corners to minimize pipe exposure. Use a good-quality tape, where necessary, to hold the insulation in place and keep the seams closed. Wrap the tape several turns around the insulation; don't just run it lengthwise along the seam. And for safety's sake, don't disturb any boiler piping that appears to have asbestos insulation on it already.

Pipe insulation is inexpensive and widely available at hardware stores and home centers. Make sure the material used on heating pipes is rated to at least 180°F, because some types will melt on heating pipes.

High-density fiberglass pipe insulation is more expensive but necessary for the high temperatures found in steam systems. Be sure to measure the pipes carefully when ordering the insulation. Due to the large, awkward fittings, it can be difficult to cover all the elbows and tees in a steam system, but do as much as you can.

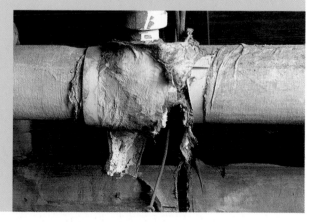

Duct or pipe insulation that contains asbestos (the material on these steam pipes) can be dangerous if it's disturbed or falling apart. Airborne asbestos fibers can lead to lung cancer and other diseases.

PRO **TIP**

If you are planning to replace an old heating system with a new, energy-efficient one, stick with the same fuel- and heat-distribution system.

WHAT CAN GO WRONG

Atmospheric vented combustion equipment depends on waste heat to carry combustion byproducts up the chimney. That waste heat is one of the major sources of inefficiency in old furnaces and boilers. New, high-efficiency equipment wastes much less heat. Cool chimneys can condense water, potentially damaging the structure and the equipment. Old masonry chimneys can be retrofitted with aluminum or stainless-steel liners, which eliminate condensation and improve draft velocity (they should be installed by a professional). Many new furnaces and boilers can be vented directly through a sidewall or band joist, eliminating the need to upgrade an old chimney. Be careful if you upgrade your furnace or boiler; an atmospheric hot water heater left alone to vent through an old chimney may also cause problems.

Air-venting systems that aren't working properly can lead to uneven heating, large temperature fluctuations, and discomfort. A tune-up can increase energy efficiency and comfort dramatically. If the air vents are too small, if there are not enough of them, or if they are clogged with mineral deposits, air gets trapped in the system, and the steam cannot reach its destination. Having a professional replace malfunctioning air vents, add extra vents to radiators, and add special high-volume air vents to large central supply pipes can improve steam-system efficiency by quickly getting the heat where it is needed. Thermostatically controlled vents can reduce the rate of steam delivery to some rooms, reducing overheating and improving overall comfort.

Two-pipe steam systems (less common in residences) have a separate condensate-return pipe.

Instead of air vents, two-pipe systems have a steam trap at each radiator. Steam-trap maintenance is critical for proper operation, and all the steam traps in a system should be replaced or rebuilt at the same time, not one by one.

In addition to the standard cleaning and tuning that every boiler or furnace requires regularly, many steam systems need periodic adjustments to the water level, which is typically done by the homeowner. Steam boilers also need regular water maintenance; periodically, boiler water should be drained to remove sediment and rust. Chemically treating steam-boiler water reduces corrosion and improves steam distribution efficiency. Steam-boiler water maintenance should always be performed by technicians with experience in local water conditions and steam maintenance.

Zoning Distribution Systems

Dividing a house into multiple heating zones, each with separate thermostatic temperature control, is often considered an energy-saving, as well as a comfort, feature. The theory is that people may lower the thermostat independently in parts of the house they are not using, reducing heat loss from those areas. Whether this saves energy depends entirely on people's habits. The simplest form of zoning is the installation of more than one heating system, each serving a section of the house with its own thermostat. In homes with electric baseboards, each room is usually a separate zone. Newer two-story homes often have a separate furnace and air conditioner to serve each floor.

Individual heating systems can be divided into separate zones with varying success. Hot water boilers can easily be zoned with separate circulator pumps and piping; residential steam systems are pretty much impossible to zone. Furnaces and heat pumps can be zoned with special dampers that block airflow to various sections of the house, but those installations typically suffer efficiency problems. All ducted heating systems, especially heat pumps, depend on adequate airflow. When only one zone calls for heat, the airflow is choked off and efficiency suffers dramatically.

One way around this problem is to install multi-speed equipment. Some high-end furnaces have modulating burners, the best heat pumps have dual-speed compressors, and both have variable-speed blowers. Those features allow the equipment to run more efficiently when there is only partial demand. They even improve the efficiency of single-zone systems by matching the equipment output to the load in mild conditions.

The vent on the left side of this steam radiator has an adjustment knob at the bottom to control how fast the steam fills the unit.

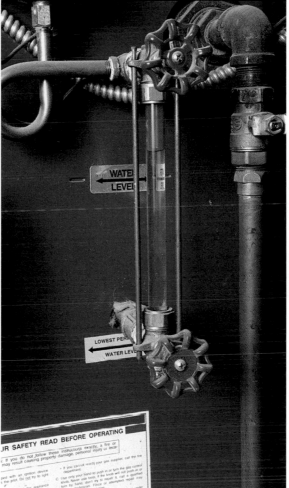

Most steam boilers require a periodic addition of water. This is done by opening a valve on the inlet water line. Like an oil dipstick in your car, this sight glass helps you monitor the water level so you can keep it just right.

Upgrading or Replacing Heating Equipment

Replacing a heating system with a newer, more efficient system is expensive, so it will typically have a long payback. However, if you have to replace a broken furnace or boiler, it is almost always cost-effective to select a high-efficiency system. Even if your existing heating system is functional but appears to be on its last legs, replacing it early can help avoid a big surprise at the worst time. Deciding, rather than being forced, to replace a system significantly reduces the panic factor and allows for a more reasoned choice. It may even reduce the cost a bit, because it won't be an emergency call.

+ SAFETY FIRST

Years ago, materials containing asbestos were commonly used to insulate pipes and ducts. Usually white and fibrous, asbestos is often fragile; if disturbed, it can release dangerous fibers into the air. If your pipes or ducts appear to have asbestos insulation, *don't touch them.* The presence of asbestos can be verified by lab tests; confirmed or suspected asbestos materials should either be encapsulated or removed by a qualified asbestos-remediation contractor.

When shopping for a new furnace or boiler, compare efficiency ratings and get the highest you can afford.

WHAT CAN GO WRONG

When replacing a heating system, size *does* matter—but bigger is definitely *not* better. A system that is much bigger than necessary is sort of like a big diesel truck engine in a compact car—inefficient, expensive, and hard to control. Any heating-system-replacement bid should include a detailed load calculation based on the thermal characteristics of the house, such as insulation levels, window types, and surface areas. The widespread practice of simply replacing an old unit with a new one of the same size perpetuates the problem. Many homes start out with systems that are much too big; if the thermal envelope has been improved, the oversizing problem becomes even worse.

If your furnace or boiler looks like this, it may be time to replace it with a more efficient one, even if it is still running.

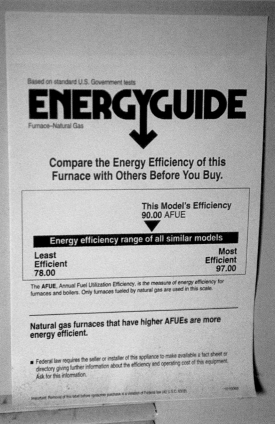

The yellow Energy Guide sticker indicates the efficiency rating of new heating equipment and provides a comparison among similar models.

Efficiency ratings

All new boilers and furnaces have standardized efficiency ratings, just like the gas-mileage ratings on automobiles. When selecting equipment, look for the highest efficiency ratings. Fuel-fired furnaces and boilers have an Annual Fuel Utilization Efficiency (AFUE) rating, which accounts for burner efficiency, pilot fuel, and off-cycle losses. New furnaces have AFUEs of 78% to 96%; boilers range from about 80% to 87%. AFUE ratings are available from manufacturers or on the Internet (see Resources on p. 194). Air-source heat pumps are rated by HSPF; geothermal, by COP (see p. 116).

The U.S. Environmental Protection Agency (EPA) and Department of Energy (DOE) maintain a listing of high-efficiency equipment on their Energy Star Web site (www.energystar.gov/products/); always look for the Energy Star label,

which indicates that the equipment meets certain above-minimum efficiency standards set by the government. Remember that the ratings apply to only the equipment. Installation problems, improper maintenance, and distribution problems (such as duct leakage) can reduce performance dramatically.

Choosing a contractor

Replacing a heating system is not a do-it-yourself proposition. Because it is a big-ticket item, you should always interview and obtain alternative bids from at least two or three contractors. Don't be tempted by the lowest bid. Consider quality, warranty service, energy savings, and customer references. Bids should include details on the equipment, accessories, installation specs, labor, and associated costs.

Most high-efficiency furnaces and boilers have special installation requirements to ensure that they work reliably and don't have problems. Find out whether bidders have experience with the specific type of installation that you are discussing. Most manufacturers offer training and technical support for newer, more sophisticated equipment, so a contractor who tries to discourage you from installing high-efficiency equipment may be unwilling or unable to read the directions.

Sizing is also important. Many contractors avoid detailed sizing calculations to save time, but the time spent calculating energy loads can easily be paid for by reduced equipment costs. If you talk to a heating contractor who gives you a price over the phone, or without measuring the thermal components of your house, look elsewhere.

When replacing a heating system, it generally doesn't make sense to switch fuels or replace an existing distribution system with a different type. The most likely exceptions to this rule are the conversion of electric-resistance baseboard heat-ing to a fuel-fired boiler with hydronic distribution and the replacement of an electric furnace with a heat pump or fuel-fired furnace. Except for changes in the distribution system for the purpose of improving comfort or efficiency (such as duct-system changes to increase airflow), there is rarely justification for the large expense of replacing distribution equipment.

Some steam-radiator systems can be retro-fitted to use existing radiators for hydronic distribution. The cost will vary considerably depending on the system and the layout of the house. Because hot water boilers are always more efficient than steam boilers, changing a steam system to a hot water system can significantly increase boiler efficiency, improve comfort control from room to room, add the possibility of zoning the house, and reduce noise. Replacing a hot water boiler, or converting from steam to hydronic, is also a good time to replace an inefficient tankless coil or stand-alone water heater with an indirect-fired model.

Hydro-Air Systems

Hydro-air systems are hybrids. They deliver heat to a house by blowing warm air through ductwork, like a furnace does, but the heat source is usually a hot water boiler. Hydro-air systems typically use only one heating appliance to produce heat and hot water for the house, improving efficiency and reducing mainte-nance. Hot water can be easily piped to several zones with separate air handlers in different parts of the house, without the problems of matching airflow to burner capacity. Hydro-air handlers can also be easily integrated with air-conditioning.

Hydro air handlers use hot water circulating through a heat exchanger, or fan coil, to heat air pushed through by the blower. The "A" coil at the bottom is for cooling. (Photo © Lin Wagner.)

Air-Conditioning

CHAPTER SEVEN

Air-conditioning—either centrally installed or mounted in a wall or window—can present a significant electrical load in many houses, but it is possible to cut your spending and still keep cool. Of course, it is important to maintain and operate any air-conditioning system properly for maximum efficiency. Simple maintenance, proper servicing, and one-time upgrades can keep your A/C system in tiptop shape. In some cases, it may be time for a new air conditioner, either as a replacement for an existing system or as a new home improvement.

Although you may not be able to pay for a new, efficient central air conditioner in energy savings alone, when you do buy one you should buy the most efficient one you can find. This chapter will help you find a contractor who can correctly size and install a new system. But first, there are a number of things you can do to reduce the cooling loads in your house and cut costs significantly.

PRO TIP

All fans generate heat. If you run ceiling fans but don't set the thermostat at a higher temperature, this heat will actually increase your cooling energy needs.

IN DETAIL

Some appliances use electricity even when you think they are turned off. Cable television decoders are a classic example: If they're plugged in, they're consuming energy whether they're being used or not. In fact, anything that turns on with a remote control draws energy continuously, staying on to receive the signal from the remote. Plug-in wall cubes, commonly used with answering machines, cordless phones, and the like, also use power whenever they are plugged in. Even when the device is off, the wall cube continues to draw about half its rated power as long as it's plugged into the wall.

This wall cube, which powers a disk drive, draws about 18 watts. The only way to shut it off is to unplug it from the wall. (Photo © Kevin Kennefick.)

Cooling Basics

Heat flows from a higher temperature to a lower one. In winter, houses lose heat; in summer, they gain it. Just as heating bills benefit by reductions in heat loss, cooling loads—and bills—benefit by reductions in heat gain. Most summer heat gain comes from three places: solar radiation, internal gains, and air leakage in the building and ducts.

Where does the heat come from?

During the heating season, the largest energy loads in most homes come from conductive heat loss through walls, ceilings, and windows. Air leakage in the building envelope and ducts are a close second. Radiation effects are minimal.

In hot weather the tables are turned. Conduction plays a minor role, because the source of most air-conditioning loads is solar radiation through windows and uninsulated roofs. The same solar heat gain that provides free heat in winter is what really drives the need for air-conditioning in summer. And it's not just a problem with south-facing windows; in fact, the majority of cooling loads is generated by east- and west-facing glass. Even conductive heat gains through a poorly insulated attic are largely driven by radiation, when the sun shining on the roof superheats the attic far above outdoor temperatures.

Internal gain is the name for heat that is generated inside a building by lights, appliances, and people. It is significant and may outstrip all other sources besides windows. Some things that we do indoors, such as cooking, dishwashing, showering, and bathing, are obvious sources of heat. Others are not hard to find. Refrigerators, televisions, and computer equipment and their accessories all give off heat. Of course, lighting generates heat, as do less-obvious sources, such as standby loss from water heaters.

Where Do the Cooling Dollars Go?

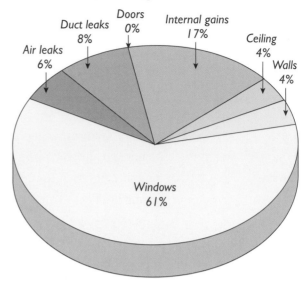

Here is a breakdown of the cooling loads of a typical Orlando, Florida, house with single-pane aluminum windows and minimal window shading. The building envelope and ducts are fairly leaky, and the ceiling and walls are moderately insulated. As the chart indicates, most of the loads come from the windows and the heat generated inside the house (internal gains).

In addition to solar and internal heat gains, air and duct leakage can also contribute significantly to cooling loads. This is particularly true in humid climates, where outdoor air leaking inside brings humidity along with heat.

How air conditioners work

Virtually all residential air-conditioning systems use a compressor-driven refrigerant vapor cycle to cool house air. The compressor cycle controls refrigerant temperatures in the condenser and evaporator coils, which absorb heat from indoor air at a low temperature, then eject it outdoors at a higher temperature. Air conditioners, heat pumps, and refrigerators all use the refrigerant vapor cycle to essentially push heat uphill, from a cooler place to a warmer place. An air conditioner pushes heat from the cool indoors to the hot outdoors, cooling the interior. In addition to sending indoor heat outdoors, an air conditioner must also eject the heat generated by the compressor. Locating the compressor outdoors near the outdoor fan coil helps with that process.

One thing that separates air conditioners from heating systems is their ability to dehumidify, as well as cool, indoor air. This happens when water condenses on the cold fins of the evaporator coil as air passes across them. As noted in chapter 1 (see the sidebar on p. 22), dehumidification is an important component in maintaining healthy indoor air quality and comfort. Humidity—evaporated water in air—contains a significant amount of heat energy, which must be accounted for in the system's design. The energy required to remove excess humidity is called *latent load,* and it can be caused by moisture sources from within the home or from humid outdoor air leaking indoors.

Reducing Loads

With cooling, just as with heating, the less load there is on a building the less energy dollars you spend. Think of the air conditioner as removing heat that builds up rather than cooling down the house. The better you are at preventing heat from building up, the less heat your air conditioner must remove and the less time it will have to run—saving you money. There are two equally valid approaches to reducing cooling loads: reducing your need for cooling, and reducing heat gains in your house.

Central Air-Conditioning System

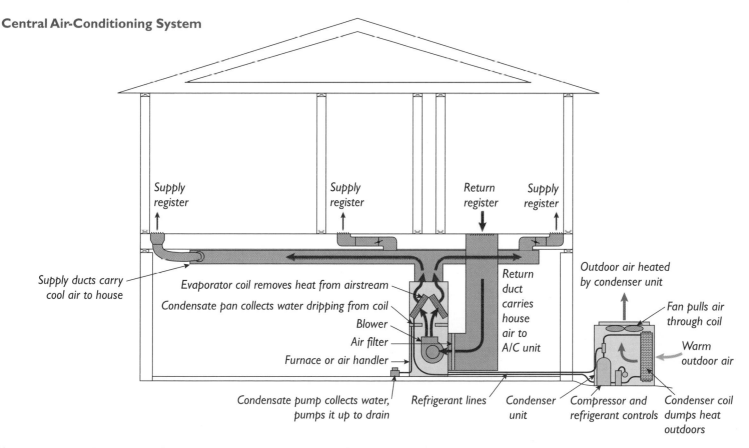

Supply register

Supply register

Return register

Supply register

Supply ducts carry cool air to house

Evaporator coil removes heat from airstream

Condensate pan collects water dripping from coil

Blower

Air filter

Furnace or air handler

Return duct carries house air to A/C unit

Outdoor air heated by condenser unit

Fan pulls air through coil

Warm outdoor air

Condensate pump collects water, pumps it up to drain

Refrigerant lines

Condenser unit

Compressor and refrigerant controls

Condenser coil dumps heat outdoors

Most central air conditioners are split systems, like the one shown here. Hot refrigerant coming from the compressor is cooled in the condenser coil, then piped into the air handler unit. The temperature of the liquid refrigerant drops rapidly as it expands into the evaporator coil, cooling the air by 15°F to 25°F as it passes through the coil. Water condensing on the coil drips into a metal pan, where it is piped to a drain or condensate pump for removal. The evaporator coil may be mounted in or above a furnace or in a dedicated air handler, or it may share the air handler cabinet with a hot water hydro-air coil.

Yellow arrow = Warm outdoor air
Green arrow = Outdoor air heated by condenser coil

WHAT CAN GO WRONG

All central air conditioners have a drain pan underneath the evaporator coil to collect water from the humid air that condenses on the coil. If the pan is out of level, or has a lot of junk in it, water can sit in the pan when the air conditioner shuts off, then evaporate into the air, undoing some of the dehumidification the system has accomplished. Standing water in a condensate drain system may also provide a breeding ground for mold, so make sure the system works efficiently.

If your A/C unit is below the house's drain system, you should have a condensate pump to collect water and pump it up into a drain. A malfunctioning pump can be a significant source of moisture in the basement or crawl space.

Reduce the need for cooling

Although I always try to emphasize energy efficiency without sacrificing comfort or utility, one surefire way to cut cooling costs is to use your air conditioner less. A house with more insulation, better windows, and less air leakage is comfortable with no air-conditioning for more of the summer. Setting the thermostat higher, particularly when the house is empty, reduces the system's run time and saves energy. A clock-thermostat can do that for you automatically, bringing the temperature to a comfortable level before you typically arrive home. Clock-thermostats are available to handle both heating and cooling setbacks (see the bottom left photo on p. 104).

Fans can also help raise the temperature at which you feel comfortable. By installing an efficient ceiling fan and keeping the air moving in occupied rooms, most people can comfortably increase the temperature setting of their thermostat by 4°F to 6°F, saving 20% to 35% on their cooling bills. Fan flow should point downward to maximize the feeling of air movement in the room. Oscillating and

Specially developed by the Florida Solar Energy Center, this super-efficient fan moves more air and uses less electricity than standard paddle fans. It also has a cool, efficient, dimmable fluorescent light; programmable temperature and motion sensors; and optional remote control. The suggested retail price of the Calloway II is $129, and the Windward II is $149. These fans are readily available at most popular home centers. (Photo © Steven C. Spencer.)

box fans can also provide portable comfort. When using any type of fan, remember that it will keep people cool only while they are in the room. Turn off fans when you are not using them, because they generate heat.

Whole-House Fans

A whole-house fan is designed to replace air rapidly, filling the house with cool, dry outdoor air. It's important to open windows or doors around the house while the fan is on. And of course, it should be run only when outdoor air is more comfortable—cooler and dryer—than indoor air. After running a whole-house fan for a couple of hours late at night or early in the morning, close windows and doors tightly to retain the cool air as the day warms up.

Unlike most whole-house ventilation fans, this one by Tamarack Technologies has a motorized, insulated cover with good weatherstripping. It's available in 700- and 1,000-cfm models ($490 and $619, respectively), both of which mount easily between two joists at 16 in. or 24 in. o.c. and are available with remote controls, including an X10 home-automation-compatible system. (Photo courtesy Tamarack Technologies.)

A simple fan can keep you more comfortable in hot weather and reduce your need for air-conditioning. But turn it off when you (or your cat) aren't in the room, because fans generate heat. (Photo © Kevin Kennefick.)

Solar Gain

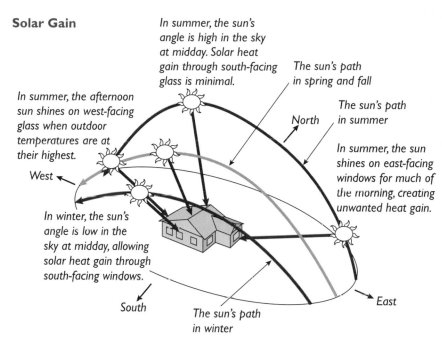

In summer, the sun's angle is high in the sky at midday. Solar heat gain through south-facing glass is minimal.

The sun's path in spring and fall

The sun's path in summer

In summer, the afternoon sun shines on west-facing glass when outdoor temperatures are at their highest.

North

In summer, the sun shines on east-facing windows for much of the morning, creating unwanted heat gain.

West

In winter, the sun's angle is low in the sky at midday, allowing solar heat gain through south-facing windows.

East

South

The sun's path in winter

The amount of solar gain coming through a window depends heavily on the sun's angle: the closer it is to a right angle (shining straight in), the more energy that enters the house. In summer, most unwanted heat gain comes through skylights and east- and west-facing windows. In winter, virtually all of the useful heat gain comes through south-facing glass. In spring and fall, solar gains are more mixed by direction, and the best strategies to minimize energy use depend on the overall climate.

The annual route of the sun's path works to our advantage in trying to control solar gains in most of North America. Moderate shades or overhangs on the south side can virtually eliminate solar gains in summer, while still admitting plenty of free solar energy during cold months, when the sun is low. To reduce unwanted gains in summer, deep overhangs, shades, or large trees are needed to avoid punishing solar radiation from the east and west.

Ceiling-mounted whole-house fans that exhaust into the attic are another popular method to reduce the need for cooling, but they must be used properly to be effective. It is critical that air leaks between the attic and house be sealed, and that the attic be well vented to the exterior, to ensure that the fan exhaust goes outdoors, not back into the house.

Another system that is often used in commercial buildings is an economizer cycle, which uses a device called an *enthalpy control* to determine when outdoor air is cooler and dryer than indoor air. Whenever the thermostat calls for cooling during those times, the enthalpy control runs the air conditioner's blower but not the compressor; it also activates a damper, so that the return air comes from an outdoor air duct rather than from inside the house. A residential economizer system, called the DuroZone Fresh Air Intake and Economizer Control Center, is available from Duro Dyne® Corporation.

Reduce heat gains

The two big sources of heat gain that create cooling loads are solar gains (through windows and the attic) and internal gains. There are several strategies to prevent solar gains from heating a house in the first place. Shade the house with trees or architectural-shading devices, reflect solar energy with light-colored roof coatings and solar-control glazing, and, of course, insulate and air-seal attics and exterior walls. Although the options for reducing internal gains are more limited, simple measures, such as changing from incandescent to compact fluorescent lighting, can make a significant difference.

Interior shades cut down on solar gain but not as well as exterior shading does. The sun still heats the window and the air between the shade and the glass—air that slowly mixes with the house air.

135

PRO TIP

Landscaping with trees or a trellis with thick vegetation can shade walls and roof as well as windows.

WHAT CAN GO WRONG

Adequate airflow is even more important with air conditioners than it is with furnaces. If, in the process of sealing large leaks in undersized ducts, you end up cutting the airflow through the system, it will decrease the system's efficiency and may even damage the compressor.

WHAT CAN GO WRONG

If you're thinking of coating an existing roof surface to gain higher reflectivity, be careful. First of all, don't ever paint or coat a roof that has gone bad. If the surface or decking is rotten, the coating won't stick to or protect it. Any low areas where water pools up must be leveled first. And don't try to apply a coating in cold or wet weather, or it will not cure properly. Finally, stay away from ceramic beads that may be sold as a paint additive. Studies have shown that they don't increase reflectivity, but they do make paint more difficult to apply and may shorten its service life.

Roofing Reflectivity

The more reflective your roofing surface, the lower your cooling bills will be. White metal, metal tiles, and elastomeric coatings have the highest reflectivity; black and gray have the lowest. Some white materials, such as asphalt shingles, have surprisingly low reflectivity. Reflectivity may decline over time, but quality products should remain at 50% or higher after several years. The Energy Star program labels roofing products (mostly coatings and commercial roofing products, as well as some clay and metal tiles) that meet minimum performance standards set by the EPA and DOE. For a list, see www.energystar.gov/products/ and look for the link to "Roof Products."

Roofing Type	Typical Reflectivity	Performance
White elastomeric and acrylic coatings	70–85%	Very good
White anodized metal	75–80%	
White EPDM rubber	75%	
White clay tile	50–60%	Good
White asphalt shingles	25%	Moderate
Gray asphalt	10–20%	Poor
Black asphalt or EPDM	5%	

Reduce solar gains. Shading the right place can have a huge impact on cooling loads. Because of the high percentage of solar gains from east- and west-facing windows, the most effective strategies in any climate involve shading those windows. Although internal curtains and roller shades can help a lot (the lighter in color and the more opaque, the better), they still allow some solar heat to come in through windows.

Large overhangs, trellises, porches, and other architectural details can significantly reduce unwanted solar gain. In mixed and cold climates, avoid large overhangs on the south side. (Photo by Roe Osborn, courtesy *Fine Homebuilding* magazine, © The Taunton Press.)

The best shading strategies are done on the exterior, preventing the sun's heat from ever reaching the glass. Architectural details, such as overhangs, awnings, and exterior shutters, all work well. Landscaping with trees or installing a trellis with thick vegetation can provide an attractive solar shield, shading the walls and the roof as well as the windows. In very hot climates, where wintertime solar gains are of minimal benefit, shading the south side of a house, as well as the east and west sides, is beneficial.

You can also prevent solar heat from entering windows with solar-control glazing or transparent solar-control films. Chapter 5 explains those features in more detail. Choose products with the lowest possible SHGC rating for east- and west-facing glass in all climates and for south-facing glass in very hot climates.

Research has shown that roof color also has a significant impact on solar gain. The most reflec-

A highly reflective roof can save substantially on air-conditioning bills in hot climates. (Photo courtesy All Weather Surfaces Hawaii, Inc.)

tive roofing materials do the best job, and they can reduce cooling loads by 20% or more when compared to dark-gray asphalt shingles (see the chart on the facing page). Although saving on cooling energy certainly won't justify replacing your roof, if you live in a hot climate, consider using reflective, light-colored sheet metal, metal tiles, or cement tiles when you do have to reroof. Don't assume that light-colored shingles are highly reflective. Only the surface granules are colored, so white composition shingles are only slightly more reflective than dark-colored ones, and they won't provide much savings.

Reflective coatings can also make a big difference, and at a much lower cost than a whole new roof. Acrylic elastomeric coatings with high reflectivity can easily be applied with a paint roller on built-up or membrane roofing materials. At $20 to $25 per gallon for high-quality products, these coatings may not be cost-effective if you consider only energy savings. However, because the roof surface will be cooler, they can significantly extend the life of existing roofing materials, which also saves maintenance expenses.

A *radiant barrier* is another attic retrofit that can save cooling energy, but it is likely to be cost-effective only in hot, southern climates. Both radiant barriers and light-colored roofs should be weighed against the benefits of installing more

Radiant Barriers

Radiant barriers are reflective surfaces—usually heavy foil or foil-coated sheet stock (mylar, kraft paper, or foam insulation)—installed between a roof deck and an insulated ceiling. The shinier the foil, the better it will work. Look for products with high reflectivity (0.9 or more) and low emissivity (0.1 or less). Costs range widely ($0.10/sq. ft. to $1.00/sq. ft.), and the inexpensive products generally work as well as the pricey ones. Some have a foil facing on only one side, which is fine, but the foil should face the attic. Radiant barriers need an airspace next

A radiant barrier attached to the bottom of roof rafters can significantly reduce attic heat gain, but don't use it as a substitute for insulation.

to the foil to be effective; that happens automatically if the material is applied to the underside of uninsulated rafters. Don't install radiant barriers on the attic floor over existing insulation, because they won't work.

TRADE SECRET

When an air-conditioning condenser coil is located in a sunny spot or on a roof, it is working at a disadvantage by trying to eject heat into air that is being warmed by the sun. Keeping a condenser coil in the shade by planting trees or tall bushes, building a trellis, or otherwise shading the area around it can help it run more efficiently. However, be careful not to interfere with the air circulation around the coil. An air conditioner needs unrestricted airflow to work efficiently.

Wall air conditioners depend on free airflow and should never be installed (like this one) in a restricted area—even if it keeps them in the shade.

This recessed-light retrofit kit from TLC attaches to a regular recessed light socket, and the reflector insert accepts a compact fluorescent bulb. In addition to saving energy and reducing heat generation, the insert is airtight-rated as well. (Photo © Kevin Kennefick.)

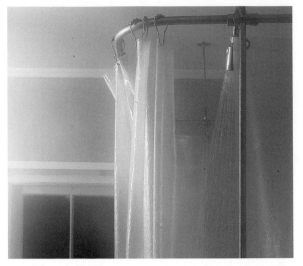

Using exhaust fans to vent moisture sources will help you save on your air-conditioning costs by reducing the latent load. (Photo © Kevin Kennefick.)

attic insulation and sealing and insulating ductwork; those tasks should always be your first priority. A radiant barrier, for example, provides about the same savings as 2 in. to 3 in. of additional loose-fill insulation, which may be cheaper to install and will save more energy during the heating season than a radiant barrier will. On the other hand, if you have cathedral ceilings or an attic with a very shallow roof slope and leaky ductwork without access for sealing, a white, reflective roof or coating could mean big savings—possibly as much as 30% to 40%.

Reduce internal gains. As shown in the drawing on p. 132, internal gains, or heat generated

Leaks in air-conditioning ducts waste a lot of money, particularly when the ducts are in an attic. Sealing connections thoroughly with mastic is vital to proper A/C operation.

This gap between the A/C return and the drywall sucks hot attic air into the air handler. It should be caulked or sealed with mastic.

by activities within a house, can be a significant component of the home's cooling energy requirements. Some internal gains, such as the number of inhabitants or the hot water usage, are difficult to change. However, replacing lights and appliances with more energy-efficient products saves energy in two ways. First, it reduces the electricity required to operate those products year-round. Second, because more efficient lights and appliances produce less heat energy, replacement also saves on cooling expenses. Chapter 10 has more detailed information on maximizing appliance and lighting efficiency; any of the steps listed there will reduce cooling energy requirements as well.

In addition to minimizing internal heat gains, it is also helpful to reduce or minimize moisture sources in the home, which add to the latent (dehumidification) loads in the building. Use exhaust fans when cooking and bathing, and take any necessary steps to reduce large moisture loads.

Duct insulation and sealing

Air-conditioning ducts have the same leakage and insulation issues as those of heating ducts (see pp. 110–115). In fact, leaks and missing insulation in attic ductwork hurt A/C systems more than

heating systems, because, during peak cooling times, attics are usually much hotter than outdoor ambient temperatures (during the heating season, ducts are rarely in spaces that are fully exposed to outdoor conditions). All air-conditioning ducts, particularly those outside the conditioned space, should be thoroughly sealed and insulated (as described on pp. 112–115).

Maintenance and Upgrades

Like most other equipment, air conditioners need regular maintenance and service. Some things you can probably do yourself, while others require a professional technician.

Replacing filters

Like heat pumps and furnaces, air-conditioning systems depend on adequate airflow to remove heat efficiently from your house. Whether you have a central air conditioner or individual room units, check the filters regularly and clean or replace them when they are dirty. Because airflow is important, do not to shut off any of the supply registers in the system.

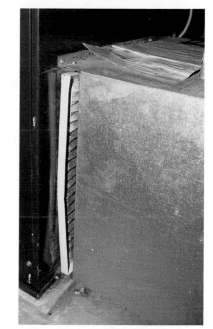

A filter slot without a cover allows an air conditioner (or a heat pump or furnace) to suck dust and dirt past the filter. It may also pull return air from places it shouldn't, such as the attic, garage, or crawl space where the unit is located.

A good filter cover should fit tightly but not require a nut driver to remove.

This air-conditioner filter can easily be rinsed, dried, and replaced to keep it running as efficiently as possible.

+ SAFETY FIRST

Don't ever turn off an air conditioner—either at the circuit breaker or at the thermostat—and then turn it right back on. The compressor may not be able to handle the heavy load when it tries to restart, so wait at least 4 to 5 minutes. Many new systems have a built-in time delay, but you risk inducing expensive damage with systems that don't. Of course, don't attempt any service on an air conditioner unless you know exactly what you are doing and have turned off the power at the circuit breaker.

IN DETAIL

In relatively hot, dry regions, evaporative coolers (or swamp coolers) provide very efficient air-conditioning. Cool water runs through a damp pad or fiber matrix, and air is blown through the pad and into the house. As water evaporates into the air, it absorbs energy and cools the air in much the same way that perspiration evaporating from the skin cools our bodies. For evaporative coolers to work, the outdoor air must be dry enough to absorb a significant amount of evaporated moisture.

Evaporative coolers like this one can provide indoor comfort at a much lower cost than air-conditioning, but they are effective only in a dry climate. (Photo courtesy Convair Cooler, Inc.)

Dirt tends to build up on the surface of the evaporator coil. To remove it, carefully insert brush bristles between the fins, then lift the dirt from behind. A technician, spraying from behind with a special coil-cleaning spray, can clean seriously clogged coils.

Cleaning air coils

When filters don't work properly or air gets around them, the evaporator coil can become clogged with dirt and dust. Depending on the system, you may need a service technician to access the coil. If you can reach it yourself, lift the

Once they have verified the proper charge, service technicians should never attach gauges or add refrigerant to a system unless its performance declines.

dirt from behind with a stiff brush. Be careful not to drive dirt further in or bend the fins.

The outdoor condenser coil should also be kept clean and free of dirt and debris. Be careful not to spray water directly at the coil, which may drive dirt deeper into the space between the fins.

Once an air-conditioner system has been emptied with a vacuum pump, the correct amount of new refrigerant can be measured with a scale (visible at right).

Other than weighing it, a proper refrigerant charge can be verified only by a superheat or subcooling test once the airflow is known to be correct.

Instead, using a long-bristle brush with soft bristles, carefully insert the bristles between the fins and lift the dirt from behind.

Regular service

Regular service calls—typically every two to three years—should include testing the controls, cleaning the blower, cleaning the condenser and evaporator coils, checking the insulation on the refrigerant lines, and checking the condensate drain system. An initial service appointment should include testing and fixing any airflow problems, and then carefully measuring and correcting the refrigerant charge. Like a heat pump, once that has been done, service technicians should *not* attach refrigerant gauges to the system, unless the system performance declines or there is other evidence that something is wrong.

Like heat pumps, an over- or undercharged air conditioner is less efficient, and systems are often improperly charged. First, airflow must be in the recommended range of 400 cfm to 425 cfm per ton before the refrigerant charge can be correctly diagnosed. In practice, though, few technicians bother to test airflow.

It is difficult to test airflow in an air conditioner, because it has no heat source. Temperature drop (measured just like temperature rise; see p. 108) can work if you know the charge is correct. However, measuring the charge properly if you haven't checked the airflow requires purging and weighing the refrigerant. Airflow should be measured near the air handler by a skilled technician with a pitot tube or anemometer, both of which can measure air velocity. (Airflow in cfm equals velocity × duct area in square feet). A flow hood can be used at the registers, but it is less accurate and will underestimate airflow by the amount of any duct leakage.

Once airflow is correct, the superheat or subcooling must also be measured carefully (which

Any air conditioner that is more than 20 years old is a good candidate for replacement with a new, more energy-efficient unit.

New air-conditioning systems are almost twice as efficient as the minimum standards of 20 years ago—some even more so.

one depends on the type of system). Alternatively, the refrigerant may be emptied with a vacuum pump, and then the correct number of ounces for the system can be weighed on a scale.

New Air-Conditioning Systems

If you live in a hot climate and have central air-conditioning that is more than 20 years old, chances are good that replacing your system with a new, energy-efficient model will pay for itself in energy savings. High-efficiency systems on the market today are nearly twice as efficient as systems from the early '80s. But before running out and replacing your system, you will first need to do to other things. Finish any upgrades on the

PRO TIP

It's better to undersize rather than oversize an air-conditioning system, because it will run more efficiently and dehumidify better.

TRADE SECRET

In an efficient house with a small cooling load, one or two room units may be a better solution than central air. If the cooling load in your house is less than 20,000 BTUs per hour, even a small central system will be too big, and it will cost more to run. And if you want to cool only some parts of your home at one time, central systems cannot be zoned easily; a few small room units are much more economical to buy and operate.

Window- or wall-mounted air conditioners have lower efficiency ratings than central systems, but there are no ducts to waste the cold air. Cooling only one or two rooms also uses much less energy than cooling an entire house.

EER vs. SEER

You can compare the energy performance of central air-conditioning systems by examining their Seasonal Energy Efficiency Ratings (SEER). Room air conditioners are rated in Energy Efficiency Ratios (EER) rather than SEERs, and the most efficient units have EERs of 11 or 12, depending on the size of the unit. SEER and EER are expressed in units of BTUs per watt, but the two measurements aren't the same, because they are measured under different outdoor conditions. EER is measured under hotter outdoor conditions than SEER is, so these ratings appear to be lower for otherwise identical performance. The most efficient central air conditioners are more efficient than the most efficient room units, but not by as much as may otherwise appear.

To find the SEER rating for central A/C equipment, look up the model number online at www.ariprimenet.org, and look for "Unitary Air-Conditioning Systems" under "Residential Certified Products." The Energy Star labeling program covers both room and central air conditioners; any product with the Energy Star label has been tested to meet higher efficiency and performance standards set by the government. Log on to www.energystar.gov and look under "Find products—heating and cooling—room air conditioners."

New air conditioners should have an Energy Guide label that shows its efficiency rating, as well as a comparison with the ratings of other units of the same type. Room units have an EER, while central systems have a SEER.

building envelope, and become familiar with air-conditioning products and installation criteria.

Of course, if you have a fairly new system (less than 10 years old), it is probably more cost-effective to maintain it and keep it running as efficiently as possible until it wears out. As always, energy-efficient upgrades always cost the least when you are fixing or replacing something anyway. If your old air conditioner is on its last legs or not operating, replace it with the most efficient unit you can find.

High-efficiency air-conditioning

New central air conditioners are rated for energy performance with a Seasonal Energy Efficiency Rating (SEER). SEER ratings are measurements under standardized test conditions of btus per hour of cooling output, divided by input watts. The higher the SEER, the more efficient the system. New central air conditioners are required to have an SEER rating of at least 10.0; the most efficient units on the market have SEER ratings of 16 or more. Some of the best high-efficiency systems have two speed compressors; the lower speed provides better, more efficient cooling and dehumidification under mild, part-load conditions.

One important consideration in replacing a central unit with a more efficient one is matching the new condensing unit to the existing indoor evaporator coil. You may be able to save some money on the installation by keeping your old coil, but be careful: The efficiency ratings of new air conditioners depend on the proper match between indoor and outdoor units.

Sizing a system

Proper sizing is important for heating systems, but even more so for air conditioners. Air conditioners always run less efficiently for the first 10 to 15 minutes of each cycle; an oversized cooling system runs for only a few minutes at a time, never reaching its potential. Oversized air conditioners cost more to buy and more to run. Even equipment that is properly sized for typical high temperatures in your area will be oversized when conditions are less extreme, and there are always more hours of moderate temperatures than there are of extremes. An air conditioner that is twice the size it needs to be at the highest outdoor temperature will be three to four times oversized for most of the summer.

Dehumidification, which depends on air flowing through the evaporator coil for enough time to extract condensed moisture, is another reason to carefully size an air-conditioning system. When an oversized system runs for only a few minutes, the moisture just starts to collect on the coils when the thermostat is satisfied. Once the unit shuts down, the moisture simply reevaporates into the house. An air conditioner that is too large by 50% to 100% will be unable to maintain a healthy humidity level in the home.

In fact, it's better to undersize an air conditioner slightly, particularly in humid climates. Sure, the

indoor temperature may creep up from 70°F to 73°F for a few hours in the afternoon during the hottest weather, but you will still be healthier and more comfortable, and at a much lower cost, than you would be with an oversized system.

There are typically two ways that most contractors select the size of a replacement system: They replace it with the same size as the old unit, or they use calculations based on the square footage of the house. These methods almost always result in air conditioners that are too big; if energy improvements were made to the building, the error would be even larger.

For example, if, on the hottest days of summer, your old air conditioner ran 40 minutes of every hour, it was already 1.5 times too large; if it ran 30 minutes of every hour, it was twice as big as it needed to be. Of course, that assumes the machine was operating properly and did not have significant duct leaks.

Correct load calculations are based on your home's window size, the glass type, and the size and R-values of the walls and roof. Those factors must be considered when sizing any air-conditioning system. If a contractor gives you a price for an air conditioner without measuring those things, or simply offers to replace the existing unit with a new one of the same size, get a bid from someone else, especially if you have made a point of describing the envelope improvements you have made in your house.

A contractor also needs to know which direction the building faces. Sometimes a 90-degree difference in orientation can cut the cooling load in half! When installing a new air conditioner, shop for value, not just for price. Other things to look for when assessing bids on new air-conditioning equipment include the warranties (from both the manufacturer and the installer), service contracts, longevity of the business, customer references, and technician knowledge.

A high-velocity duct system is another option for retrofitting central air-conditioning in a house with no ducts. The narrow ducts can easily be snaked through places where conventional ductwork would never fit. (Photo courtesy Spacepak, a MESTEK company.)

✔ According to Code

Many states have new construction energy codes that require sizing calculations for air-conditioning equipment. Codes specify the use of statistical design temperatures, which are not the most severe temperatures ever seen in a given location. The calculation procedure allows for a generous margin of safety; other margins do not need to be built in to the calculations. Unfortunately, few building inspectors pay attention to these code requirements, even where they have been adopted in their states. However, they are a critical foundation for a good system design, both in new construction and in existing homes.

Heating

CHAPTER EIGHT

Hot Water

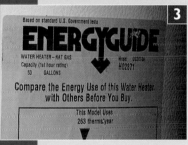

Hot water, like heat, is a necessity in all modern homes. In very efficient homes, water heating can even be a larger load then heating, air-conditioning, or electrical appliance use. The annual cost to heat your hot water is driven by two factors: usage and efficiency. Reducing the amount of hot water you use can impact your utility bills as much as, or more than, improving the efficiency of your water heating equipment, and at a lower cost.

This chapter shows you ways to reduce water heating loads by cutting down on hot water consumption. It outlines basic procedures for maintaining standard water heaters for longevity and efficiency and describe some do-it-yourself projects to help reduce efficiency losses. It also discusses how and when to replace or upgrade your water heating equipment for the best efficiency possible.

If the flow rate of a shower is more than 4 GPM, it is well worth replacing it with a new low-flow 2.5-GPM showerhead.

WHAT CAN GO WRONG

Installing a low-flow shower-head can increase the back pressure in the water supply lines. This can cause the pipes to spring a leak; more frequently, it can cause or increase leakage in a faulty diverter valve (the valve that shuts off the flow to the bathtub faucet when the shower runs). I have measured water flows as high as 9 GPM from a tub faucet while the shower was running. Fixing a leaky diverter may be as easy as changing a washer, or it may involve replacing the entire mixing valve.

A low-flow showerhead doesn't save hot water if the faucet keeps running. The diverter valve in this shower needs to be rebuilt or replaced.

Hot Water Conservation

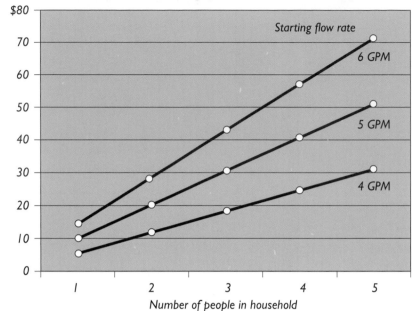

Potential Annual Savings from Low-Flow Showerheads

Starting flow rate

6 GPM

5 GPM

4 GPM

Number of people in household

Because most Americans shower every day, reducing a showerhead's flow can save a lot of water and money. Depending on the flow rate at which you start—in gallons per minute (GPM)—and the number of people in the household, your yearly savings can be substantial. These numbers assume a water heating efficiency of 55%, daily 5-minute showers for each person in the house, and a natural gas price of $0.80/therm. If you heat your water with electricity, the savings may be significantly larger; if your water heater's efficiency is higher, the savings will be smaller. Remember that you won't just be saving fuel costs: For every $10 in water heating savings, you will also save about 3,000 gallons of water per year.

Hot Water Conservation

One of the themes in this book is conservation without deprivation, or paying for the functionality you need or want but not paying for waste. Hot water is a good example of that concept: If the various jobs that use hot water can be done equally well with less water, you will save money. There are a number of ways you can reduce hot water usage and consumption.

Low-flow showerheads

When I first got into the energy-efficiency field in the early 1990s, low-flow showerheads had a bad reputation. If you haven't had one in your house, you've probably been in a hotel room with one of those sleek little silver barrels: They produce wet air, cold feet, billowing shower curtains, and lots of steam, but nothing resembling a satisfying shower. Many of them also had little shutoff buttons, allowing the user to cut the flow while

soaping up. I suspect that few people used those buttons. In my experience, the valves tended to clog up and become inoperable.

Over the past decade, as plumbing regulations for new construction have required showerheads with ratings of 2.5 gallons per minute (GPM) or less, a much wider array of useful products has emerged, ranging from simple spray heads to multifunction shower-massage spectaculars. Shop around. If your existing showerhead was made prior to 1993, any new product that you install will produce significant savings—and not at the expense of a good shower.

There are two tricks when upgrading your old showerhead: removing the old one without breaking the shower arm and installing the new one without marring it. Usually, you'll be able to unscrew the old showerhead by hand and replace it with a new unit. Just be sure to support the shower arm carefully when trying to loosen the old head; too much leverage may cause an older arm to break off inside the wall. Or worse, it

Most replacement low-flow showerheads have spongy rubber gaskets and can be hand-tightened to be watertight.

Trying to unscrew an old showerhead without breaking off the shower arm may be more trouble than it's worth. If the shower arm is old, it is often easier to replace the entire assembly along with the showerhead.

could create a leak in the wall that may go unnoticed until it has caused substantial damage.

If the old showerhead doesn't come off easily, it may be better to replace the entire arm. Use a pair of pliers to get a firm grip on the old arm and unthread it carefully from the fitting inside the wall. Before installing the new arm, be sure to wrap a few turns of Teflon® tape around the threads.

Wrap the end of a new shower arm with several turns of Teflon tape before threading it in place. Don't forget to put the trim cover on the new arm before wrapping the threads.

Measuring Flow

If you're not sure what the flow rate of an existing showerhead is, you can measure it easily. Get a 1- to 2-gal. bucket, and make sure you know exactly how much it holds (1 gal. is 16 cups). Find a helper and a stopwatch or a clock with a second hand. Turn on the shower, and have the helper start timing as you put the bucket into the stream of water. Stop timing when the bucket is full, and then calculate the flow rate in gallons per minute. The water flow equals the bucket capacity (in gallons) times 60 (time in seconds divided by the number of seconds it took to fill the bucket). If the flow rate of a shower is more than 4 GPM, it is worth replacing your showerhead.

IN DETAIL

The temperature markings on a water heater dial (if it has them) are notorious for bad calibration. To find your actual water temperature, use a good-quality thermometer with a scale of up to at least 150°F. Choose a time when no one has used hot water for at least an hour, then run water at full hot from a tap for a few minutes, until the temperature has stabilized. Reduce the flow to the size of a pencil, and run the water into a small glass with a thermometer in it. Wait until the thermometer reading has stabilized, and that's your hot water temperature.

This inexpensive probe-type digital thermometer is good for measuring hot water temperature.

Faucet aerators

Like showerheads, new kitchen and lavatory faucets have had maximum-flow ratings of 2.5 GPM since the mid-1990s. Some vintage fixtures don't have standard screw-in aerators and cannot be retrofitted easily, but, in most cases, a new aerator in an existing faucet can further reduce hot water usage.

Besides the simple cartridge type of aerator, there are also add-on units that give you more control over water flow. If you are planning to replace a kitchen faucet, an integrated faucet/ retractable sprayer unit can provide flexible spray patterns and low water flow in one attractive package.

Replacing an old aerator with a 2.5-GPM aerator is a simple step that can save a lot of money. In this case, the old aerator (left) did nothing to reduce the flow of water.

For convenience *and* efficiency, many kitchen faucets have built-in sprayers and selectable spray patterns. All new faucets are rated at 2.5 GPM or less.

This kitchen aerator not only reduces water flow to 2.5 GPM but also has a small lever that slows water to a trickle. That can be handy when washing dishes, because you can set the water temperature where you want it and then control the flow with a flip of your finger.

When the lever is pushed up, the flow slows to a dribble.

Other appliances

Two other home appliances use substantial amounts of hot water: clothes washers and dishwashers. New, horizontal-axis washers consume one-quarter to one-third of the hot water and electricity used by conventional washing machines (see the sidebar on p. 190). Regardless of your washing machine type, you can easily save hot water by being conscious of your usage. Use warm or cold cycles when hot is unnecessary, and set the fill level appropriately to the size of load.

Dishwashers are a little more complicated. Older units generally depend on an incoming hot water temperature of 130°F or higher to work properly. Many new models have built-in booster heaters, which locally heat the wash water to 140°F to 145°F. Not only do they use less hot water, but they also allow you to reduce the temperature setting on your water heater (see the photo on p. 150). In general, to save hot water, use the energy-saving "Normal" or "Light" setting, and always fill the dishwasher to capacity before running it, because it will use the same amount of hot water whether it's empty or full. (For more information on dishwasher efficiency, see pp. 190–191).

Maintenance and Efficiency Upgrades

The vast majority of homes in the United States have stand-alone water heaters. These are independent hot water storage tanks with their own heat source, with the sole function of providing domestic hot water. In some cases, homes that are heated with a boiler may have a tankless coil or an indirect-fired storage tank (those systems are covered on pp. 158–161.)

Components of a Gas Water Heater

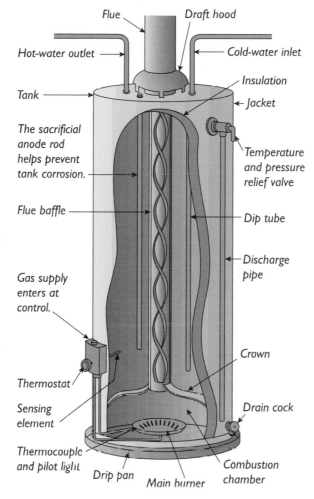

Flue · Draft hood · Hot-water outlet · Cold-water inlet · Tank · Insulation · Jacket · The sacrificial anode rod helps prevent tank corrosion. · Temperature and pressure relief valve · Flue baffle · Dip tube · Discharge pipe · Gas supply enters at control. · Crown · Thermostat · Sensing element · Drain cock · Thermocouple and pilot light · Drip pan · Main burner · Combustion chamber

A typical gas water heater has a sheet-steel tank with a flue in the center for venting combustion gases. The burner is mounted at the base of the tank, which is crowned to distribute the heat. As hot water is drawn off the top of the tank, cold water enters from the bottom by way of a dip tube. The cooler water is sensed by the thermostat, which then turns on the gas at the burner—provided the safety thermocouple senses the presence of a pilot flame. Gas water heaters must be properly anchored in seismically active areas (not shown).

WHAT CAN GO WRONG

The recommended temperature for any storage water heater is somewhere between 120°F and 140°F. A temperature setting below 120°F may increase the risk of *Legionella pneumophilia* bacteria growth and is not recommended. If you have a dishwasher without a booster heater, a tank temperature of 130°F to 135°F may be necessary to get your dishes clean.

This tank is insulated with urethane foam. A tank with insulation rated R-10 or higher won't benefit much from an insulation wrap.

Standard water heaters are cheap and inefficient. They are typically expected to last only 5 to 10 years, so most people do not invest much money in them. One reason is that replacing a water heater tends to be an emergency event, full of stress because the old water heater has suddenly failed. Proper maintenance can significantly extend the life of a water heater, and some efficiency improvements can be made to existing tanks with minimal investment. If your present water heater appears to be near the end of its useful life, now is the time to do research on the right type of replacement unit. Then you will be well prepared, whether you decide to wait until the old one goes or to replace the tank at your convenience.

Two types of tanks: gas and electric

Stand-alone water heaters come in two basic types: gas and electric. Gas water heaters, fired with piped natural gas or propane, are the most common. They are typically more expensive to install but, because of their lower fuel cost, are usually much cheaper to operate than electric tanks.

Gas water heaters are usually smaller than electric water heaters, because their burners produce more heat than an electric heating element. A

+ SAFETY FIRST

The draft hood is a critical component of a standard atmospheric water heater. It provides space for the room's air to be drawn into the flue to help carry combustion gases up and out the chimney. If the draft hood is blocked, removed, or otherwise restricted, the result could be carbon monoxide poisoning, or even fire. To reduce fire risk, never store items on the floor, on top of, or leaning against a water heater.

Typically, gas water heaters don't have degree markings, but the recommended temperature of 120°F to 130°F is usually between "Warm" and "Medium." It may take some trial and error to find the setting that's just right.

capacity of 40 to 50 gallons is typical for most houses.

Electric water heaters in single-family homes often hold 80 gallons or more. Electric water heaters have the advantage that they don't require fuel combustion in the house. Because of the convenience, they are a much more common choice for homes where piped natural gas is not available.

Setting the temperature

The temperature of many hot water heaters can be lowered without any noticeable reduction in the hot water supply. Lowering the temperature of stored hot water saves energy by reducing the conductive heat loss through the tank jacket, called *standby loss*. Standby losses depend on the location of the tank (how cold it is outside the tank), how well the tank is insulated, and how much hot water you use. The better insulated the tank and the greater your hot water use, the less savings a temperature setback will provide.

Components of an Electric Water Heater

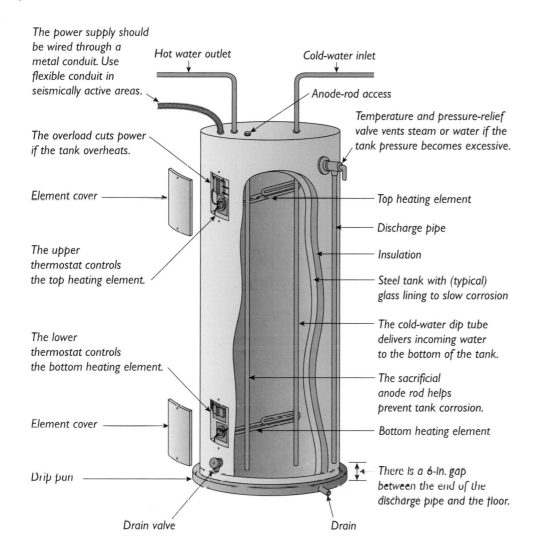

The power supply should be wired through a metal conduit. Use flexible conduit in seismically active areas.

Hot water outlet

Cold-water inlet

Anode-rod access

Temperature and pressure-relief valve vents steam or water if the tank pressure becomes excessive.

The overload cuts power if the tank overheats.

Element cover

Top heating element

Discharge pipe

Insulation

The upper thermostat controls the top heating element.

Steel tank with (typical) glass lining to slow corrosion

The cold-water dip tube delivers incoming water to the bottom of the tank.

The lower thermostat controls the bottom heating element.

The sacrificial anode rod helps prevent tank corrosion.

Element cover

Bottom heating element

Drip pan

There is a 6-in. gap between the end of the discharge pipe and the floor.

Drain valve

Drain

An electric water heater makes hot water with a pair of heating elements. The bottom element does most of the work. The top one kicks in when the hot water in the tank becomes depleted. Note the dip tube, which delivers incoming water to the bottom of the tank. This ensures that the hottest water in the tank is always available to be drawn off the top. The controls are designed to ensure that only one heating element at a time can be energized, which prevents overloading the electric circuit.

Reducing the temperature setting by 10°F may save 2% to 5% of your water heating costs. The investment is $0, and it's easy to readjust it later if you turn it down too much. In addition to energy savings, a lower tank temperature significantly reduces scaling and corrosion and increases the life of the tank.

The thermostat knob on a gas water heater is usually located at the front of the gas valve. Look carefully at the markings; on many gas water heaters, counterclockwise rotation *increases* the temperature setting.

Electric tanks have two thermostats—one for each element—located behind metal covers near the bottom and the top of the tank. Because there is exposed wiring inside, shut off the circuit breaker before unscrewing the covers. Set both elements to about the same temperature, or set the top element just slightly cooler so the bottom element activates first.

Insulation wraps

To further reduce standby losses, cover your water heater with an insulation blanket. On a cheap, poorly insulated tank, a vinyl-faced wrap can double or triple the insulation level, cutting the standby losses by up to half and reducing total water heating costs by up to 10%. However, if

PRO **TIP**

A well-insulated water tank won't benefit from extra insulation, but insulating a cheaply made tank can save up to 10% on your water-heating bills.

TRADE SECRET

It's a popular myth that installing a clock timer to shut off an electric water heater for periods of low usage can save a lot of energy. Energy in a water heater goes to consumed hot water and standby losses. The timer won't reduce hot water consumption. Standby losses through the tank wall will be reduced only if the temperature of the water dropped significantly during the off period. If the tank is well insulated, the temperature remains high for many hours, negating the effect. If the tank is poorly insulated, it is cheaper and easier to add an insulation wrap than to add a timer. (It *is* worth shutting off the tank when you go away for a week or more.)

The thermostat on an electric water heater is usually adjustable with a small screwdriver. Setting the temperature usually requires a bit of trial and error, because the thermostat markings are often inaccurate.

your tank is already well insulated, there is little or no benefit to adding the wrap. If the tank has 1.5 in. or more of foam insulation, or the label states that the R-value is 10 or more, a tank wrap won't help very much.

When insulating a water heater, carefully follow the directions on the tank-wrap kit. For electric heaters, cut away the wrap over both heating element covers to provide access and pre-

+ SAFETY FIRST

The worst thing you could do to tank insulation on a gas or electric water heater is to wrap it *over* a temperature and pressure (T & P) relief-valve lever. If the thermostat were to malfunction and the tank overheat, any interference with the T & P valve could literally cause a huge explosion. If the discharge pipe is too close to the tank to fit the insulation under it, then cut out a section of the wrap with several inches of clearance around the T & P valve (see the bottom photo on the facing page).

An insulation blanket can reduce by almost half the standby losses of a poorly insulated tank. When insulating an electric water heater, wrap the insulation snugly around the unit.

vent the electrical components from overheating. Similarly, wraps should not cover the gas valve or access panel of gas water heaters. Also, don't insulate the top of gas water heaters. Some manufacturers place stickers on their products warning against tank wraps. Take heed, because installing one may void the tank's warranty.

Insulating hot water pipes

Hot water pipes lose energy in two ways: through conductive losses in pipe walls while hot water is running and through thermosiphon effects (see the sidebar on the facing page). Both can be reduced by insulating hot water pipes, and thermosiphoning can be reduced or eliminated by adding heat traps to hot and cold water pipes.

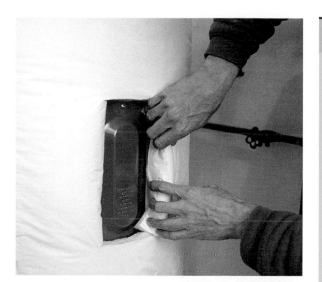

At each access panel, cut an "I" shape with a utility knife. The top and bottom of the "I" should outline the top and bottom of the panel. Then fold under the sides to expose the cover.

The simplest heat trap consists of a "loop the loop" of pipe, which can be made with a flexible connector attached to the heater's hot and cold water connections. The trap stops thermosiphoning with basic physics: Hot water will not flow down, unless it is pushed through the pipe by water pressure. The loop should have a 5-in. to 6-in. radius and be insulated with pipe wrap. Alternatively, special heat-trap couplings can be installed at the tank connections. Some high-efficiency tanks have built-in heat traps.

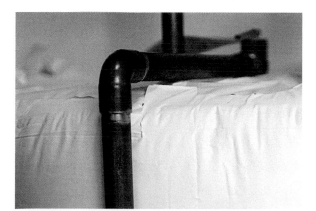

Insulation wrap should always be tucked under T & P discharge pipes so it doesn't interfere with relief-valve operation. Or the wrap can be cut back at least 3 in. from the valve.

How Water Pipes Lose Heat

Conductive heat loss through pipe walls robs energy from hot water, increasing your wait for hot water at each fixture (wasting water, as well as hot water). Heat loss also reduces the delivery temperature at the tap, which means you will mix in more hot water to get the desired temperature. *Thermosiphoning* is the constant, convective circulation of hot water from the water heater into hot *and* cold water pipes. Heat is emitted, and the cooler water sinks back into the tank; this happens when water is not running through the pipes.

Heat loss from conduction and thermosiphoning can happen in both hot and cold water pipes. The effects occur for the many hours every day that no hot water is being drawn. Thermosiphoning stops when someone begins to draw hot water; so do the conductive losses on the cold side, because the pipe fills with incoming cold water. However, conductive losses on the hot side increase when the pipe you draw is filled with hot water on the way to its destination.

Hot Water Heat Loss

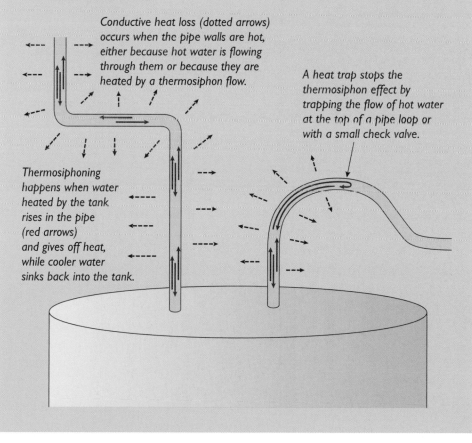

Conductive heat loss (dotted arrows) occurs when the pipe walls are hot, either because hot water is flowing through them or because they are heated by a thermosiphon flow.

A heat trap stops the thermosiphon effect by trapping the flow of hot water at the top of a pipe loop or with a small check valve.

Thermosiphoning happens when water heated by the tank rises in the pipe (red arrows) and gives off heat, while cooler water sinks back into the tank.

153

PRO TIP

If your ceiling is too low to remove the old anode rod without breaking it, get a flexible-linked rod that can be slipped in from the side.

IN DETAIL

A *tankless coil* is a heat exchanger mounted in a boiler; water running through it is heated on its way to a hot water tap or shower. Tankless coils are inexpensive to install (about $200 added to the cost of a new boiler) but very inefficient. A tankless coil depends on the boiler staying hot year-round, so it can supply hot water whenever it's needed. Therefore, the boiler chimney and jacket losses waste money all summer and add unnecessary heat to the house.

This tankless coil should be replaced with an indirect storage tank when the boiler is replaced.

A flexible pipe connector may be all you need to create a simple heat trap loop. Hot water rises by thermosiphon to the top of the loop and stops there. These pipes still need to be insulated. (Photo by Charles Miller, courtesy *Fine Homebuilding* magazine, ©The Taunton Press.)

This water heater has a built-in heat trap. The loop is built into the tank, so hot water can't thermosiphon *up* into the pipes. (Photo © Kevin Kennefick.)

The most common pipe insulation is made from polyethylene and is widely available at hardware stores and home centers.

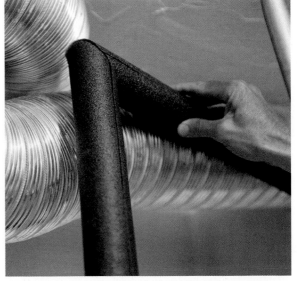

Pipe insulation should be measured in place and mitered carefully at the corners with a knife or scissors to ensure a tight fit.

Minerals from water (mostly calcium and magnesium) are deposited on the tank's walls and internal flue, flaking off over time and landing on the bottom. This creates an insulating layer that slows heat transfer from the burner to the water. (Photo © Rex Cauldwell.)

Circulating Loops

Hot water circulating loops, common in hotels, are sometimes installed in larger homes to provide fast hot water at every fixture. Hot water is pumped continuously from the storage tank, to all the fixtures, then back again. Hot water circulating loops can save a lot of water from going down the drain but can also be a big energy hog. If your house has a loop, it should be carefully insulated to reduce heat loss. A timer that shuts off the circulating pump during low-use hours can also help.

If you have to wait a long time for hot water, or if you have an existing recirculating hot water loop, a product is available that can save energy and water. The Metlund® "D-Mand System" consists of a small pump and a zone valve that operate on demand (by pushing a button) to draw hot water quickly into the supply pipes. It reduces water waste, because it sends the water back into the cold-supply pipe rather than down the drain. As a replacement for a continuous recirculation loop, it saves energy by pumping only when needed and by eliminating standby losses from the recirculation loop when hot water is not being used.

This system quickly brings hot water to all plumbing fixtures on the hot water supply line without sending any down the drain. Various models range from $330 to $490, depending on the size of the home and the need for wireless remote push buttons. (Photo courtesy ACT-Inc. Metlund Systems.)

Insulate hot water pipes after doing any necessary plumbing modifications. Pipe insulation is readily available at most home centers and hardware stores and is easy to install. The biggest benefit from pipe insulation occurs within the first 10 ft. of the tank, but it is usually easy and inexpensive to insulate all accessible hot water pipes.

Don't bother insulating a pipe run that is dedicated to only a washing machine; it won't save anything, because the washer will always draw the same amount of hot water regardless of its delivery temperature. Be sure to choose the right diameter for the pipe insulation for your hot water pipes; most homes have a mixture of ½-in. and ¾-in. pipes, so it's a good idea to measure how much of each you will need.

Maintenance

There are two basic maintenance operations that can increase a tank's life span. One is to regularly flush out debris and scale, which can also improve the efficiency of your tank by improving heat transfer. Annually flushing water through the drain valve at the bottom can help wash away the crud.

PRO TIP

While solar water-heating systems are expensive, they are cost-effective in many areas, particularly when compared to electric-resistance water heating.

TRADE SECRET

An electric on-demand water heater rarely makes sense for an entire house, because electricity is expensive. However, for a single bathroom or kitchen sink that's far from the nearest water heater, a small tankless electric unit can be inexpensive to install. In that application, long waits while running hot water (and the waste associated with it) can be virtually eliminated.

IN DETAIL

The energy factor, or EF rating, is based on a standardized test that takes into account burner efficiency, pilot usage, and jacket losses for typical hot water usage. EF ratings for gas, oil, and electric water heaters can be found in the *Consumers' Directory of Certified Efficiency Ratings for Heating and Water Heating Equipment,* by the Gas Appliance Manufacturers Association (GAMA). Log on to www.gamanet.org and follow the links to "Consumer Directory." The directory also shows first-hour ratings and recovery efficiency, which is the burner's efficiency.

At least once a year, flush out the sediment at the bottom of your water heater by opening the drain at the bottom. You don't need to turn off the water supply to the tank or empty the tank—just open the valve and let it rip.

A ball valve installed with a pipe nipple is much more effective at flushing out sediment than is the stock drain fitting found on most water tanks. To prevent disaster, don't try to remove the stock fitting from an old tank. (Photo by Charles Miller, courtesy *Fine Homebuilding* magazine, ©The Taunton Press.)

An old anode rod sacrifices its life to save the tank. Replacing the rod with a new one every few years will increase the life of the tank. (Photo by Charles Miller, courtesy *Fine Homebuilding* magazine, ©The Taunton Press.)

There's no need to completely drain the tank; the force of the cold water pressure helps flush out the material.

Unfortunately, most drain valves that are installed at the factory don't allow much sediment to pass through, so it's better to replace it with a full-flow ball valve. This is also much more effective if the tank has a dip tube with a curve at the bottom that swirls incoming water around the base of the tank.

The other thing that should be done to extend the life of a water heater is to replace the anode rod when necessary. The anode rod, typically made of magnesium formed around steel wire, is a sacrificial device designed to corrode before the tank itself. Once the magnesium material has decomposed or is covered with scale, the anode rod stops working and the tank will start to deteriorate.

Anode rods are designed to last for about 5 years (depending, of course, on the water), typically just a little longer than the tank's warranty. You will probably need a heavy-duty socket wrench with a breaker bar to unthread the anode rod. Don't try to remove it until you have a new replacement rod handy. And be very careful not to damage the tank or the water fittings when removing the rod. Replacement anode rods are available at plumbing supply houses for $20 to $40. Of course, you will need to shut off the tank and the incoming water supply, and empty the tank before replacing a drain valve or anode rod.

Replacing Hot Water Systems

When it is time to buy a new hot water heater, it makes sense to install the most efficient replacement system possible. Which type will work best for you depends on the type of hot water and heating systems in your house. If you have a furnace, then you will need some type of independent, stand-alone water heater. If you have a hot water boiler, it probably makes sense to use it for water heating, especially if you have recently installed an efficient boiler. If you heat your house with electric resistance or a heat pump, chances are that you have an electric water heating tank; in that case, you would probably benefit the most from a solar water heating system (see the sidebar at right).

Water heater efficiency

Water heaters suffer from three kinds of losses that reduce their efficiency: chimney losses (or burner efficiency), pilot losses, and standby losses through the sides of the tank. Every new stand-alone water heater—whether a tank or an instantaneous

Solar Hot Water Systems

Solar water heating systems can be a good option almost anywhere in the U.S. At an installed cost of between $2,000 and $3,500, a solar water heater is often a cost-effective solution. If you currently heat water with electricity or propane, you can usually expect a reasonable payback (5 to 10 years) from a well-designed solar water heating system. Depending on your location, hot water needs, and fuel costs, solar may even be cost-competitive with oil or natural gas.

Solar water heaters most often use flat plate collectors mounted on a roof or freestanding frame. In an open-loop system, the home's potable hot water runs through the collector. An open-loop system is typically used in mild climates or, in cold climates, drained in winter, because it is prone to freezing. A closed-loop, or indirect, system has a piped loop of water or antifreeze that is separated from the potable hot water supply by a heat exchanger. Most closed-loop systems use an antifreeze solution (typically nontoxic glycol). In a drain-back system, the fluid is stored in a separate storage tank to avoid freezing when the sun isn't shining, so plain water can be used.

Before installing a solar water heating system, the site should be carefully evaluated by a professional installer for solar access and local weather conditions. Solar collectors must be carefully sized to a family's needs. To be efficient and have a long service life, the storage tanks must be adequately sized to match the collector area.

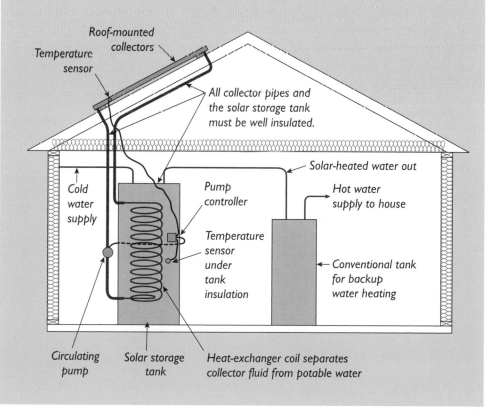

Roof-mounted collectors

Temperature sensor

All collector pipes and the solar storage tank must be well insulated.

Solar-heated water out

Cold water supply

Pump controller

Hot water supply to house

Temperature sensor under tank insulation

Conventional tank for backup water heating

Circulating pump

Solar storage tank

Heat-exchanger coil separates collector fluid from potable water

IN DETAIL

One of the thorniest problems in hot water efficiency is the waste of all the heat in the water that goes down the drain. One product on the market, the Gravity Film Exchange (GFX) system, can recover up to 60% of that heat. The unit can't recover much heat from appliances that use hot water in batches, such as clothes washers and dishwashers. When properly piped into the drain that serves the largest number of showers in the house, it can not only save energy but also effectively increase the first-hour rating of the water heater.

(Photo courtesy T. R. Strong Building Systems, Inc.)

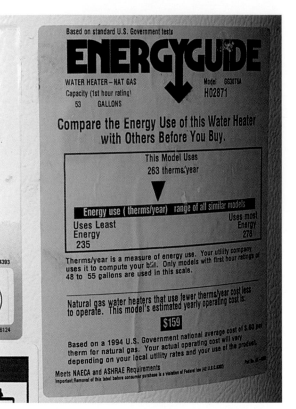

All new water heaters are required to have an Energy Guide label, which compares the energy use of this model to that of similar models. Buyers beware: "Energy Saver" is a common name found on water heaters, but it can be almost meaningless. I've seen that name on units that were near the bottom of the scale of energy efficiency for their size. Unfortunately, few water heaters have their EF rating listed on the tank, but you can look it up in the GAMA directory or ask the supplier.

heater—has an efficiency rating (called an Energy Factor, or EF, rating) that takes all of these types of losses into account.

High-efficiency water heaters typically have efficient burners, electronic pilots, and high levels of built-in insulation. Try to get a water heater with the highest EF rating for the type of application you need.

Condensing water heaters

The most efficient gas water heaters on the market are condensing heaters; they typically have EF ratings of 90% or higher. The best ones have stainless-steel tanks and high firing rates—typi-

cally around 90,000 to 120,000 btu/hour, or two to three times that of a typical tank.

Compared to standard gas water heaters, condensing water heaters are expensive—in the range of $1,500 to $2,500—and may be more appropriate for supplying whole-house heating as well as hot water. Because of their high heat output, they are well suited for supplying a hydro-air system (see the sidebar on p. 129). A hydro-air handler used in conjunction with a condensing gas water heater is probably one of the most efficient replacements for an old, inefficient gas furnace and a standard electric or gas water heating tank.

Instantaneous heaters

On the other end of the spectrum is the instantaneous, or tankless, water heater. The premise of a stand-alone tankless water heater is to save energy by eliminating the storage tank and its associated standby losses, providing hot water only when you need it. However, a tankless water-heating coil that's run from a boiler wastes far more energy by keeping the boiler hot all year.

Stand-alone instantaneous water heaters have a slightly higher range of efficiencies than conventional water heaters. They are not listed in the GAMA directory (see In Detail on p. 156), but most manufacturers do list the EF ratings for their products. Some instantaneous water heaters are fired by gas or propane. Units with electronic ignitions have much higher EFs, typically 20% higher, than do those with standing pilots. Most operate by sensing a drop in water pressure when someone opens a tap. Better models regulate the burner output to maintain a constant output temperature regardless of the flow rate. Electric tankless heaters are also available. Prices for stand-alone instantaneous water heaters range from $750 to $1,500, not including installation.

In addition to a higher efficiency, tankless heaters have the advantage of producing hot water

HOW MUCH HOT WATER DO YOU NEED?

No one likes to run out of hot water. When you replace a water heater, it's a good idea to evaluate the size of the new unit. Water-heater capacity is more than the number of stored gallons. What matters is that it can provide enough hot water for the household. The standard measurement of water heating capacity is called *first-hour rating*; all manufacturers publish the first-hour ratings of their products. To determine the first-hour rating for your household, use the chart below to calculate your peak-hour demand. Then look for a water heater with a first-hour rating that is at least as large.

As you draw hot water, the burner (or electric element) starts heating the incoming water, providing additional volume beyond the tank's storage. Therefore, the ability of a water heater to supply hot water is a tradeoff between the storage volume and the firepower. Smaller tanks can be balanced by higher BTU firing rates or vice versa. Electric tanks, for example, have relatively slow heat input, so their storage volumes tend to be larger.

A jetted bathtub needs to be filled quickly, so it throws off the rules a bit. Generally, a jetted tub needs at least 80% of its capacity in storage; for example, a 60-gal. tub requires a 48-gal. tank. Water temperature also affects the balance; higher temperatures provide longer showers or fill bigger bathtubs, because you need less cold water mixed in. Higher settings won't affect the hot water draw of automatic equipment, such as clothes washers or dishwashers, but they will reduce the efficiency of those appliances by increasing the standby and piping losses.

To calculate your peak-hour hot water use, fill in the number of times someone in your home is likely to engage in each activity during the hour of maximum hot water use (only fill in uses that will happen in the same hour). Multiply that by the number of gallons shown in the appropriate column to obtain the subtotal of hot water consumption for each use; add those together to obtain the total. Look for the highest efficiency model you can find with a first-hour rating at least as large as your total.

Gallons of Hot Water Used (Approx.)

Use	Standard fixtures/ appliances	Low-flow fixtures/ efficient appliances	Times Used during Peak Hour (Fill In)	Gallons Used during Peak Hour
Shower	20	15		
Bath	20	20		
Hand/face wash	2	2		
Dishwasher	15	15		
Hand dishwashing	4	4		
Clothes washer	32	21		
Food prep	5	3		
			Total	

Sources: Gas Appliance Manufacturers Association *Consumers' Directory*; excerpted by permission from Chapter 48, Table 4, ASHRAE 1999 Handbook—HVAC Applications (www.ashrae.org); American Society of Heating, Refrigerating and Air-Conditioning Engineers, Inc.

VENTING A GAS WATER HEATER

Direct-Vent Water Heater

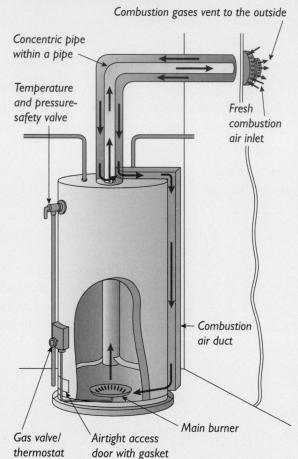

Combustion gases vent to the outside

Concentric pipe within a pipe

Temperature and pressure-safety valve

Fresh combustion air inlet

Combustion air duct

Main burner

Gas valve/ thermostat

Airtight access door with gasket

In a direct-vent water heater, outside air for combustion is brought directly to the fire, usually through a larger-diameter pipe that surrounds the combustion vent pipe, and then through a duct to the burner. These sealed-combustion water heaters can be vented through a sidewall or through the roof, depending on the manufacturer and the model. Most can be ordered with extension kits for longer vertical or horizontal vent-pipe runs. Be sure to follow the manufacturer's instructions for maximum allowed lengths. There are also clearance guidelines for the space between the outdoor vent termination and other features, such as windows, decks, vertical walls, and so on. Follow the manufacturer's instructions, and check local codes for clearance requirements. Other details of tank construction are similar to those of a standard gas water heater (not shown for clarity).

A standard gas water heater uses atmospheric venting to carry flue gases up the chimney. Like an atmospheric-vented heating system, it requires adequate combustion air to ensure safe and efficient combustion (see the sidebar on p. 111). That means they depend on a significant amount of waste heat to carry flue gases up the chimney and out of the house; that waste is a source of inefficiency.

Gas water heaters are also prone to backdrafting, because of their relatively low heat output. When it's time to replace a water heater, consider getting an induced-draft system, which has a small blower that ejects combustion byproducts, or a sealed-combustion, direct-vent water heater, which brings combustion air directly to the burner. Both types are typically vented through a sidewall, eliminating the need for a chimney and the possibility of backdrafting.

The vent on this induced-draft water heater, sometimes called a power vent, has a small fan at the top that ejects flue gases through a PVC pipe.

Induced-draft and sealed-combustion direct vent water heaters bring combustion air directly to the burner and are typically vented through a sidewall, eliminating the need for a chimney and the possibility of backdrafting.

continuously, as long as you keep drawing it. Their biggest limitation has always been capacity. In the past, standard models have been able to produce only 2 to 3 GPM at a reasonable temperature. That is only enough for one shower at a time, which is not adequate for many families. To get 6 GPM—enough for two showers at once, with a little to spare—from 50°F incoming to 110°F delivered at the tap, you need about 175,000 btu/hour. There are a couple of units on the market in that range, such as the Takagi T-K2. Because of its very high btu output and first-hour rating, the unit is suitable for both space heating and water heating in most climates. Although not quite as efficient as a condensing water heater, it has the advantage of taking up very little space.

Indirect-fired tank (with boiler)

If you heat your house with a hot water boiler, indirect-fired water heaters can generate hot water much more efficiently than tankless coils or most stand-alone units (see the sidebar on p. 163). The storage tank contains a thermostat that requests heat from the boiler, just like a separate heating zone. The boiler should be configured to shut down (or maintain a very low level of heat) when there is no call for space or hot water heating. If the boiler is sized fairly close to the heating load, a control can be added to give water heating a 30-minute priority over space heating, which ensures adequate hot water, even on a cold morning.

Many indirect-fired tanks have a built-in heat exchanger. Boiler water is pumped through the heat exchanger, heating water in the tank without mixing boiler water with the potable water supply. Alternatively, almost any type of insulated storage tank can be combined with an external heat exchanger to produce hot water from a boiler.

This high-efficiency gas water heater has a stainless-steel tank and an efficiency of 95%. It features a sealed-combustion burner. (Photo by Bruce Harley, © Conservation Services Group.)

An external heat exchanger requires two circulating pumps, adding a small electrical load. But when the unit is properly sized, the heat transfer is very efficient. All piping between the boiler and the storage tank, as well as the external heat exchanger (if used), should be thoroughly insulated to minimize conductive heat loss.

✓ According to Code

If you understand sweating copper pipe joints, you may be comfortable connecting the water lines of a new tank. Only a qualified contractor, however, should do gas line hookups. Check with your local plumbing inspector's office to see what restrictions there may be and which permits are required for any water heater insulation. If you're going to install a water heater with a venting system that differs from the previous unit, be sure to follow the manufacturer's instructions and local codes for installation details.

PRO TIP

If you're replacing a hot water heater, consider your annual fuel costs as well as the initial installation cost.

IN DETAIL

Indirect water heaters cannot be tested for standard efficiency ratings, because without the boiler they are not an entire system. To estimate the efficiency of a well-insulated indirect tank for comparison purposes, multiply the AFUE rating of your boiler by 0.9. For example, if you have a boiler with an AFUE rating of 85%, the hot water efficiency with an indirect tank is 0.9 × 85%, which equals 77%. That is not as good as an instantaneous water heater with an EF rating of 80%, but it is much better than a stand-alone water heater with an EF of 60%.

This external plate-frame heat exchanger can be used to heat domestic hot water from a boiler, or to create hydronic heat from a standard water heater, without mixing the two water supplies.

Choosing a contractor vs. doing it yourself

Replacing a water heater is somewhat easier than installing a heating or air-conditioning system. If you simply replace a conventional gas or electric stand-alone tank with a new unit of the same type (but with a higher efficiency), you may be able to make most of the connections yourself. If you want to change the water heating equipment to a completely new type, or if the water heating is integrated with the space heating system, you should hire a professional contractor.

When choosing a contractor, consider factors such as energy savings, quality, warranty service, and customer references, as well as price. Bids should include details on the equipment, installation specs, labor, and associated costs. Always choose a contractor who is familiar with the equipment and has a track record installing it, particularly if you want to install something out of the ordinary.

New water heater installations should include heat traps (either built into the tank or added separately). And don't just think about installation costs and efficiency; fuel costs can be a major factor as well. If you have an electric water heater, it may make sense to switch to gas or propane. I don't recommend oil; stand-alone oil water heaters are expensive and inefficient, have a short life expectancy, and require frequent service.

Comparing Operating Costs

Even though propane is expensive, it may be a better water-heating choice than electricity if piped natural gas is not available in your area. This chart shows that even with the additional cost of conversion, the $250 increment will be reclaimed in about two years through lower operating costs (assuming typical fuel prices). The numbers are similar to those for a heat-pump water heater, though the long-term reliability of those systems has not yet been established.

Medium Efficiency	EF	Estimated Installed Cost	Fuel Price (Rate)	Annual Water Heating Cost for a Family of Four
Electric	90%	$450	$0.10/kWh	$490
Natural Gas	58%	$650 (including conversion)	$0.75/therm	$195
Propane	58%	$700 (including conversion)	$1.20/gal	$340

Water Heating Alternatives

It is common to heat a house and its hot water supply with separate systems, such as a furnace and a hot water heater. Integrated systems use the same appliance for both space and hot water heating, which can have several benefits. First, there is only one combustion device, which eliminates the backdrafting risk of one appliance, eradicates the need for one chimney flue or venting system, and reduces regular service needs. It can save space in the house, too. And, if the appliance that produces heat is very efficient,

Often referred to by their generic brand names, such as Boiler Mate or Super Stor, indirect-fired water heaters can generate plenty of hot water and offer high efficiency and long service life.

This heat-pump water heater produces hot water at a savings of nearly 50% when compared to conventional electric water heaters. Although it is priced at about $600, the added cost over a conventional electric water tank should be recouped in just a year or two. Some early product designs have had reliability problems; I recommend staying away from units designed as an add-on retrofit to an existing tank. (Photo courtesy Triad Marketing Group.)

integrated systems, like an indirect-fired tank, are usually the least expensive ones to operate.

One promising new system for inexpensive electric hot water heating is the heat-pump water heater. That system uses electricity to extract heat from the air and uses it to heat water in much the same way that a heat pump works (see pp. 116–120). The unit has more than twice the efficiency of conventional electric water heaters and performs best in warm climates, where it cools and dehumidifies the air around it. It is less efficient in cold temperatures, and in cold or moderate climates, it shouldn't be installed in a garage or another location where the temperature often drops below freezing.

Renovations

CHAPTER NINE

1 Air-Sealing, p. 166

2 Insulation, p. 168

The best time to invest in an energy-efficient upgrade is when you are already planning to buy a product or make improvements to your home. Because you are making a substantial investment during a renovation project, you have a rare opportunity to significantly improve the energy efficiency of your entire house. On the other hand, if the opportunity is missed, renovations carry the potential for energy, comfort, and air-quality disasters.

3 Built-Up Walls and Roofs for High R-Values, p. 172

4 Moisture Control, p. 178

Of course, a renovation can mean a simple change in wall or roof cladding, or it can mean a total gut/rehabilitation project. It can involve one room, or it can involve an entire home. Additions to houses provide their own unique set of opportunities and potential pitfalls.

5 Mechanical Systems (Heat, A/C, Hot Water, Ventilation), p. 182

IN DETAIL

In any building project, it's important to keep in mind the *continuity* of the thermal envelope. Your insulation and your air barrier should be aligned and should surround the entire house without interruption. It's much easier to visualize this before you put up any drywall. In fact, while you are contemplating exactly where the insulation should go, think about how thorough the air barrier is. There should always be a solid air barrier in line with every insulated surface.

Air-Sealing

After the demolition and framing dust settles in any renovation project, the temptation is to get the space insulated quickly so that the finishing work can begin. It's important to resist that temptation and take a little time to seal air leaks properly. This will be the best opportunity (really, the only one) you'll have to find and seal any cracks and holes in the thermal envelope, and it doesn't take much time or money—just awareness and attention to a few important details.

Look for leaks

Of course, the most important place to seal leaks is between insulated surfaces and the outdoors. However, the most commonly missed leaks are joist bays and wall-stud cavities that need draftstopping where they run from interior floors and walls into attics, crawl spaces, or other unconditioned areas (see chapter 2). And don't forget to seal any leaks between an addition and the rest of the building.

Before you insulate a house, walk around with a foam gun and seal all wiring and plumbing penetrations between wall cavities and unconditioned spaces (attic, basement, or crawl space). Also, seal around window and door jambs, being careful not to spray too much foam in large gaps. Pay attention to any areas that need draftstop blocking, and

Sealing all penetrations during a renovation or building project is much easier when the wall cavities are open. (Photo © Kevin Kennefick.)

fill them with blocks of wood or foam board that are caulked in place. You can use the same techniques outlined in chapter 2, except that it will be a lot easier to reach everything before the insulation and drywall are installed.

Creating a super air-seal

If you live in a cold climate, you can create super airtight walls and ceilings without breaking your budget, though the process is somewhat labor-intensive. One way to do it is by installing well-sealed, 6-mil polyethylene sheeting on the interior, both as a vapor barrier and as an air barrier. (With most types of insulation, this would usually be installed after the insulation is in place).

All the seams in the poly must be taped with a high-quality tape (such as 3M's builder's sealing tape or Tyvek Sheathing Tape, readily available at most lumberyards) or sealed with acoustical sealant to create an effective air barrier. You will also need to enclose electrical outlets on exterior walls with poly pans or use airtight outlet boxes (see the photos on the facing page).

In all climates, I recommend thoroughly sealing the exterior sheathing at the sill plate and at all

> ✔ **According to Code**
>
> Although any blocking or draftstops installed between a heated space and an attic area will help slow the spread of fire, some codes require that blocking be made of specific materials to qualify as firestopping. Spraying foam around wiring holes may also be forbidden; check with your local building inspector before you start sealing holes.

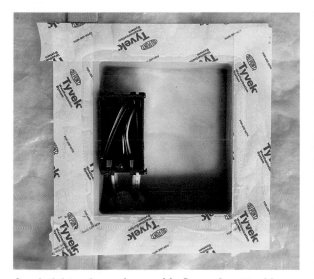

An airtight poly pan has a wide flange for attaching a vapor barrier. This one is made by Lessco (available from EFI and other suppliers). (Photo © Kevin Kennefick.)

A gasketed electrical box provides an airtight seal on exterior walls, whether or not you use poly as an air barrier. (Photo © Kevin Kennefick.)

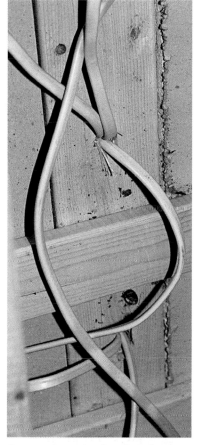

As top plates (and end studs of partition walls) dry and shrink, the gap between the wood and the drywall will end up being anywhere from $\frac{1}{32}$ in. to $\frac{3}{16}$ in. along both sides of the framing.

sheathing connections with caulking or high-quality tape (or both). *Don't* put polyethylene on the interior surfaces of exterior walls in hot climates.

Some builders and drywallers regularly slash a poly vapor barrier with a knife before putting up drywall. They believe that moisture will be trapped between the drywall and the poly, causing sagging drywall and mildew. Although it's true that if the insulation is installed poorly, water vapor can condense on the poly, but that happens only if the poly gets cold. If the vapor barrier is kept warm—by installing insulation properly and by sealing cracks at the wall's exterior so wind can't penetrate the wall cavity—it's impossible to trap water with a poly vapor barrier. After all, the primary purpose of a vapor barrier is to keep the water vapor on the warm side of the insulation, where it *won't* condense.

The ceiling plane can be a little bit more difficult. One of the trickiest places to seal well is the junction between partition walls and insulated ceilings. Particularly difficult are newly framed walls, because the top-plate material shrinks as it goes from 15% or higher moisture content when you buy it to an equilibrium of 6% to 8%. In a

cold climate, if you're putting a poly vapor barrier on the ceiling, let the edge of the poly hang down 2 in. to 4 in. on all sides of each room, so it can overlap the top plates. Then squeeze a bead of acoustical sealant on the top plate, behind the poly, and embed the poly in it.

You can use a similar approach where the end studs of interior partitions meet exterior walls. If you're using poly as the air barrier on a ceiling, use poly pans or airtight electrical boxes for any mounted ceiling fixtures.

Note that it is not important to seal partition-to-ceiling connections between a first and second

Condensation in Hot Weather

In mixed and hot climates, it is best to focus on sealing the exterior sheathing and drywall well and avoid the use of an interior vapor barrier altogether. The concern is that outdoor moisture can be drawn in to the cool inside surface of the poly in hot weather, where it may condense. This situation is particularly likely with brick veneer or other types of exterior cladding that may hold water, which can be driven inward by solar radiation. It can even happen in northern climates, particularly in air-conditioned homes. In this situation, kraft facing is a better interior vapor barrier.

PRO TIP

In order to achieve their full R-value, fiberglass batts must be carefully installed, without gaps or compression.

IN DETAIL

In general, I recommend better thermal performance for building components than current energy codes demand. (See the chart above right.)

TRADE SECRET

If you're planning to blow in cellulose insulation, leave a 4-in. space in the center of the wall between the sheets of drywall, as shown below. The gap makes it easy to insert a fill tube to insulate each wall cavity. Once insulated, fill the space with a strip of $3/8$-in.-thick drywall, then mud and tape the entire seam.

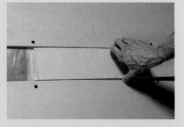

(Photo © Kevin Kennefick.)

Insulation Recommendations

	Walls	Ceilings	Floors	Windows
Cold Climates	R-25–R-40	R-50–R-70	R-30–R-40	U-0.25–U-0.3
Mixed Climates	R-20–R-30	R-40–R-60	R-20–R-30	U-0.3–U-0.35, with an SHGC of 0.3–0.5.
Hot Climates	R-15–R-20	R-30–R-50	R-20–R-30	U-0.4–U-0.5, with an SHGC of 0.2–0.3

One way to ensure an airtight seal across the top of each partition wall is to embed the poly vapor barrier in a bead of acoustical sealant. As an alternative, you can tape the edge of the poly to the top plate with high-quality tape. (Photo © Kevin Kennefick.)

floor; here, you want to focus on sealing the band joist at the exterior walls. Another area to watch out for is any change in ceiling height, from one room to another, in an insulated ceiling. Those transitions usually need blocking (see the sidebar on p. 33), which is much easier to install when the walls are open. Also, if you are installing recessed lights in any insulated ceiling areas, be sure to use airtight light fixtures (see the top right photo on p. 38).

Insulation

If you are demolishing drywall or plaster in one room or many, the temptation is to slap some fiberglass batts in the empty wall cavities and say, "good enough," before refinishing. If the wall was uninsulated to begin with, that will certainly be a big improvement, but carefully choosing and installing insulation at this point will pay big thermal dividends for years to come.

Attic Air-Sealing in Hot Climates

If you live in a hot or mixed, humid climate, the last thing you want to do is install a vapor barrier on the inside of your ceiling insulation. One option is to use airtight drywall for the ceilings, between the top plate and the wall drywall, and at the end studs where each partition intersects the exterior wall. Use EDPM rubber gaskets or adhesive at every top plate. (For this to be effec-

tive, you must use gasketed, airtight electrical boxes in all ceilings and exterior walls as well.)

Another option in hot climates, particularly in homes that have ductwork in the attic, is to "cathedralize." Insulate and seal the roof and attic gable ends with sprayed foam, instead of trying to insulate and seal the attic floor and all the ductwork.

**Installation Defects and
Fiberglass Batt Performance**

**The Effect of Gaps and Spaces on
Batt Insulation Effectiveness**

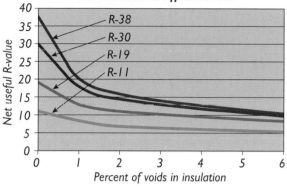

*The performance of insulation suffers dramatically when
there are gaps and spaces in the installation. As this chart
indicates, very small voids have a surprisingly large impact
on batt performance. Other typical installation defects
including compression; rounded corners; gaps and spaces
at the sides and ends of batts; side-stapled faced batts;
and a combination of compression and space around wiring,
plumbing, blocking, or other obstructions. Also, notice that
higher R-value batts suffer a significantly greater degradation
in performance than lower R-value batts.*

Use a putty knife or a 6-in. taping
knife to tuck the back corners of
batts into place to help prevent
the corners from rounding.
When fiberglass batts are
properly installed, you'll get
much closer to the R-value for
which you're paying. (Photo by
Charles Bickford, courtesy *Fine
Homebuilding* magazine, © The
Taunton Press.)

Fiberglass batt insulation

Because fiberglass batts are so vulnerable to instal
lation defects, it's extremely important that they
be installed very carefully. For example, batts
should be fluffed up to their full loft, or thickness,
and tucked into cavities with no compression or
rounding of corners. They must fill cavities completely, without gaps or spaces, so they need to be
carefully cut and trimmed to the proper size and
shape. They also should be cut around obstructions and split over any wiring or plumbing pipes
that run through cavities.

If you have an unsheathed wall that opens into
an attic space (such as a kneewall), it's important
to enclose the insulation on all sides. When a wall
cavity is left open on one side, cold air can circulate through the batt, as well as through small gaps
at the framing, reducing its effectiveness. If you live
in a cold or mixed climate, the open side of the
wall should be sheathed with vapor-permeable

The rounded shoulders and gaps
that are typical in batt installations can result in substantial loss
of R-value. Batts should be cut to
fit neatly around all obstructions
and should fill the entire cavity.
(Photo © Kevin Kennefick.)

WHAT CAN GO WRONG

Most vinyl-siding salespeople will tell you that the ¼-in. or ⅜-in. layer of foam board that they install under the siding will improve the insulation performance of your walls. But in reality, it's wishful thinking that the stuff adds R-value. The reason they use that "backer board" is to create a nice flat surface over the existing siding. If you're replacing your siding, it makes more sense in just about any climate to add a 1-in. to 2-in. layer of rigid foam, which will really make a thermal impact.

The backerboard that's installed underneath vinyl siding is more for the convenience of the installer than it is for insulation. (Photo © Kevin Kennefick.)

housewrap or semipermeable insulation, such as extruded polystyrene. Polystyrene provides the benefit of adding R-value to the wall assembly. In a hot, humid climate, the exterior side of the wall should be covered with a polyethylene vapor barrier or foil-faced insulation.

Sprayed- or blown-in products

Generally, my first choice for insulating wall cavities is cellulose, either as an open-cavity damp spray or as a dry dense-packed application. Damp-spray cellulose is not a do-it-yourself type of application, because it requires specialized equipment and training to do well.

Depending on your area, sprayed cellulose may be 10% to 40% more expensive than fiberglass batts (installed by a contractor). At about R-3.4 per in., you get only a little more R-value than batt insulation. In terms of performance, you'll get much more for your money with cellulose, because it is not subject to the same types of installation defects that plague fiberglass jobs.

In a hot climate, the back of an exposed kneewall can be covered with a vapor-barrier material, such as this foil-faced bubble wrap.

The penalty for improper batt installation is even greater in attics and cathedral ceilings than it is in walls. Whenever possible, use loose fill or sprayed types of insulation to avoid those problems. (Photo © Kevin Kennefick.)

Low-density, spray-applied foams such as Icynene or Demilec are the most common residential products; they range in price from about $1.25 to $2.00 per square foot, installed in a 6-in. cavity. (Photo by Steve Culpepper, courtesy *Fine Homebuilding* magazine, © The Taunton Press.)

Damp-sprayed cellulose installs quickly, completely fills wall cavities, and is more impervious to air movement than fiberglass batts.

Immediately after spraying the damp material, a worker scrubs off any excess with a special rotary brush, leaving the wall perfectly flat.

✓ According to Code

Building codes don't allow you to use combustible materials to seal leaks around chimneys, so metal flashing is usually the preferred material. If you are gutting a building or constructing an addition, you may want to consider installing steel framing with top and bottom plate channels up against the chimney. The steel is non-combustible, and the channels provide a good air-seal at the top of the chase.

Steel studs with steel-channel top plates provide an easy way to stop air from leaking through the chimney chase. Caulk the top plates to the chimney with high-temperature silicone. (Photo by Bruce Harley, © Conservation Services Group.)

Professional Spray Foams

There are a number of very useful contractor-applied spray-foam products that, when used in the right places, can save a lot of work. Although expensive, they provide high R-values and control most air leaks in one easy step. They are particularly useful for finishing an attic area that has sloped ceilings and dormers. Because the foam conforms exactly to the shapes of the rafter bays, you can cover the entire roof surface with nearly perfect insulation and air-sealing. Spray foams can be applied directly on the underside of roof sheathing, so they are also helpful when venting a roof is impractical (check local codes).

Two low-density, water-blown foams—with no hydrochlorofluorocarbon (HCFC)–blowing agents—include Icynene and Sealection®. Other types of foam that have a higher density (and that are probably slightly more expensive per R-value) include Comfort Foam® and Corbond®, among others.

TRADE SECRET

If you apply drywall directly over rigid-foam board insulation that is thicker than ½ in., you may soon see a lot of nail (or screw) pops. It's better to cover the rigid foam with 1×3 furring strips before installing the drywall. Attached with screws at 16 in. o.c., either at right angles to or directly over the framing, 1×3 furring provides a solid nailing base that won't wreak havoc with your taping job.

When insulating walls or ceilings with thick foam board, use furring to provide a solid, stable base for the drywall. (Photo © Kevin Kennefick.)

Damp-Spray Cellulose

Although an effective insulation material, damp-spray cellulose is not typically a do-it-yourself project. Still, there are a few things you should know if you are planning to use this type of insulation. First, moisture content is critical in a damp-spray-cellulose application. If too little water is mixed with the cellulose fiber, the material will be crumbly and won't stick well. If too much water is added, it will slump away from the top plates. Basically, if you pick up a handful of freshly sprayed material and squeeze it hard, no water should drip out. When checked with a moisture meter, after a day or two of drying, the moisture content should be at or below 25% before the cavity is enclosed with drywall.

Also, sprayed cellulose can't be used in walls more than 6 in. thick or in cathedral ceilings. If you have an overhead application, or if you wish to build thicker walls for higher R-values, consider covering the wall (or ceiling) first and using dense-packed cellulose (see p. 80). You can blow in the cellulose behind unfinished drywall, then patch the drywall while you do the rest of the taping.

Despite the beneficial qualities of damp-sprayed cellulose and foil-faced foam board, don't sandwich damp-spray cellulose between an interior poly vapor barrier and an exterior foil-faced foam. Even at a moisture content of 25%, that's a lot of water to trap between two very effective vapor barriers. To avoid problems, leave off the interior vapor barrier or use extruded polystyrene on the exterior.

If your remodeling project doesn't include opening the walls, or if you want to install the insulation yourself, dense-packed dry cellulose is probably your best bet. This is essentially the same process as blowing cellulose into uninsulated walls in any house, which is covered in chapter 4. Even if you are gutting the walls and replastering, you can hang the wallboard first, then fill the cavities with cellulose. Use a fill tube, if possible, for best results. Install the cellulose before taping and finishing the wall, so that you won't have to add another step to the finishing process.

Insulating floors and ceilings

If you are insulating an open attic area or a flat ceiling with an attic above, refer to chapter 4; the issues are exactly the same, and the same techniques apply. Resist the temptation to put fiberglass batts between the joist bays while the ceiling is open; instead, install loose-fill insulation after the drywall is up.

For floors and enclosed cathedral ceilings, my preference is first to sheath the joists or rafters, and then install dense-pack cellulose. Be sure to note with a pencil any obstructions or blind cavities as you install plywood sheathing or drywall so you will not miss them while blowing the insulation. If you do choose fiberglass batts, install them with as much care as possible.

Built-Up Walls and Roofs for High R-Values

If you are insulating an older house but not remodeling or changing the surface finishes, the level of insulation you can achieve is limited by the existing structure. During moderate to substantial remodeling, however, you have much more latitude in determining the level of insulation.

Using a remodeling opportunity to improve the thermal performance of your house can give you more bang for your insulation buck. With some planning and foresight, you can substantially beef up the insulation levels in walls, roofs, and floors without adding tremendously to the cost of the project. Here is a look at some approaches, ranging from layers of foam board to built-up, double-stud construction.

Adding foam board

Depending on the thickness of your walls and the overall desired R-value, you can add a layer of rigid-foam board on the inside or the outside of walls, cathedral ceilings, or floors. There's not much point in adding it on flat ceilings, where you can simply blow in more insulation. Extruded polystyrene and foil-faced polyisocyanurate board are both good choices for interior or exterior applications, regardless of the climate.

For the same R-value, rigid-foam board gives you more benefit than cavity insulation, because it covers the thermal shortcuts of wood framing. In cold climates, 2 in. of foam board applied outside exterior sheathing helps keep the sheathing warmer, reducing the likelihood of condensation. In fact, some residential codes now allow for unvented roof assemblies, as long as 40% or more of the total R-value is made up of rigid-foam insulation on top of the roof deck.

One issue with built-up interior walls is that of electrical boxes, which will need to be remounted to account for the new wall plane. Another complication that you will have to deal with if you add thickness to a wall, whether with foam board or some other technique, is the need for extension jambs around window and door openings. This is fairly easy to do from the interior, either by extending the window frames with wooden strips or by adding drywall returns.

If the thickness is added to the exterior, you will have to push the window and door frames out to the new exterior wall surface. Of course,

More appropriate in a modern-styled house, drywall returns provide an attractive and inexpensive solution to window openings in thick walls. A wooden stool and apron provide a nice window shelf. (Photo © Kevin Kennefick.)

Side extension jambs set at an angle can turn a window opening in a thick wall into a miniature bay window, which looks attractive even in a fairly traditional house.

WHAT CAN GO WRONG

Although housewraps such as Typar® and Tyvek are marketed as air barriers, they have some inherent limitations. If you're re-siding an old house with plank sheathing, housewrap can certainly help tighten the walls, but it must be carefully taped at all seams. Unfortunately, the places where housewrap is not usually properly detailed are the places where the exterior envelopes of houses leak the most anyway: around window and door openings; at cantilevers or other transitions in exterior walls; and especially where exterior walls meet attic, garage, or other unconditioned spaces. Housewrap functions best as a secondary drainage plane that provides moisture protection in exterior walls.

Adjustable Electrical Boxes

When installing interior foam board, it is often difficult to properly mount electrical boxes. The Adjust-a-box® comes in a single- or double-gang box and has an adjustable bracket that allows for the increased thickness of interior wall sheathing. Note that the box is not airtight, but you can place it in a poly pan or caulk the knockouts in the back and caulk it to the foam board for a good air-seal.

With the turn of a screw, the bracket on this adjustable electrical box can position the front of the box up to 2 in. away from the face of the stud, allowing for up to 1½ in. of foam board, plus drywall. It's also great for interior wood paneling or other nonstandard interior finishes. (Photo © Kevin Kennefick.)

One way to reduce lumber and improve insulation at the outside corners of an exterior wall is to use 1×3 stock or plywood nailers for drywall backing, as shown. (Photo by Scott Phillips, courtesy *Fine Homebuilding* magazine, © The Taunton Press.)

if you are installing new windows anyway, that will not be much of a problem. In either case, pay careful attention to proper window- and door-flashing details (see pp. 178–179).

Cross-strapping walls or ceilings

Another technique for providing a thicker cavity to accommodate extra insulation is to nail 2×3 cross strapping, or other framing of substantial thickness, across the studs or rafters. Cross-strapping works best when you start with a 2×6 wall, because you are adding only an extra 1½ in. of insulation. Although carefully installed fiberglass batts can work well with this type of wall, spray foam or damp-spray or dense-pack cellulose works better. Those products have a higher R-value and interrupt the thermal-bridge effect (except where the framing members cross, which is a relatively small area).

Electrical boxes can be mounted directly to the cross strapping. If you are doing the work yourself, including the cellulose installation, the cross-

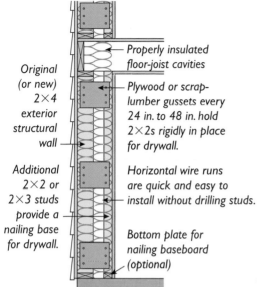

Original (or new) 2×4 exterior structural wall

Additional 2×2 or 2×3 studs provide a nailing base for drywall.

Properly insulated floor-joist cavities

Plywood or scrap-lumber gussets every 24 in. to 48 in. hold 2×2s rigidly in place for drywall.

Horizontal wire runs are quick and easy to install without drilling studs.

Bottom plate for nailing baseboard (optional)

Gusseted Wall

This type of wall is much faster and less expensive to build than a double-stud wall. The interior framing members are smaller and, with gussets prenailed to them, go in place quickly. In a remodel, the interior studs can also be set plumb and straight to correct problems with the original wall framing.

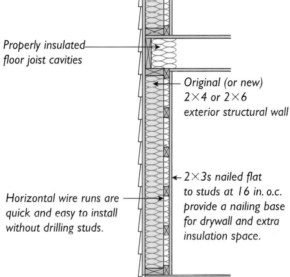

Properly insulated floor joist cavities

Original (or new) 2×4 or 2×6 exterior structural wall

2×3s nailed flat to studs at 16 in. o.c. provide a nailing base for drywall and extra insulation space.

Horizontal wire runs are quick and easy to install without drilling studs.

Cross-Strapped Wall

Adding 2×3s at right angles to the wall studs or rafters provides a thicker cavity and covers most of the framing with a couple of inches of insulation to provide a thermal break. In most cases, this costs less than covering the wall surface with rigid foam.

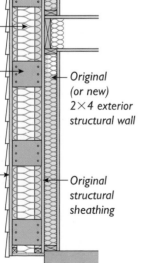

Insulation-filled truss completely covers joist.

Nonstructural vertical trusses built from 2×2s with plywood gussets attached vertically at 16 in. or 24 in. o.c.

Exterior sheathing provides a nailing base for siding and protects insulation from wind-washing.

Original (or new) 2×4 exterior structural wall

Original structural sheathing

Larsen Truss

A Larsen truss can be added to the exterior of a house with little disruption to the inside wall surfaces. Windows and doors should be installed at the new exterior wall surface, with extension jambs to the interior trim. As with any exterior wall, window and door flashing is critical, as is a drainage plane of housewrap or felt paper under the exterior sheathing.

IN DETAIL

Cedar and redwood owe much of their weather resistance to chemicals called *surfactants*—the same chemicals that make soap effective. Research has shown that unprimed cedar or redwood that are in direct contact with plastic housewrap or felt paper can significantly reduce its water repellency. Those woods should always be back-primed if they are applied directly over housewrap or felt. An airspace, such as a rain screen, is even more effective. In addition, portland-cement stucco is alkaline and also degrades housewrap, so stucco coatings on wood frame buildings should be applied over two layers of #15 felt, not over housewrap.

The most important role of housewrap is to keep out water that gets past the siding. However, all too often I see applications that are prone to trapping water. Look under the window to the left—the lower piece overlaps the upper one!

strapping approach should be substantially cheaper than foam board—especially when compared to interior-applied foam board with furring.

In the past, designs for superinsulation often featured double-studded walls to contain a lot of insulation. However, the extra framing is expensive and usually structurally unnecessary. Instead, walls and rafters can be built to any thickness with pieces of plywood or other scrap material (which are called *gussets*). The gussets, typically installed on 2-ft. to 4-ft. centers, tie a nonstructural interior member, such as a 2×2, to the wall studs or rafters. A gusseted wall can be made as thick as you like for maximum R-value (see the top drawing on p. 175).

Lightweight trusses of any thickness, commonly called *Larsen trusses*, can also be built out of 2×2s and plywood gussets, then nailed to the building's exterior. Of course, the depth of a Larsen truss is limited by the eave and rake-end roof overhangs, which must cover the top of the wall. And keep in mind that doors and windows will need to be reset to the new exterior wall plane, which will also need to be re-sided.

To provide a watertight seal, slip a piece of housewrap or building paper into a slit above the window or door and over the head nailing flange or flashing. (Photo by Roe A. Osborn, courtesy *Fine Homebuilding* magazine, © The Taunton Press.)

Drywall Clips

Cracks and nail pops are a major drywall headache. Gypsum board is flexible to a point, but it is often tightly nailed into every corner, leaving no room for it to flex. As the wood members move relative to each other (particularly while drying), the drywall cracks. Many problems can be avoided simply by using fewer fasteners, especially in corners.

The Gypsum Association recommends using no screws within 11 in. to 12 in. of corners where walls meet ceilings. At wall-to-wall inside corners, the association suggests fastening to only one stud. Those details allow the gypsum to "float," so it can flex slightly when the framing moves. Of course, corners still need solid support behind the drywall with framing or clips. In fact, you can eliminate extra framing and improve the drywall installation by using drywall clips. Some are stapled or nailed directly to the framing, while others are slipped onto the first drywall sheet while it's being installed. Eliminating the extra studs also makes it easier to run wiring.

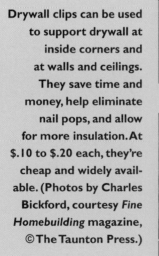

Drywall clips can be used to support drywall at inside corners and at walls and ceilings. They save time and money, help eliminate nail pops, and allow for more insulation. At $.10 to $.20 each, they're cheap and widely available. (Photos by Charles Bickford, courtesy *Fine Homebuilding* magazine, © The Taunton Press.)

When installing housewrap, pretend that it won't be covered with anything. It should be able to shed water on its own.

WHAT CAN GO WRONG

Don't assume that caulking, tape, or sealants will stop water over a long period of time. Those products depend on chemistry to adhere one material to another. Sooner or later, the adhesives fail, the caulking dries up, and water starts to seep in—usually unnoticed. Taping the flange is better than just nailing it on over the housewrap. However, if the adhesive tape at the top of this window fails, water can sneak in behind the housewrap, seep under the nailing flange, and leak into the wall.

(Photo © Mike Guertin and Rick Arnold)

Preparing a Window or Door Opening

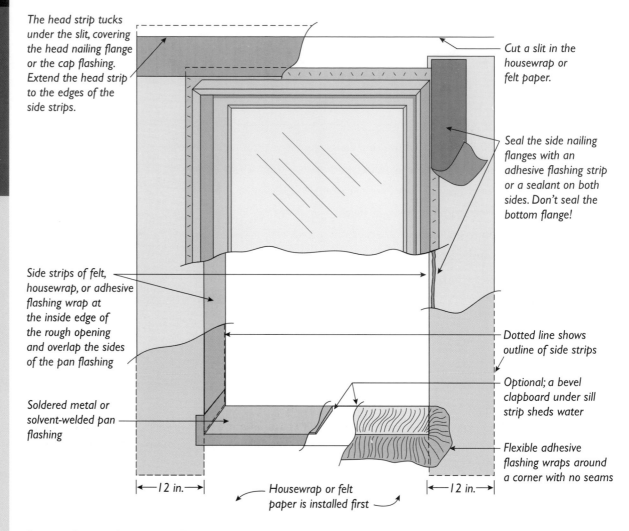

The head strip tucks under the slit, covering the head nailing flange or the cap flashing. Extend the head strip to the edges of the side strips.

Cut a slit in the housewrap or felt paper.

Seal the side nailing flanges with an adhesive flashing strip or a sealant on both sides. Don't seal the bottom flange!

Side strips of felt, housewrap, or adhesive flashing wrap at the inside edge of the rough opening and overlap the sides of the pan flashing

Dotted line shows outline of side strips

Optional; a bevel clapboard under sill strip sheds water

Soldered metal or solvent-welded pan flashing

Flexible adhesive flashing wraps around a corner with no seams

|←— 12 in. —→| |←— 12 in. —→|

Housewrap or felt paper is installed first

Sooner or later, window and door frames leak. To make a window or door opening really waterproof, so water doesn't get into the building frame, carefully prepare each rough opening before installing the unit. Don't depend on adhesive strips stuck on picture frame–style over nailing flanges—water will leak behind them through the sill, and adhesives fail. Attach the sill strip or pan flashing and the side strips after the housewrap or felt paper is in place, then install the window or door according to the manufacturer's instructions. You can use tape, adhesive flashing strips, silicone, or urethane caulk to seal the side nailing flanges, but leave the bottom flange open to shed water easily. Cut a slit in the housewrap or felt above the head flange, tuck in the head strip, and you're all set. You can cover the seam with a piece of good-quality tape or adhesive strip, but water repellency won't depend on it.

Note: Bituminous adhesive strips should not be applied over plastic housewraps, and butyl rubber strips should not be used with asphalt-impregnated felt, unless chemical compatibility is verified. Generally, you should apply bituminous strips only over wood framing or asphalt-impregnated building papers and use compatible adhesive tapes, such as 3M's 8086 Builder's Sealing Tape, or Tyvek Sheating Tape with plastic housewraps.

Moisture Control

Whether you're recladding a house or building an addition, the most important issue to consider is moisture control. In fact, good moisture control is much more important than energy improvements. Remember: When buildings were uninsulated and leaky, they dried out easily, whether the source of moisture was from indoors or out. Now that houses are built tighter and are better insulated, walls often do not dry quickly, which can lead to serious structural damage or mold growth. Controlling moisture from both the interior and the exterior is important; interior moisture issues are covered in chapters 1 and 3; this section will focus on exterior moisture control.

Drainage planes

A large number of building failures in recent decades have been traced to poor exterior water-management details. Siding and flashing details have traditionally focused on shedding water but have largely ignored the fact that wind and capillary action can drive water uphill through exterior siding. Unless you live in an extremely dry climate, it's best to assume that water *will* get past the exterior cladding, particularly in and around window and door frames.

If you accept that no siding system keeps out all water, the solution is pretty easy: Apply a layer of building paper, either housewrap or felt paper, behind the siding. This will act as a redundant drainage plane to keep water that penetrates behind exterior siding from soaking into the wall.

To be effective, the drainage layer must be waterproof (or at least water resistant) and be overlapped to shed water running down under the force of gravity. It also must be detailed properly around window and door openings (see the drawing on the facing page). While you install it, pretend that you're not going to cover it with anything—you should create an effective weather barrier that will shed rain on its own.

The use of building paper as a drainage plane, including the installation details around window and door openings, is nothing new. But somehow, in our acceptance of the marketing message that housewraps are primarily for energy efficiency, those basic details have largely been forgotten.

In addition to window and door openings, pay close attention to where a roof connects to a taller, vertical wall. A gable roof that dies into a wall is always vulnerable to water intrusion. Applying a layer of one of the new flexible adhesive flashings

Regular adhesive flashing strips are an alternative to flexible adhesive flashing membrane or metal or plastic pan flashing. Install a small patch over the corner, then adhere the main piece over it before installing the side strips. (Photo by Roe A. Osborn, courtesy *Fine Homebuilding* magazine, © The Taunton Press.)

This housewrap was mostly applied properly, because it is *over* the roof shingle step flashing and adhesive membrane. But the job was not done perfectly. Note the lower corner (center of photo), where the membrane is installed over the housewrap. That detail may leak when the adhesive fails.

WHAT CAN GO WRONG

You may think that the combination of passive solar heating with in-floor radiant heat will provide a super-efficient house, but the thermal lag of radiant heating systems can work against solar design. After a cold night, the slab will already be charged with heat when the sun rises in the morning. The heating thermostat will shut off, but the already-warm slab will not absorb much of the solar gain, and the space may overheat. If you turn down the thermostat at night to let the slab cool, it may take a long time to bring the house back to a comfortable temperature on a cloudy day. If you want to combine radiant floor and passive solar heating systems, reduce the amount of south glazing to less than 7% of the floor area to avoid overheating.

WHAT CAN GO WRONG

You don't want to use an electric hot water heater for supplemental heating. Even though its rating (energy factor) may look more efficient, the fuel is expensive and (most important) the heating capacity is too small for most loads.

Even wood shingles can be installed rain-screen style. The furring runs horizontally, and a gap of ¼ in. to ½ in. at the end of each strip helps drain any bulk water. In addition, water dries easily through the gaps between the shingles. (Note: The horizontal board covering most of the second course is a temporary spacer.) (Photo © Roland W. Kohl.)

Horizontal clapboard siding can be installed on vertical furring strips mounted 16 in. o.c. Wet siding dries into the airspace, which is screened at the bottom to keep out insects. (Photo by Zachary Gaulkin, courtesy *Fine Homebuilding* magazine, © The Taunton Press.)

underneath the roofing and siding can help, but, if it's stuck on over the housewrap, it's a chemistry solution. To make matters worse, there can be chemical compatibility problems between adhesive membranes and various building papers, including asphalt-impregnated felt paper. If the membrane is installed under the roofing and building papers,

then it's a last line of defense. It's still important to install the other materials properly.

For a better physics solution, make sure the housewrap or building paper on the wall overlaps the water and ice shield. Better yet, it should also overlap the roof's step flashing to keep water above the roof. If the step flashing is installed after the

Detailing a Rain-Screen Wall

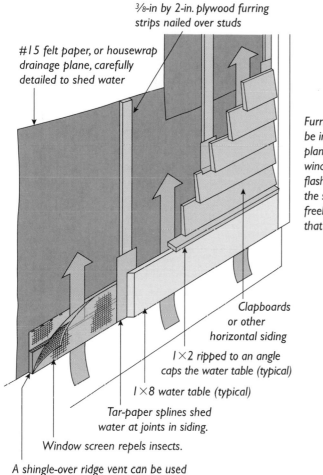

⅜-in by 2-in. plywood furring strips nailed over studs

#15 felt paper, or housewrap drainage plane, carefully detailed to shed water

Furring strips and siding should be installed after the drainage plane is complete, including all window, door, and roof counter-flashing. The vent space behind the siding allows water to drain freely, reducing vapor pressure that can drive paint from a wall.

Clapboards or other horizontal siding

1×2 ripped to an angle caps the water table (typical)

1×8 water table (typical)

Tar-paper splines shed water at joints in siding.

Window screen repels insects.

A shingle-over ridge vent can be used between furring strips to pad a window screen and still allow water to drain.

housewrap or building paper, simply cut a slit a few inches above the top edge of the step flashing, then tuck in a piece of counter flashing that overlaps the step flashing, just as you would above window and door openings (see the bottom photo on p. 176).

Rain screens

If you live in a wet climate (one with 40 in. or more of annual rainfall), or simply want a more effective cladding system, you can dramatically enhance the drainage plane by installing a vented drainage space behind the siding. This is called a *rain screen system*, and the airspace provides multiple benefits. First, the airspace provides a place for water to drain when it leaks past the siding. Second, the airspace creates a

pressure drop across the siding, cutting the pressure of wind-driven rain against the drainage plane. Once past the siding, water tends to fall instead of being driven farther into the wall. Finally, it equalizes the humidity on both sides of wood siding. That can be a money saver, because it reduces moisture-related cupping, checking, and paint failure.

Rain screens can be used with horizontal siding of any type, as well as with panels and even shingles. They are less important with vinyl siding, which tends to drain well and does not have paint-durability issues. Synthetic stucco finishes should be applied over wire lath that is held off of the building paper by wood strips or special furring nails—never applied directly over plastic housewraps.

WHAT CAN GO WRONG

I recently did an energy consultation for customers who were doubling the size of their house by adding a second floor. The plumber had already taken the hot water boiler away, even though it was fairly new and efficient, saying that it would never be big enough to heat the expanded house. It's too bad, because my calculations showed the heat loss on the finished house to be less than 35,000 btu/hour—*less* than the original, uninsulated house of half the size. To top it off, the new boiler was only slightly more efficient than the original; if they were going to spend the money, they should have at least gotten a high-efficiency model.

Mechanical Systems (Heat, A/C, Hot Water, Ventilation)

If you are investing in remodeling and improving the energy features of your house, you should probably consider replacing heating and air-conditioning systems at the same time (if they are more than 10 years old). Chances are good that they are oversized. After you improve the house's energy performance, the loads will be significantly reduced and the inefficiency of oversized systems will appreciably cut into your savings— this is especially true with air conditioners. Even if you're building an addition and not making thermal improvements to the existing house, old equipment may have been oversized. Make sure the installing contractor does a careful heating and/or cooling load calculation as part of the proposal.

Another common issue, particularly with additions, is heating and cooling distribution systems. If you are improving the thermal efficiency of the rest of the house while building an addition, one option is to reconfigure some of the old distribution system to supply the new living space. The amount of distribution that you need in each room (ducts or baseboard) is directly proportional to the heating or cooling load, so significant thermal improvements can free up a substantial number of duct runs. Of course, any distribution system in an unconditioned space should be well insulated, and all new ductwork should be thoroughly sealed with mastic during assembly.

Supplemental heating and cooling systems

Because of space constraints, foundation access, or other reasons, it is often easier to install a separate, new heating or cooling system in an addition; consider supplying heat with one or more independent wall-mounted heaters (see the sidebar on p. 122).

Another option is to install a high-efficiency gas hot water heater, which can provide *both* heat and hot water for a well-insulated addition or even for an entire, remodeled home (see the sidebar on the facing page). The newer, high-output gas-fired tankless heaters also work well.

In my experience, there's not much conflict between heat and hot water needs if you use a water heater to supply both heat and domestic hot water. The storage tank eliminates the hot water priority control that is needed with a boiler. When a heating zone calls for heat, the hydronic return water temperature quickly warms to between 70°F and 90°F, so the tank temperature does not drop dramatically. However, if you turn down the space heat thermostat at night, make sure the room temperature comes back to a comfortable level before "shower hour." The added load of bringing a house up to temperature after a setback can drop the tank temperature for a while—especially if it's used with radiant floor heating.

Heat can also be distributed through ducts with a fan coil. Some fan coils are rated for potable water, so they don't require heat exchangers. This approach also allows for air-conditioning with the same air handler. Alternatively, a separate room air conditioner can provide cooling for a new space.

Planning ventilation

If you're gutting a significant part of your house or adding a lot of new space, don't forget to think about ventilation. This is a good opportunity to improve a home's ventilation system or add one that doesn't exist already. Although it is fairly easy to retrofit a high-quality bath fan and timer or a return makeup air system (see chapter 3), a high-quality central ventilation system does the best job of delivering fresh air where you need it. The relatively high cost of retrofitting ductwork for a central system in an existing home is likely to be reduced during a remodeling project, when walls are already open.

USING A WATER HEATER FOR HYDRONIC HEAT

People are often surprised to learn that I heat my entire house—2,400 sq. ft. in southwestern Vermont—with a 40-gal. propane water heater. It's the *load* that matters, not the size of the house. From a well-insulated addition to a large superinsulated house, a standard water heater can easily handle a heating load of 15,000 to 45,000 btu/hour. Using a water heater for the dual function of providing heat and hot water is much more efficient than using either a water heater or a boiler by itself. The installation can save space and money, and it can be used for hydronic heating distribution or for heating a hydro-air coil (see the sidebar on p. 129).

How can water heaters provide reasonably efficient space heating, even though their efficiency ratings are much lower than boilers? The energy factor (EF rating) of a hot water tank includes the standby losses when the burner is off. When you add a second function (space heating) to a water heater, those losses are spread out over many more hours of burner use, resulting in higher net efficiencies for both functions. Water heaters are better suited to small heating loads than boilers are, and they are not subject to the thermal shock that can damage grossly oversized boilers.

The lower temperatures found in hot water heaters are great for radiant floor heating, and they don't need the injection valves often required with a boiler. They also provide safer, lower surface temperatures for old cast-iron radiators. For baseboard applications, I plan for 140°F (an exception to the 120°F–setpoint recommendation in chapter 8). The output of fin-tube baseboards is usually 40% to 50% lower at 140°F than at typical 180°F boiler temperatures. That is rarely a problem in renovations, because existing baseboards tend to be oversized (even before energy improvements), but the situation should be taken into account when installing new baseboard.

For heated spaces with a calculated heat load of 45,000 btu/hour or less, choose a tank with a btu/hour input rating at least 50% higher than the heating load *and* with a storage capacity (in gallons) between 80% and 110% of the required first-hour rating for water heating (see the sidebar on p. 159). The larger the heat load, the higher the tank's storage capacity should be. If the heating load is greater than 50,000 btu/hour, I recommend a specialized, superefficient tank, such as Polaris or Voyager.

Using a Hot Water Heater for Space and Water Heating

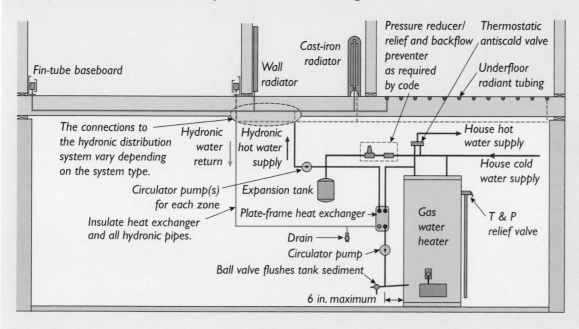

Fin-tube baseboard

Wall radiator

Cast-iron radiator

Pressure reducer/ relief and backflow preventer as required by code

Thermostatic antiscald valve

Underfloor radiant tubing

The connections to the hydronic distribution system vary depending on the system type.

Hydronic water return

Hydronic hot water supply

House hot water supply

House cold water supply

Circulator pump(s) for each zone

Expansion tank

Plate-frame heat exchanger

Gas water heater

T & P relief valve

Insulate heat exchanger and all hydronic pipes.

Drain

Circulator pump

Ball valve flushes tank sediment

6 in. maximum

In many homes, a standard gas water heater can provide both heat and hot water. An external plate-frame heat exchanger (separates the potable hot water supply from the hydronic system. Alternately, a water heater with a built-in internal heat exchanger makes the plumbing simpler and eliminates the second circulator pump. (Note: The combustion venting system and some plumbing components are not shown for clarity. Check local plumbing codes for required shutoffs, boiler drains, and so on.)

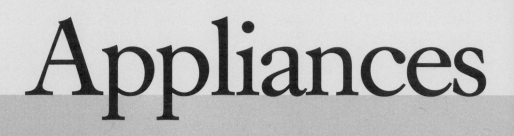

Appliances

CHAPTER TEN
and Lights

Appliances and lighting represent a significant part of the average family's energy budget, or about 45% of the residential energy dollars spent annually across the country. Although the actual electrical consumption of most individual lights and appliances is small, most houses have a lot of them, which can add up. In addition, every house has a few major appliances that account for a large share of the total electricity consumption. Here is where thoughtful planning about how you use appliances and lights—and some inexpensive controls—can make a big difference.

Smart shopping can also help. Whenever you buy an appliance, select a product that offers the same degree of performance but uses less power. An energy-efficient lightbulb can save from $20 to $50 over its lifetime. This chapter will discuss where and how to get the most for your energy dollar from the appliances and lighting in your home.

185

PRO TIP

Most household electricity is consumed by small loads that run continuously, and by medium or large appliances that cycle on and off.

WHAT CAN GO WRONG

People with high electric bills sometimes ask whether their meter is broken. In my experience—and that of utility company employees—a meter's record is pretty accurate. Standard mechanical electric meters are almost always right on, and if they do wear a little after decades of service, they tend to slow down a bit, rather than speed up. If you think your bill is too high, look more closely at things that use electricity in your home.

Determining Consumption

Technically speaking, most appliances and lights are not a fixed part of a house. But if you are thinking about making energy improvements to your house, you should include them in your plan, both for environmental and for economic reasons. Appliances and lights use about 26% of the raw energy consumed in households across the United States, while home heating uses about 50%. However, because electricity costs much more per unit than other fuels, the amount of money spent on appliances and lighting is about 45% of the total. Efficient appliances and lights not only save electricity (and money) while you use them, but they also save on the expense of

air-conditioning your home. Because of their higher efficiency, they produce less waste heat.

It is also worth noting that reducing home-appliance energy use is a significant way to reduce environmental impact. Research has shown that lights and household appliances rank 5th out of 130 categories of consumer activities with the most environmental impact. Home-appliance energy use is almost on par with the 4th-ranking category— heating, water heating, and air-conditioning— in contributing to greenhouse-gas emissions and air pollution.

How much am I using?

We tend to be fairly aware of a home's heating or cooling system, because we can feel when it's running (or not). We can see when a light is turned on or when the dryer is used. But many appliances operate quietly in the background, chugging away and using electricity without really being noticed. What matters most with any elec-

National Energy Use: Household Annual Expenses

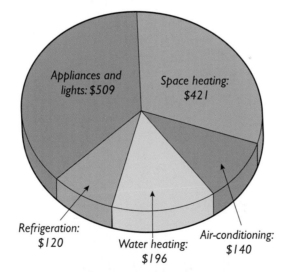

Although refrigeration, lighting, and appliances represent only 26% of all energy used by residences nationwide, they consume 45% of the energy dollars of the average household (including apartments). The actual percentages may vary substantially, depending on the climate and habits of an individual family, but these figures still leave significant room for improvement.
(Source: U.S. Department of Energy, Residential Energy Consumption Survey [RECS], 1997.)

How Much Electricity?

The amount of electricity used by any appliance (or light) depends on its power in watts and on the amount of time it operates. Our overall consumption, or usage, is measured in kilowatt-hours (kWh) at the electric meter, which equals power (in thousands of watts) × hours. For instance, a hair dryer that uses 1,200 watts and runs for 15 minutes each day uses 1.2 kW × 0.25 hr = 0.3 kWh per day. At a rate of $0.09/kWh, that adds up to only about $0.80 per month (0.3 × 0.09 × 30). Compare that to a 60-watt lightbulb that runs all day. In that case, 0.06 kW × 24 = 1.44 kWh/day, or $3.90/month.

Home-Appliance Electrical Use

The amount of energy a particular appliance uses varies significantly with wattage and the amount of time it's used each day. This chart shows the typical usage range of most common household appliances.

		Watts (low)	Watts (high)	Hours/day (low)	Hours/day (high)	kWh/month (low)	kWh/month (high)
Big Users	Swimming pool pump[1]	300	1,000	8	24	72	720
	Dehumidifier[1]	450	900	4	24	54	648
	Electric space heater[1]	1,200	1,500	1	12	36	540
	Hot tub (or sauna)[2]	300	1,500	8	10	72	450
	Refrigerator or freezer	350	1,000	4	8	42	240
	Waterbed	0	350	0	18	0	189
	Electric oven/range[3]	1,200	2,500	0.5	1.5	18	113
Moderate Users	Dryer (electric)[3]	3,500	5,000	0.25	1	26	150
	Sump pump[1]	200	500	0.5	10	3	150
	Aquarium[3]	25	300	16	16	12	144
	Clothes washer [4]	350	1,000	1	4	11	120
	Well pump	750	2,000	0.5	1.5	11	90
	Color TV	30	200	3	12	3	72
	Computer	50	200	4	12	6	72
	Printer/fax	25	200	4	12	3	72
	Dishwasher[3,4]	200	1,200	1.5	1.5	9	54
	Ventilation fans[1]	25	200	1	8	0.75	48
	Microwave oven	750	1,500	0.2	0.75	5	34
Heating Auxiliary Electric[1] (Electric components of gas or oil heating system)	Oil furnace	250	600	2	12	15	216
	Gas furnace	150	400	2	12	9	144
	Oil boiler	150	400	2	12	9	144
	Gas boiler	50	200	2	12	3	72

[1] Typically used seasonally; amounts shown are during appliance operation.

[2] An outdoor hot tub in winter may use 1,000 kWh/month or more, depending on climate.

[3] Wattage varies significantly, depending on equipment, cycle, or setting. Wattage range shown may be a composite.

[4] Does not include hot water heating input.

(Sources: Massachusetts Appliance Efficiency Education Service Manual, 1995; Central Vermont Public Service Auditor Manual "What It Depends On," 1995)

TRADE SECRET

Unless you are using them for hours on end, small appliances (like kitchen gadgets, hair dryers, irons, garage-door openers, power tools, and battery chargers) and electronics (answering machines, cordless phones, and computer equipment) generally don't use much electricity. A TV or stereo doesn't use much, but the components in a large home-entertainment system can add up, especially if they are always on.

Electronic components can leak electricity 24 hours a day, even if you hardly use them. Choose components with an Energy Star label, and plug the items you use less often into a power strip that can be switched off. (Photo © Kevin Kennefick.)

trical appliance or lighting use is the overall consumption of electricity, or *usage*.

Usage is defined by the size of a load and the amount of time it runs. The size of an electrical load is the amount of power it uses at a given moment—for example, 10 watts, 200 watts, or 1,200 watts. Large loads that run for very short periods (a few seconds or minutes at a time) may actually consume very little electricity. Small loads that run continuously can add up to a lot. The really big consumers are medium or large loads that run for many hours. If you want to figure out where your electricity dollars are going every month, estimate the power consumption and run time of each appliance. You may be surprised at some of the results (see the chart on p. 187).

Appliances

Once you have identified your big electricity consumers, you can use three basic approaches to reduce your appliances' energy usage: reduce the run time of appliances, improve the energy efficiency of your existing appliances, or buy new appliances that are more energy efficient.

Reducing run time

Reducing appliance run time may be as simple as turning things off when you don't need them. However, some of the big users, such as pool pumps and dehumidifier, typically run full-time in the background, where you are not usually aware of them. In some cases, it may be possible to add a simple control to turn the appliance on only when it is needed.

For example, many pool pumps run 24 hours a day. However, for proper filtration and circulation, 6 to 8 hours a day is usually adequate. You can have a 24-hour timer installed in the pump circuit for about $200; the savings can be as much as $50 per month when the pool is operating. In fact, energy codes in many states require

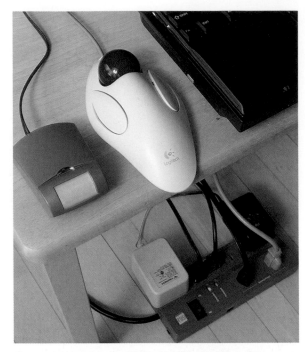

One way to save electricity is with the Watt Stopper, a power strip that has a motion sensor with an adjustable time delay. When you leave a room, it shuts off six of the eight outlets, leaving on two so that critical equipment—such as a computer's main processing unit, a fax machine, or a VCR and cable box—won't be interrupted. (Photo © Kevin Kennefick.)

timers on new pool installations. Of course, if you have a heated pool, an insulated cover can also save a lot—provided you close it when the pool isn't in use.

To reduce the operating time for a dehumidifier, monitor the humidity level in the air and don't run it more than necessary. Indoor relative humidity should be kept between 30% and 50% for optimum health, so get a humidity gauge and adjust the dehumidifier control to maintain those levels.

Reducing run time can also be a matter of planning ahead. For example, instead of using the microwave (and extra electricity) to defrost food, put frozen food in the refrigerator well in advance of when it will be needed. When you're cooking, use the microwave instead of the oven whenever you can—it uses much less energy for the same tasks.

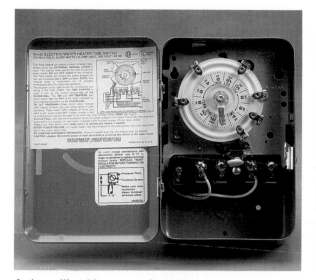

A timer like this one can be set to operate a swimming pool pump, or another large electrical load, for several on/off cycles per day. Check the timer's ampere rating to make sure it's adequate for the load it's controlling. (Photo © Kevin Kennefick.)

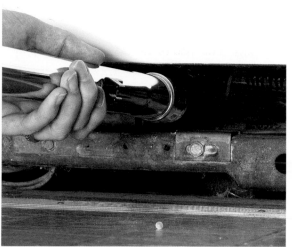

Cleaning the refrigerator coils keeps an old fridge running as efficiently as possible. You can use a vacuum wand or buy a specialized refrigerator brush (available from EFI and other suppliers) to help reach between the coils. (Photo © Kevin Kennefick.)

Old refrigerators use more energy; those from the 1970s are typically the least efficient models ever built.

Improving efficiency

It's also important to learn how to improve the efficiency of your appliances. Efficiency can often be increased by simple cleaning and maintenance or by choosing the proper settings when using appliances.

Refrigeration. Just about everyone has a refrigerator, and this is one appliance that you can easily maintain to achieve better efficiency. The first thing is to ensure adequate air circulation around the unit. Keep it a few inches away from the wall, and don't box it in with cabinets. Cleaning the coils periodically with a vacuum cleaner and a brush can also help.

Make sure the door seals are tight, keep the unit away from heat sources (don't put it next to the stove or dishwasher), and watch the temperature setting. The refrigerator compartment should stay between 36°F and 38°F, and the freezer between 0°F and 5°F. If you have a power-saving switch, turn it on. Typically, the switch disables the internal heaters that prevent condensation. Turn it off only if condensation occurs. It may not be needed at all, or it may be needed only in humid weather.

Finally, keep refrigerators, and especially freezers, reasonably full; they are much less efficient when they are nearly empty. Eliminate an extra fridge that you may keep in the garage or basement for overflow (or the odd six-pack). Or just unplug it until you need it to stock up for that holiday gathering. Buying a new, highly efficient refrigerator won't save any energy if you keep the old one running.

Laundry. Doing the laundry uses energy in three ways: washers and dryers have electricity-consuming motors that move clothes and water; washers use hot water, which is typically heated with gas or electricity; and dryers heat clothes, also with gas or electricity. When you run a wash, pay attention to the washer settings. Always use a cold water rinse, and use a warm or cold wash for loads where that's appropriate. A warm/cold cycle uses about half as much total energy as a hot/cold cycle!

Also, pay attention to the size of the load. You get the most efficiency if you fill, but don't overload, the machine. And if you do run a smaller load, set the wash level appropriately. The settings

Don't use indoor dryer vents like this one. In addition to the moisture load, if you have a gas dryer you may dump carbon monoxide indoors. To reduce dryer energy, buy an efficient washer instead.

PRO TIP

Even the most ineffi-cient new models of household appliances typically use much less energy than appliances that are 10 or more years old.

IN DETAIL

The EPA and DOE work together with appliance manufacturers to set standards for high-quality products that use significantly less energy than standard products of the same type. As of this writing, appli-ances in the Energy Star labeling program include clothes wash-ers, dishwashers, refrigerators, dehumidifiers, and many categories of consumer electronics and computer/ office equipment. See the Energy Star Web site at www.energystar.gov for more information, including model numbers of labeled products.

This dryer vent outlet is clogged with lint. Anything that interferes with the airflow of the dryer hose or outlet reduces its efficiency.

on your washer also affect drying time. Always use the fastest spin setting, unless it's a "gentle" load, to remove the most water.

For dryer efficiency, keep the lint filter clean, and check the outlet periodically for lint that may be clogging the vent. If your dryer hose is kinked

or twisted (or too long), replace it with as short and direct a run as possible, preferably with a straight, sheet-metal duct instead of a flexible vinyl or an aluminum duct. Try to do multiple loads in a row to take advantage of the dryer's retained heat, and fill, but don't overload, the machine.

Dishwasher. This appliance uses both elec-tricity and hot water. You can minimize energy use by paying attention to the settings. Don't use the "Heavy" or "Pots and pans" cycle unless you really need to. Prerinse only the dishes that are heavily soiled, so you can take advantage of the "Light" setting for the entire load. Wait until the machine is full before turning it on. It uses the same amount of energy whether you wash one dish or thirty. Note that some new dishwashers have particle sensors that stop the machine as soon as the dishes are clean.

If you don't have to take the dishes out right away, you can run the machine with the "Air-dry"

Horizontal-Axis Washers

Horizontal-axis clothes washers have been common in Europe for many years, but they have just started to gain in popularity in the U.S. They save energy by using less water and by employing gravity instead of brute force to help agitate the clothes. They also spin out more of the water, further saving energy by reducing drying time. In addition, they do a better job of cleaning while using less detergent, and they're easier on clothes, too. Because it loads from the front, the top of the washer can be used to sort laundry or to stack the dryer. Although it costs more than a regular washer, you can recover the extra expense in energy savings in 4 to 8 years.

Horizontal-axis (or H-axis) washers can be identi-fied by their front-loading feature. They use less water, save energy, and are easier on your clothes.

setting (sometimes called "energy saver"). If your dishwasher has a booster heater inside, turn down the temperature setting on your hot water heater to 120°F or as low as you can for the other hot water needs in the house.

Smart shopping for new appliances

Minimum efficiency regulations for new appliances have increased over the years, so even the least-efficient new models typically use much less energy than appliances that are 10 or more years old.

In most cases, it's not cost-effective to go out and buy new, energy-efficient products just to save energy. Two exceptions to this rule are old refrigerators and dehumidifiers. If you have old models of either of those units, go out and purchase an Energy Star–labeled model. You'll start saving money right away. For other appliances, look for the most efficient products available when you do have to go shopping—and always choose an Energy Star–labeled appliance at a minimum.

Also, keep your eyes open for utility rebate programs or other promotions. Local electric utilities often provide financial incentives for consumers to buy more efficient appliances. Incentives may range from coupons, mail-in rebates, or point-of-sale discounts to programs that pick up and dispose of older, inefficient appliances, such as refrigerators.

Lighting

There are two basic approaches to making the lights in your home more efficient: eliminating unnecessary usage and using the most efficient products available. Many of us heard the message "turn off lights when you're not using them" while we were growing up. Of course, how much lighting you need is a matter of eyesight and per-

sonal taste; turning off the light isn't always a practical solution.

One of the best ways to eliminate unnecessary lights is to use controls. Regularly used indoor lights can be put on timers or occupancy sensors so they aren't left on for hours when no one is using them. Exterior walkway or security lighting can be put on timers, motion sensors, or photocell controls (or a combination) to minimize their usage while ensuring that they are on whenever needed.

Compact fluorescent lamps

To maximize the efficiency of your existing light fixtures, replace the lightbulbs with compact fluorescent lamps (CFLs). Although they are more expensive than incandescent lamps, they save about two-thirds of the electricity for the same amount of light, and they last about 10 times longer than regular lamps. That saves money in the long run, and it can also save a lot of hassle replacing lamps in fixtures that are difficult to reach.

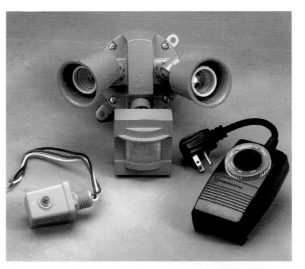

Controls such as photocells, motion sensors, and timers (left to right) can automatically turn indoor or outdoor lights on and off when needed, reducing waste. Most are available at hardware stores and home centers for hard-wiring or plug-in applications. (Photo © Kevin Kennefick.)

TRADE SECRET

Over the years, CFL manufacturers have tended to overstate the equivalent incandescent wattage that a bulb or fixture replaces. CFLs do provide the same amount of light at a much lower wattage, but be cautious. I recommend using a 3-to-1 ratio to be safe. If your favorite lamp has a 75-watt bulb, replace it with at least a 25-watt CFL, regardless of what the package says.

Compact fluorescent lamps come in many shapes and sizes and range in price from $5 to $20 each. Look for units with electronic, rather than magnetic, ballasts. Note the package on the right, which indicates that the lamp will work with a dimmer switch. (Photo © Kevin Kennefick.)

The popular torchère-type floor fixtures, which typically come with 300-watt halogen lamps, not only use a *lot* of electricity but also can be a fire hazard. Many types of CFL torchères are available, and some come with dimmers. This one has a three-way switch with a maximum wattage of 85 on its "high" setting. (Photo © Kevin Kennefick.)

Many of the CFLs that were on the market even a few years ago were big, clunky, and difficult to fit in fixtures. They often flickered or had a strange, greenish cast to the light. But CFLs have improved rapidly, and today's CFL lamps are smaller and more reliable and have much better quality of light. Although they start more quickly than older CFLs, even the best of them can take a little time—up to a minute or so—to reach their full brightness. But this is typically not an issue for lights that are used for long periods. There are also more options than ever before, including lower and higher light outputs, dimmable lamps, and three-way lamps.

+ SAFETY FIRST

Never put a CFL in a fixture that has a dimmer switch, unless it is rated for dimmer use. It can be a fire hazard. Lamps that have a "night-light" function, and some electronic security timers, can also be a problem with standard CFLs. Dimmable CFLs are safe in those applications.

Because of their high up-front cost and long life, CFLs save the most money when they replace lights that are used for at least a couple of hours at a time. Typically, the greatest light usage is in the kitchen, living or family room, and outdoor areas. Indoor lamps that are on a security timer are good candidates, too. Depending on your habits, hallways, circulation areas, work areas, and children's bedrooms or study areas may also be good choices. In most homes, it doesn't make much sense to use CFLs in closets, bathrooms, basements, or garages. If you do have lights in those areas that are regularly left on for hours (on purpose or by accident), and controls won't work to change that, it's worth replacing the bulbs with CFLs.

Efficient light fixtures

In addition to screw-in CFLs, you can also purchase fixtures with special built-in CFLs. CFL fixtures typically include a ballast (an electronic component that runs the fluorescent light) and a plug-in pin base for the lamp inside. The pin-base lamps are usually less expensive than the screw-in types, because they don't need a built-in

Most lighting manufacturers offer interior CFL fixtures in a wide variety of styles. Look for the Energy Star logo on all fixtures, which is a reliable indicator of quality, reliability, and energy savings. (Photo © Kevin Kennefick.)

A typical Energy Star light fixture uses special CFLs. Note the built-in ballast (the gray rectangle between the two lamps). (Photo © Kevin Kennefick.)

ballast like the screw-in CFLs. CFL fixtures are good candidates to replace any high-use lighting fixtures in the home, particularly ones that you are planning to update anyway. They can also replace high-use fixtures for which you can't find a CFL screw-in bulb that fits properly.

CFL fixtures come in hundreds of styles and sizes, including wall sconces, ceiling dome fixtures, pendant lights, recessed cans, exterior-wall fixtures, and floodlights. Prices are typically $20 to $30 higher than an equivalent standard light fixture, and styles range from utilitarian economy models to some pretty fancy ones. Many of the major lighting manufacturers make them, including Progress, Seagull, Juno®, Brownlee, General Electric®, Kichler®, Maxlite®, and others. You probably won't find a big selection of them at your local home center, but specialty lighting stores should be able special-order them if they don't have them in stock. And beware of CFL fixtures that don't have the Energy Star label. Although they may save energy, some tend to be cheaply made and are unreliable.

One type of fixture that I haven't yet seen with CFLs is a chandelier. Although CFLs are getting smaller and more compact, they simply aren't available in the tiny incandescent candle type of bulb that chandeliers typically use (though I bet someone's working on it).

Energy-efficient lighting—both lamps and fixtures—is an area that utility companies tend to promote heavily, so watch for rebates or promotions, or call your electric company to find out what they have to offer.

Many types of wall-mounted exterior fixtures are also available with built-in CFLs. (Photo © Kevin Kennefick.)

+ SAFETY FIRST

Keep in mind that most compact fluorescent lamps take a little longer to start when the weather is cold. Although their technology has improved dramatically over the past few years, they may still remain rather dim for several minutes in very cold conditions (below 25°F). That may be hazardous if you use them for exterior lighting—for instance, if you flick on the light just to run out on an icy sidewalk to grab the newspaper or round up the dog.

Resources

General Products

ACT, Inc. Metlund Systems®
3176 Pullman Avenue, Suite 119
Costa Mesa, CA 92626
Phone: (714) 668-1200
Toll Free: (800) 638-5863
Fax: (714) 668-1927
www.metlund.com
*"D-Mand System" instant hot
    water system*

AM Conservation Group
430 Sand Shore Road, Suite 7
Hackettstown, NJ 07840
Phone: (908) 852-6464 or
    (800) GOOD-BUY
    (800) 466-3289)
Fax: (908) 852-6444
E-mail: amcg@nac.net
www.amconservationgroup.com
*Water-saving and weatherization
    supplies*

American Water Heater
    Company
P.O. Box 1597
Johnson City, TN 37605
Phone: (800) 999-9515
Fax: (800) 999-5210
www.americanwaterheater.com
Polaris high-efficiency water heater

Aqua Therm®, First Co.
8273 Moberly Lane
P.O. Box 270969
Dallas, TX 75227
Phone: (214) 388-5751
Fax: (214) 388-2255
E-mail: sales@firstco.com
www.firstco.com
Hydro-air handlers

Aube Technologies Inc.
705 Montrichard Avenue
Iberville, Quebec
Canada J2X 5K8
Phone (450) 358-4600 or
    (800) 831-AUBE
Fax: (450) 358-4650
E-mail: service@aubetech.com
www.aubetech.com
*Model T1033A—Single-pole
    ventilation controls*

Comfort Foam®, a division of
    Foam Enterprises, Inc.
13630 Watertower Circle
Minneapolis, MN 55441
Phone: (800) 888-3342 or
    (763) 559-3266
Fax: (763) 559-0945
www.comfortfoam.com
Contractor-applied spray foam

Commercial Construction
    Products Division of
    ChemRex®
889 Valley Park Drive
Shakopee, MN 55379
Phone: (952) 496-6000 or
    (800) 433-9517
Fax (952) 496-6062
www.chemrex.com/thoro
*Waterproof coating for foundation
    capillary break—Thoroseal*

Corbond® Corporation
32404 Frontage Road
Bozeman, MT 59715
Phone: (406) 586-4585 or
    (888) 949-9089
Fax: (406) 586-4584
E-mail:
    corbond@corbond.com
www.corbond.com
Contractor-applied spray foam

CP Films, Inc.
P.O. Box 5068
Martinsville, VA 24115
Phone: (276) 627-3204 or
    (800) 746-8661
Fax: (276) 627-3500
www.cpfilms.com
Window films

Demilec Inc.
870 Cure Boivin
Boisbriand, Quebec
J7G 2A7, Canada
Phone: (450) 437-0123
Fax: (450) 437-2338
E-mail: demilec@swbell.net
www.demilec.com
*Sealection® contractor-applied
    spray foam*

Doucette Industries, Inc.
701 Grantley Road
York, Pennsylvania 17403-3525
Phone: (800) 445-7511
Fax: (717) 845-2864
E-mail: johnl@
    doucetteindustries.com
www.endlessshower.com
Drainwater heat-recovery system

Dow Chemical Company,
    Customer Information Group
Midland, MI 48674
Phone: (800) 441-4369
www.dow.com
*Styrofoam Wallmate—slotted insu-
    lation for interior finishing with
    furring strips*

Duro Dyne® Corporation
130 Route 110
Farmingdale, NY 11735
Phone: (631) 249-9000
Fax: (631) 249-8346
Toll Free: (800) 899-3876
www.durodyne.com
*Dyna-fresh ventilation controls,
DuroZone residential econo-
mizer controls, DuroZone
dampers*

Energy Federation, Inc. (EFI)
40 Washington Street,
Suite 3000
Westborough, MA 01581
Phone: (800) 876-0660
Fax: (888) 655-6767
E-mail: info@efi.org
www.efi.org
*General supplier of energy-
efficiency supplies, lighting,
and ventilation*

Enviromaster International, LLC
5780 Success Drive
Rome, NY 13440
Phone: (800) 228-9364
Fax: (800) 232-9364
E-mail: cmi@enviromaster.com
www.enviromaster.com
*Heat pump water heaters, efficient
boilers, mini-split AC systems*

Fantech
1712 Northgate Boulevard
Sarasota, FL 34234
Phone: (800) 747-1762
Fax: (800) 487-9915
info@fantech-us.com
www.fantech-us.com
Ventilation fans

Heat Transfer Products, Inc.
P.O. Box 429
120 Braley Road
East Freetown, MA 02717
Phone: (800) 323-9651 or
(508) 763-8071
Fax: (508) 763-3769
E-mail: sales@htproducts.com
www.htproducts.com
*Voyager® high-efficiency
water heater*

Hoyme Manufacturing, Inc.
3843-44 Ave.
Camrose, Alberta
Canada T4V 3T1
Phone: (780) 672-6553 or
(800) 661-7382
Fax: (780) 672-6554 or
(800) 661-8065
E-mail: hoyme@hoyme.com
www.hoyme.com
Ventilation dampers

Icynene Inc.
5805 Whittle Road, Suite 110
Mississauga, Ontario
Canada L4Z 2J1
Phone: (888) 946-7325 or
(905) 890-7325
Fax: (905) 890-7784
www.icynene.com
Contractor-applied spray foam

J&R Products, Inc.
4695 East 200 North
Craigville, IN 46731
Phone: (800) 343-4446
Fax: (800) 518-4446
www.jrproductsinc.com
Insulating supplies

LESSCO® Low Energy
Systems Supply
Company, Inc.
W1330 Happy Hollow Road
Campbellsport, WI 53010
Phone/Fax: (920) 533-3306
E-mail: lchlessco@excel.net
www.lessco-airtight.com
*Airtight electrical-box
mounting system*

Lipidex Corporation
50 Franklin Terrace
Duxbury, MA 02332
Phone: (781) 834-1600
Fax: (781) 834-1601
E-mail: info@lipidex.com
www.lipidex.com
AirCycler® ventilation control

Low Energy Systems, Inc.
2916 S. Fox Street
Englewood, CO 80110
Phone: (800) 873-3507 or
(303) 781-9437
Fax: (303) 781-3608
E-mail: sales@
tanklesswaterheaters.com
www.tanklesswaterheaters.com
Instantaneous water heaters

The Millennium Group
165 Virginia Drive, Suite 12
P.O. Box 1848
Estes Park, CO 80517
Phone: (800) 280-2304
Fax: (800) 335-9151
www.thenailer.com
The Nailer; drywall clips

Positive Energy
    Conservation Products
P.O. Box 7568
Boulder, CO 80306
Phone: (800) 488-4340
Fax: (303) 444-4340
E-mail:
    info@positive-energy.com
www.positive-energy.com
*General supplier of weatherization
    and ventilation supplies*

Prest-On Co.™
312 Lookout Point
Hot Springs, AR 71913
Phone: (800) 323-1813
Fax: (501) 767-5173
www.prest-on.com
Prest-On Clips™ drywall clips

Shelter Supply, Inc.
17725 Juniper Path
Lakeville, MN 55044
Phone: (800) 762-8399
Fax: (952) 898-4555
www.sheltersupply.com
*General supplier of
    energy-efficiency supplies and
    ventilation equipment*

Simpson Strong-Tie® Co.
4120 Dublin Blvd, Suite 400
Dublin, CA 94568
Phone: (800) 999-5099
Fax: (925) 833-1496
www.strongtie.com
DS Drywall Stop drywall clips

Spacepak
260 North Elm Street
Westfield, MA 01085
Phone: (413) 564-5530
Fax: (413) 568-9613
www.spacepak.com
*Compact high-velocity
    HVAC and ductwork*

Tamarack Technologies Inc.
P.O. Box 490
11A Patterson's Brook Road
West Wareham, MA 02576
Phone: (800) 222-5932 or
    (508) 295-8103
Fax: (508) 295-8105
E-mail: info@tamtech.com
www.tamtech.com
*Ventilation equipment and controls:
    Airetrak™, Tamarack Whole
    House Fan™*

3M® Construction and Home
    Improvement Markets
3M Center Building 223-5S-07
St. Paul, MN 55144
Phone: (800) 364-3577
Fax: (800) 447-0408
http://www.3m.com/US/
    arch_construct
Window films

Truefoam Ltd.™
11 Mosher Drive
Burnside Industrial Park
Dartmouth, NS B3B 1L8
    Canada
Phone: (902) 468-5440
Fax: (902) 468-4691
E-mail: info@truefoam.com
www.truefoam.com
*TrueWall panels; Parge-Plus
    insulation coating*

V-Seal®: Schlegel Systems, Inc.
1555 Jefferson Road
Rochester, NY 14623
Phone: (716) 427-7200 or
    (800) 204-0863
Fax: (716) 427-9993
www.schlegel.com

The Watt Stopper
2800 De La Cruz Blvd.
Santa Clara, CA 95050
Phone: (408) 988-5331
Fax: (408) 988-5373
www.wattstopper.com
*Isole® IDP-3050; motion-sensor
    power strip*

Health-Related Resources

American Lung Association's
    "Health House®"
490 Concordia Ave.
St. Paul, MN 55103-2441
Voice: (651) 227-8014
Toll-Free: (877) 521-1491
Minnesota Toll-Free:
    (800) 642-5864
Fax: (651) 281-0242
www.healthhouse.org

The Building Science Corp.
    and Asthma Regional
    Coordinating Council of
    New England
www.buildingscience.com/
    resources/mold/
    Design_Build.pdf
*Free download of recommendations
    for healthy buildings*

Environmental
    Protection Agency (EPA)
www.epa.gov/iaq/radon/
    index.html
*Radon information and contacts
    from the Environmental
    Protection Agency (also avail-
    able at (800) 767-7236).*
www.epa.gov/iaq/asbestos/
    index.htm
*Information on asbestos programs
    in your state*

The Healthy House Institute
430 North Sewall Road
Bloomington IN 47408
Phone/Fax: (812) 332-5073
E-mail:
    healthy@bloomington.in.us
www.hhinst.com

Books

Bower, John. *The Healthy House: How to Buy One, How to Build One, How to Cure a Sick One.* 4th edition; paperback; ISBN 0963715690. The Healthy House Institute, 2000.

Bower, John. *Understanding Ventilation: How to Design, Select and Install Residential Ventilation Systems.* Hardcover; ISBN 0963715658. The Healthy House Institute, 1995.

Brower, Michael, and Warren Leon, *The Consumer's Guide to Effective Environmental Choices: Practical Advice from the Union of Concerned Scientists.* Paperback; ISBN 060980281X. Three Rivers Press, Random House, 1999.

Recommended Specifications for the Application and Finishing of Gypsum Board, GA-216. Gypsum Association, 2000.

Web Sites (General)

Energy Star
www.energystar.gov/
Listing of high-efficiency equipment and appliances

Home Energy magazine
www. homeenergy.org
Searchable database of past articles, free access to most materials

Rocky Mountain Institute
www.rmi.org
Resource for technology, energy policy, and advocacy

www.ariprimenet.org/
ari-prog/direct.nsf/
webpages/product+types
Heat Pump ratings.

www.gamanet.org/consumer/
consumer.htm.
AFUE ratings of residential furnaces and boilers; EF ratings of water heaters

Web Sites (Solar Water Heating and Solar Electric)

American Solar Energy Society (ASES)
www.ases.org

American Wind Energy Association (AWEA)
www.awea.org

Center for Renewable Energy and Sustainable Technology (CREST)
www.crest.org

Department of Energy (DOE)
Energy Efficiency and
    Renewable Energy
    Network
www.eren.doe.gov

Florida Solar Energy Center
www.fsec.ucf.edu
Consumer-oriented information on solar hot water, pool heating, as well as photovoltaics.

National Renewable Energy
    Laboratory (NREL)
www.nrel.gov

Real Goods
www.realgoods.com
Basic design information for renewable energy systems from a large product dealer

Solar Rating and Certification
    Corporation (SRCC)
www.solar-rating.org.
Rates solar collectors and complete water heating systems for compliance with established standards

List of Contributors

For written resources and inspiration: Michael Brower, John Krigger, Warren Leon, and Alex Wilson.

For giving generously of your time to help create the images for this book: Rich Baldassini and Sergio Gonzales at IMC Heating and Cooling; James Clinton, Alan Connolly, Dino Cunningham, Johnny Lamarre, Ian Nadeau, Joe Sheridan, and Ray Williams at Energy Guard; Bryce Clark, Todd Dustin, Jim Godin, Joe Ricard, and Shawn Tibbetts at Quality Insulation; Jonathan Goncalvez, Paul Goncalvez, Bill Joyal, and JoBo Santos at Royal Thermal View; and Steve Bonfiglioli.

For photography: RB Crotreau, John Curtis, Kevin Kennefick, and Sheri Riddell.

For images and equipment: Peter Baddeley at Convair; Edith Buffalohead at ECR; Kevin Zarzecki at Triad Marketing Group; Larry Carlson at DEC Thermastor; John O'Connell and Gary Church-Smith at Energy Federation; Bruce Spallone at Duro Dyne; Bill Kennedy and Tom St Louis at GFX; Gary Nelson and Frank Spevak at the Energy Conservatory; Kate Raymer at Tamarack Technologies; Victor Flynn at Panasonic; Ted Doyle at Space Pak; Larry Acker at Metlund; Karen McSherry at Harmon Stove Company; Mark Weissflog and Kevin Soucy at KW Management; and Lori Nelson at Columbia Paint and Coatings.

Index